Bureaucracy in
Canadian Government
Second Edition

Bureaucracy in Canadian Government

Second Edition

Selected Readings
edited by

W.D.K. Kernaghan

Brock University

Methuen

Toronto • London
Sydney • Wellington

Library of Congress Catalog Card Number 75-89951

ISBN 0-458-90980-7

77   76   75   74   73   1   2   3   4   5

Printed and bound in Canada

Preface

The complexity and turbulence of the milieu in which contemporary governments operate is reflected in rapid changes in the structures and processes of public bureaucracies. Since the publication in 1969 of the first edition of this book, the Canadian bureaucracy has continued to alter its organization and procedures to keep pace with the constantly increasing burden of government responsibilities. This revised edition focuses on the structures, politics, and issues of Canadian public bureaucracy at a time of profound challenge and swift social change.

The overall purpose of the book is to demonstrate to students of Canadian government the importance of the study and practice of public administration. To take account of recent developments and shifting emphases, the book has been substantially reorganized, and more than half of the articles are new. Other selections have been revised and updated.

The essays in the first of the six chapters serve as an introduction to the environment and the problems of public administration in Canada. Chapter Two sets within Canada's political and legal framework the internal management of the federal public service in the areas of organization, personnel and finance. Chapter Three is concerned with the relationships between senior public servants on the one hand, and elected politicians, notably Cabinet ministers, on the other. In Chapter Four, the essays centre on the various sources of influence and advice on the public policy views of both politicians and bureaucrats. The selections in Chapter Five examine the means by which public servants may be held responsible for their exercise of powers of a legislative and judicial nature. These five chapters lay a foundation for a discussion in the final chapter of public policy issues of particular relevance to the Canadian bureaucracy.

A selected bibliography is attached to each chapter to assist students wishing to read more extensively on a particular topic. For a *comprehensive* bibliography, students should refer to *Canadian Public Administration Bibliography,* compiled by W.E. Grasham and G. Julien and published by the Institute of Public Administration of Canada.

To include an appropriate number and selection of subjects in this book, substantial editing of several articles was necessary. I extend deep appreciation to all authors whose writings are reprinted here and particular thanks to those who permitted abridgement of their work.

W.D.K.K.
October, 1972.

Contents

Chapter Five
Administrative Responsibility

Chapter Six
Issues in Canadian Public Administration

Chapter One

Introduction to Canadian Public Administration

During the past twenty-five years, research on Canadian government and politics has centred largely on political parties, voting behaviour, foreign policy, and, particularly since 1960, on the financial, linguistic and cultural aspects of Canadian federalism. Public administration, which had long enjoyed a prominent position in the study of Canadian government, suffered a relative decline of academic interest during this period. Scholars tended to relegate the examination of administrative problems to the status of "research of last resort". In recent years, however, recognition of the increasingly important role of the bureaucracy in the political and policy process has reawakened concern among academics and practitioners for the study of public administration. Moreover, the Institute of Public Administration of Canada has greatly stimulated interest and improvement in Canadian public administration through its research activities, publications, conferences and seminars.

The first selection in this chapter explores the implications of the growth and influence of the public service for democratic government in Canada. It also introduces many of the subjects to be discussed in detail in subsequent chapters. The second article assesses the status of research and teaching in Canadian public administration, and examines in the Canadian context the issue of whether public administration is part of "political science" or part of "administrative science".

1

The Role of the Public Service in the Canadian Democratic System*

W. D. Kenneth Kernaghan

During this century, and particularly since the beginning of the Second World War, there has been an enormous expansion of the activities of Canadian governments. Moreover, all projections for the future indicate that this rapid growth will continue. The present scope and the continuing expansion of responsibilities at all levels of Canadian government — whether federal, provincial, or municipal — have a great impact on the daily lives and future prospects of Canadian citizens. The degree of happiness and prosperity or misery and poverty experienced by Canadians is affected by the countless decisions made each day by our governments. The range of governmental activities includes the traditional functions of administration of justice, the conduct of external relations, and the defence of the country as well as such newer responsibilities as medicare, environmental protection, and atomic energy research.

I

The two major areas of government action are the provision of *services* and the enforcement of *regulations*. The *service* functions include the maintenance of streets and highways, the mail delivery, and grants and loans for new housing and for urban renewal. Among the *regulatory* functions are the setting of standards for food and drugs, the prevention and restraint of restrictive trade practices, and the enforcement of fair housing and employment regulations. In order to carry out these and other responsibilities as effectively as possible, governments are actively engaged in *research* on matters ranging from the inspection of food and drug products to scientific and medical research. Virtually every government department and agency is involved in research related to its service or regulatory functions. Research activities are a costly, but essential, component of the total responsibilities of government.

*W.D. Kenneth Kernaghan, "The Role of the Public Service in the Canadian Democratic System," *The Quarterly of Canadian Studies* (Winter II, 1972), pp. 184-97. Reprinted and revised by permission of the author and publisher.

Very few Canadians are aware of the importance and the magnitude of our governments' operations. Canadians, like citizens of other countries, tend to be conscious of only those government activities which affect them directly and significantly — for example, the collection of taxes, the provision of family allowances, or the payment of unemployment insurance benefits. Many other important functions of government, such as the preservation of internal law and order or the administration of justice, are taken for granted unless the services are discontinued or disrupted for some reason. An excellent recent example of this situation was the awakened public concern about postal operations when the normal service was disrupted by labour disputes between postal workers and their employer, the Government of Canada.

In addition to awareness of the enormous scope of government activities, it is important to consider the transformation during this century of the environment within which modern governments operate. A number of interrelated developments affecting the nature of government activities should be noted. Rapid population growth in Canada (from 5,371,000 in 1901 to almost 22,000,000 in 1972) has been accompanied by a movement of Canadians from the rural-agricultural areas of the country to urban-industrial centres. The percentage of the Canadian population living in rural areas has declined from about 65 per cent in 1900 to about 20 per cent in 1973. Even more significant than this migration to urban centres is the fact that over 70 per cent of Canadians now live in cities, towns, or villages of 1,000 or more persons. Moreover, it is expected that by 1980 approximately 81 per cent of the population will live in such urban areas and that as many as 60 per cent of all Canadians will live in 29 major cities, each with a population of more than 100,000 persons. This "urbanization" of the Canadian population has already brought enormous problems in such areas as air and water pollution, inadequate housing, and archaic transportation systems. These critical problems can only be resolved by close and continuing cooperation between all levels of government and by the expenditure of large amount of money.

The environment within which contemporary governments work has also been greatly affected by technological developments. A few illustrations will be sufficient. The problems for government arising from the invention and widespread use of such earlier inventions as the automobile, the airplane, and television have become more critical as transportation routes have become snarled, airports have become too small for huge jetliners, and intercontinental television transmission has become possible. The opportunities brought about by more recent technological developments involving automation, computers, and atomic energy have created such problems as technological unemployment, invasion of privacy, and possible misuse of atomic energy. Future scientific and technical advances, such as increasing numbers of human transplants, test-tube babies, and instruments of instant communication pose even more challenging issues for government concern and involvement.

In addition, Canadians have seen during this century the growth of huge industrial and commercial organizations (e.g. General Motors, I.B.M.) and of large and powerful labour organizations (e.g. the United Automobile Workers, the Canadian Labour Congress.) Employer-employee disputes over wages, fringe benefits, and the effect of technological change on existing jobs can result in lengthy strikes. Such strikes may not only bring much personal strife and misfortune to those directly involved in the dispute but may also have an injurious impact on innocent third parties and on the economy as a whole. To protect the public interest, governments have been increasingly obliged to regulate the activities of business and labour organizations and to arbitrate disputes between them.

All these developments — new and expanded service, regulatory and research responsibilities, population movements and urbanization, technological and scientific developments, and the growth of large business and industrial organizations — have made the operations of governments extremely complex. Governments must provide rapid solutions to urgent current problems while planning for the solution or avoidance of future problems. They must be conscious of the widespread ramifications of major governmental decisions on various sectors of Canadian society. For example, the federal government must assess the probable impact on Canada of changes in the economic policies of other nations and decide how to counteract the adverse effects these changes may have on provincial and municipal governments, on the level of employment, on the prosperity of businesses, and so on. Once an evaluation of the likely consequences has been made, the government may be forced to alter its existing plans and programmes to take account of these changes. Clearly, governments operate in a constant state of flux and must have the capacity and the inclination to adapt quickly to change.

II

The expansion in the scope and complexity of government activities has been accompanied by a striking growth in government expenditures and in the number of government employees or public servants. (In this essay, the term "public servants" is used to describe government employees at all levels of government, including "civil servants" at the provincial level and "municipal employees" at the local level.) Expressed as a percentage of the Gross National Product (i.e. the total output of final goods and services without allowance for depreciation on capital), government expenditures at all levels of Canadian government have risen from about 31.5 per cent in 1961 to 35.5 per cent in 1970. As shown in Table 1, the relative percentage of total government expenditures spent by the various levels of government has altered substantially during this century.

Analysis of these figures demonstrates that before the outbreak of the Second World War, at which time the federal government took control of the economy to promote the war effort, each of the three levels of government spent about the same amount of money on the provision of goods and services to the public. By the end of the war, federal expenditures of public funds had risen as high as 82 per cent of total government expenditures. During the post-war period, the total amount of money spent by all levels of government has of course increased greatly. The federal percentage of total expenditures, however, has declined steadily while provincial and municipal expenditures have increased. The substantial increase in expenditures by the ten provincial governments combined is a result of the increased demand for services within the constitutional jurisdiction of the provinces, particularly in the areas of education, health, and highways.

Table 1

Year	Federal	Provincial	Municipal
1926	38%	20%	42%
1930	33	25	42
1935	35	34	32
1940	57	22	21
1945	82	9	8
1950	52	26	22
1955	58	20	22
1960	51	25	25
1965	43	31	26
1970	40	35	25

Source: Economic Council of Canada, *Eighth Annual Review,* September 1971, p. 10.

It is understandable that most Canadians are interested in knowing what the various levels of government do with the money they receive from tax-payers rather than what percentage of total expenditures is made by each level of government. To illustrate the primary areas of government spending, Table 2 shows the expenditures of Canadian governments according to the major activity or function performed for the years 1961 and 1967. The average annual rate of growth in each major area of expenditure is also shown. All figures are expressed as a percentage of G.N.P. It is important to observe that the largest increase in government expenditures between 1961 and 1967 was in the areas of education and health and that the average annual rate of growth in these areas is correspondingly high. Expenditures on defence, as a percentage of G.N.P., have declined substantially and the average annual rate of growth is very low.

Table 2

Function	Percentage of G.N.P.		Average Annual Rate of Growth
	1961	1967	1961-1967
Defence	4.2	2.7	1.3
General government	1.5	1.6	10.6
Education	4.5	6.4	15.7
Health	2.6	3.5	14.1
Social assistance	5.3	5.5	9.8
Others	13.4	13.0	8.5

Source: Economic Council of Canada, *Eighth Annual Review,* September 1971, p. 11.

The rapid increase in total government expenditures at all levels of government has been accompanied by a related growth in the number of public servants required to fulfill government responsibilities. In Canada, approximately one out of every six members of the labour force is employed by government. Table 3 shows the growth in the number of public employees at each level of government since the Second World War. As in the case of provincial government expenditures, the number of provincial public servants has increased dramatically.

Table 3

Year	Federal	Provincial	Municipal	Total
1946	116,657	50,041	56,760	223,458
1950	95,120	63,630	53,640	212,390
1955	149,360	103,700	99,850	352,929
1960	186,800	154,943	142,780	484,523
1965	214,859	237,574	196,860	649,293
1970	259,495	378,643	296,220	884,358

Source: Canada Department of National Revenue, *Taxation Statistics,* for 1946, 1950, 1955, 1960, 1965, 1970 (fiscal years).

The projections of the number of public employees required in the future are equally striking. By 1981 the number of government employees in Canada is expected to rise to approximately 1,500,000. This means that the total of public employees will have more than doubled between 1965 and 1981. Furthermore, over 80 per cent of this increase in government employees will be required at the provincial and municipal levels of government.[1]

Related to this growth in the number of government employees is the variety and change in the occupational composition of the public service. Virtually every occupation, trade and skill can be found in the public service. The Royal Commission on Government Organization in Canada (called the Glassco Commission) noted that the occupations in the federal public service range "from actuaries and anthropologists through bee keepers, dry dock riggers, map compilers and pharmacists, to veterinarians and x-ray operators. An element of mystery is created by listing of such intriguing operations as insect sampling,...receivers of wreck,...strippers and layouters."[2] Clearly, a wide variety of job opportunities is available to those who aspire to become Canadian public servants.

The increasingly complex and technical nature of government operations noted earlier has brought about a significant qualitative change in the public service. The percentage of highly educated or highly trained personnel falling into the administrative, professional, scientific, and technical categories now threatens to exceed the percentage of employees in the traditional clerical and operational categories. Indeed, in some provincial governments, the number of employees in the former categories is already greater than 50 per cent of the total employees.[3] This change in the occupational makeup of the public service means that students must not only expect to spend a longer time in school in order to obtain the education necessary for appointment to the public service but must return to school in later years to keep themselves informed about new developments affecting their jobs.

To fulfill the growing responsibilities of government, new administrative units have been created in the form of new departments, new sections of existing departments, and new agencies, boards, and commissions enjoying varying degrees of independence from political (i.e. Cabinet and Parliamentary) control. Among the twenty-six federal government departments today are the Departments of Agriculture, Consumer and Corporate Affairs, External Affairs, Industry, Trade and Commerce, Justice, Labour, National Defence, National Health and Welfare, and National Revenue. Among the government agencies, boards and commissions, of which there are about eighty,

---

[1] J.E. Hodgetts and O.P. Dwivedi, "The Growth of Government Employment in Canada", *Canadian Public Administration,* vol. 12, no. 2 (Summer, 1969), p. 234.

[2] Canada, *Report of the Royal Commission on Government Organization,* vol. 1 (Ottawa: Queen's Printer, 1962-63), p. 21.

[3] J.E. Hodgetts and O.P. Dwivedi, "Growth of Government Employment," pp. 230-33.

are such crown corporations as the Canadian Broadcasting Corporation, the Canadian National Railways, and Air Canada, and such regulatory agencies as the Canadian Radio-Television Commission and the Canadian Transport Commission. The degree of independence from political control which these various agencies enjoy depends largely on the kind of functions they perform and the amount of money they receive from the government. These agencies have such a variety of organizational forms and such a diversity of responsibilities that they cannot be dealt with adequately in this brief essay. The rest of this article, therefore, will focus solely on the regular departments of government. Moreover, discussion will centre on the federal level of government.

III

The enormous expansion of government activities and the accompanying changes in the size and operations of the public services have important implications for the nature of democratic government in Canada. At the beginning of this century, the conduct of governmental responsibilities was much simpler than it is now. Canadians used to be able to assume that their elected representatives usually understood the implications of the laws they passed; that these laws were then implemented or enforced by public servants; and that the regular courts would judge any dispute over the interpretation of these laws and impose any necessary penalties. None of these assumptions are valid for the present operations of Canadian governments.

The subject matter of many laws passed today is very technical (e.g. atomic energy) and very complex (e.g. tax reform). Moreover, the implications of major laws are widespread and their full consequences are unpredictable. As a result of this situation, our elected representatives are obliged to pass laws which are written in very general, and sometimes very vague, language and to delegate to public servants the authority to interpret, implement, and enforce these laws. Thus, government employees—who are appointed, not elected— possess powers both of a legislative and judicial nature. These are powers which have traditionally been exercised by the legislatures and the courts. Just as our elected representatives do not have adequate time or knowledge to enact laws written in specific language and providing for all contingencies, so judges have neither the time to consider all the cases which involve interpretation of the law nor the knowledge required to understand and to interpret correctly laws involving very technical matters. Thus Parliament delegates to public servants the power to pass "regulations" with the force of law, to enforce those regulations, and to impose penalties on persons, groups, or organizations who do not obey the regulations.

Much debate has centred on the issue of whether it is necessary or desirable for public servants to possess such extensive powers. It is now generally agreed, however, that if modern governments are to carry out their enormous responsibilities, much power of a discretionary nature must be granted to public servants. Government activities are too large and too complex for all powers to be exercised by our elected representatives and the courts. The Special Committee of the House of Commons on Statutory Instruments, which reported to Parliament in 1969, furnished solid evidence of the extent to which public servants in Canada possess authority to pass regulations. The Committee found that "four hundred and twenty of the 601 Acts of Parliament examined by the Committee (constituting substantially all of the statutes now in force) provide for delegated legislation".[4]

Perhaps of even greater significance than the public servants' powers of a legislative and judicial nature resulting from delegated authority is their power to influence the very content of laws. Under Canada's parliamentary system of government, the political party with the largest number of elected representatives in Parliament becomes the governing party. The leader of this party becomes the Prime Minister and he chooses the Ministers of his Cabinet from among other Members of Parliament belonging to his party. Cabinet Ministers play a dual role, then, as Members of Parliament on the one hand and Ministers of the Cabinet on the other. Each Cabinet Minister usually heads one of the various government departments. Laws related to the activities of one or more departments are considered by these Ministers and by the Cabinet before they are introduced in Parliament. The complex and technical nature of most laws means that the experience and expertise of public servants is essential for the writing or drafting of proposed laws before they are considered by the Cabinet and by Parliament. Since Ministers do not have as much knowledge as public servants about the subject-matter or the administrative and technical implications of the many laws that are proposed, they must rely heavily on the expert advice of the public servants in their departments. It is still the Ministers' responsibility, of course, to assess the potential *political* implications of proposed laws and to defend these laws in Parliament.

It has been demonstrated that public servants have significant powers to advise elected politicians on government policy and to make regulations affecting the rights and activities of Canadians. It is reasonable to ask, therefore, how we can ensure that public servants do not abuse their powers. Politicians can be thrown out of office at election time if they do not act responsibly. Since public servants are appointed rather than elected, however, they must be controlled in a different manner than politicians. What means, then, are available to ensure the responsible behaviour of public servants?

IV

There is a wide variety of restrictions or constraints on the decisions and actions of public servants. Some of these are *formal controls* exercised over

---

[4]Canada, House of Commons, *Report of the Special Committee on Statutory Instruments,* 3rd Report (Ottawa: Queen's Printer, 1969), p. 4.

public servants by persons or institutions—for example, by a public servant's administrative superior or by the courts. Other limitations on administrative behaviour are better described as *informal influences* in the sense that no person or institution has formal authority to direct the activities of public servants but can influence their activities in an informal way through suggestions and criticisms. Examples of informal influences are the views and comments of a public servant's administrative colleagues or public opinion as expressed through polls or the mass media of communication. It is notable also that some controls or influences on public servants come from *outside* the public service — as in the case of the courts or public opinion; others come from *within* the public service itself — as in the case of orders from an administrative superior or advice from administrative colleagues. There is such a great assortment of controls and influences affecting the responsible behaviour of public servants that it is possible in this brief essay to discuss only the major constraints.

The primary *controls* exercised from *outside* the public service are those of the Prime Minister and his Cabinet, Parliament, and the courts. The principal means by which the Prime Minister and the Cabinet control the activities of public servants is through the determination of government priorities, policies, and programmes. Depending on the need for the service provided by a department and the effectiveness of a department's operations, the Cabinet, chaired by the Prime Minister, can expand or reduce the financial, personnel, and material resources available to that department. The Cabinet can also control public servants working in a government department by rejecting policy proposals emerging from that department or by spurning the administrative and technical advice presented by public servants on a new policy or on the implementation of existing policies. We shall see later that the Cabinet is assisted in these tasks by the Prime Minister's Office, the Privy Council Office, and the Treasury Board.

Parliament controls the activities of public servants in several ways. It enacts the very laws which set out the organization and general responsibilities of government departments. Individual Members of Parliament exercise an important control over public servants by investigating citizens' complaints about poor service or lack of service provided by government departments.

The role of the Opposition parties in Parliament is especially important in that Cabinet Ministers must answer to Parliament for the administration of their departments. One of the means by which the Opposition tries to embarrass the government is by demonstrating to the Canadian public that government programmes are not being administered effectively. The opportunities available for Members of Parliament to comment critically on departmental administration include the daily Question Period, debate on proposed laws, debate on the Speech from the Throne, debate on the budget, debate during the Supply or Opposition days, and so on.

One of the most important Parliamentary controls on administrative activities is the use of committees. Public servants frequently appear before

Parliamentary committees (e.g. Agriculture, External Affairs and National Defence, Justice and Legal Affairs) to provide expert advice on certain subjects or to explain and defend their department's operations. Parliament has the responsibility to help ensure that government departments spend the taxpayers' money honestly and efficiently. Each year, Ministers place before Parliament the Estimates of the amount of money their departments wish to spend on various programmes during the next year. The Estimates of each department are considered in detail by one of the standing committees before being approved by Parliament as a whole. The Auditor General, who is an official responsible to Parliament, reviews the expenditures of government departments to see whether proper financial records have been kept and whether the money has been spent as Parliament intended when it approved the departments' programmes. The Auditor General presents an annual report to Parliament on the results of his investigation and draws attention to any inappropriate or illegal expenditures of public funds. His report is subsequently examined in more detail by the Public Accounts Committee of Parliament. Although this Committee, assisted by the Auditor General, makes recommendations to Parliament as to how public funds could be better spent, the government has tended to ignore these recommendations. The result is that the potential effectiveness of the Auditor General and the Public Accounts Committee as controls over the public service is not realized.

We noted above the necessity for public servants to exercise powers of a judicial nature largely because of the technical and complex character of many laws and the vast number of cases to be considered. It is important to note that some "judicial" decisions made by public servants or by administrative tribunals in a particular department may be appealed to other persons or bodies at a higher level in the department, including the Minister himself. In most cases, however, a citizen does not have the right to appeal to the regular courts against a decision made by a public servant, by an administrative tribunal, by an appeal board within the department, or by the Minister. Thus, the majority of decisions taken within government departments are final.

Moreover, the courts will not review a discretionary judgement of a public servant, even if that judgement is clearly a bad one, as long as the public servant has exercised his discretion within the bounds of authority delegated to him. The courts will quash an administrative decision, however, if the public servant acts outside the law by exceeding his authority. In addition, the courts may review a public servant's decision if the administrative procedure followed in reaching the decision conflicts with the principles of "natural justice", e.g. if the citizen did not have the opportunity to present his side of the case. Generally speaking, however, the courts do not provide very effective safeguards against possible abuse of administrative power.

Limitations on the actions of public servants are imposed from within the public service itself. Although Cabinet Ministers exercise external controls on Public servants when acting as Members of the Cabinet, they also impose internal controls as the heads of government departments The relationship between the Minister as the *political* head of the department and the Deputy Minister as the *administrative* head is very close. The Deputy Minister, as the leading public servant in his department, advises the Minister on the formation and implementation of policy but must abide by the Minister's decision as to what should be done. Starting with the Minister and the Deputy Minister, who stand at the top of the department, there is a chain of command or line of authority to the bottom of the department. The department has a hierarchical or pyramidal shape with each person accountable for his actions and decisions to a superior and having authority over a number of subordinates.

As noted earlier, the Prime Minister and Cabinet are assisted in their control of public servants by the Prime Minister's Office, the Privy Council Office, and the Treasury Board Secretariat. The Prime Minister's Office is composed of officials appointed by and responsible to the Prime Minister. These political advisers provide the Prime Minister and the Cabinet with an alternative source of policy advice to the public servants and point out the *political* implications of government action as opposed to the strictly administrative and technical advice provided by public servants.

The Privy Council Office and the Treasury Board Secretariat, by way of contrast, are composed of public servants appointed on the basis of merit. The Privy Council Office, which works closely with the Prime Minister's Office, is concerned primarily with coordinating the policy suggestions emerging from government departments and providing staff assistance to the Cabinet and the Cabinet committees. The Treasury Board, made up of six Ministers headed by the President of the Treasury Board, is a Committee of Cabinet and is assisted by a Secretariat of public servants. The responsibilities of the Treasury Board are very broad but its major functions are to promote administrative integrity and efficiency and to review the expenditure plans and programmes of the government departments. The Treasury Board, through its Secretariat, exercises very substantial control and influence over the financial, managerial, and personnel operations of departments.

Another important agency of government which controls the activities of public servants is the Public Service Commission. The Commission's primary responsibility is the staffing of the public service. It ensures that appointments to the public service are made so far as possible on the basis of the merit of the candidates rather than on such other bases as friendship or support for the party in power. The Commission is also involved in training and development programmes for government employees, including an extensive language-training programme to promote bilingualism in the public service.

The impact on administrative responsibility of *influences* as opposed to *controls* is difficult to measure because influences on administrative action are of an informal nature. No formal or legal sanctions are imposed on public servants. Among the informal influences affecting the behaviour of officials from *within* the public service are the tradition of political neutrality, standards of ethical conduct, and desire for the respect of one's colleagues. Significant influences from *outside* the public service include "lobbying" by pressure groups, public opinion, and the media of mass communication.

In carrying out their activities, "responsible" public servants are expected to promote the "public interest" or the "general welfare." Admittedly, it is very difficult to discover exactly what the public interest is in any situation, but public servants have a duty to serve the general welfare rather than their personal interests or the narrow, selfish interests of particular individuals or groups. The ideal situation for the public servant is one where his perception of the public interest coincides with most of the various controls and influences affecting his decision.

V

Despite the variety of constraints on administrative action outlined above, many people believe that even more safeguards against possible administrative abuse are necessary to protect the rights of Canadian citizens. The most popular of the numerous institutional and procedural safeguards that have been suggested is the Ombudsman. A large number of countries around the world have adopted the institution to help deal with the problem of ensuring citizens' rights in the face of a rapidly growing public service. An Ombudsman has now been appointed in six of the ten Canadian provinces (Alberta, New Brunswick, Quebec, Manitoba, Nova Scotia and Newfoundland).

The major function of an Ombudsman is to investigate complaints of citizens about improper, illegal, unfair, or discriminatory administrative treatment. He usually has access to the government documents necessary to inquire into citizens' grievances. If he believes that certain complaints are justified, he will request the public servants involved to remedy the mistakes that have been made. The Ombudsman is responsible to the legislature and presents an annual report to the legislature describing the cases that have been brought to his attention and the progress he has made in redressing any administrative wrongs that have been committed. Clearly, the Ombudsman can serve a very useful purpose in controlling and influencing administrative action as well as demonstrating the government's concern for the rights of Canadian citizens.

In conclusion, it is important to note that despite the many constraints on public servants that now exist or could be devised, public servants will continue to possess a large measure of discretionary power. The success of Canadian governments in preventing misuse of administrative powers depends to a large extent on the quality and the conscience of the individual public servants. If there is a high level of morality and a firm commitment to democratic principles among the Canadian population generally, public servants will carry over these attitudes into the administrative sphere. There will then be less need for popular vigilance and for new safeguards to guarantee the responsible conduct of Canada's public servants.

2

Identity, Pedagogy and Public Administration: the Canadian Experience*

W.D. Kenneth Kernaghan

The impact of external forces on domestic governmental institutions and processes is manifest in British and American influences on public administration in Canada. Indeed, it is customary to explain the evolution of Canadian public administration as an adaptation of selected elements of the British and American administrative systems to the unique political, social, economic and physical environment of Canada. In recent years, a broader range of influences — notably from France and Sweden — has had substantial impact on the discussion of administrative reform in Canada. This change is in part a consequence of the emphasis of the comparative public administration movement on cross-national analysis of public bureaucracies. It is primarily the result, however, of the sheer necessity for all modern governments to seek new structural and procedural devices to cope with the continually accelerating rate of change and the increasing burden of responsibilities. At the same time as this broader spectrum of external influences on domestic analysis of administrative reform has developed, the relative influence of the British administrative model has diminished and the American model has clearly emerged as the predominant external influence on Canadian public administration.

What is particularly relevant in this context is that the influence of the United States on the *study* of public administration in Canada has always been, and continues to be, greater than on administrative structures and processes. Political scientists and other scholars in Canada have relied heavily on intellectual ferment in the United States for theoretical developments affecting the study of public administration. This dependent status is regrettable in that understanding of Canadian public administration has been retarded. The absence of theories of Canadian public administration at either the macro or micro level inhibits also the full understanding of the Canadian political system which rests in part on knowledge of the role of the bureaucracy in the policy process. The literature on public administration in the United States often strikes a discordant

*W.D. Kenneth Kernaghan, "Identity, Pedagogy and Public Administration: the Canadian Experience", *Public Administration (Australia),* vol. 32, no. 1 (March, 1973). Reprinted and abridged by permission of author and publisher.

rather than a responsive note in Canada because much of this literature is inapplicable or irrelevant to Canada's unique political and administrative system.

Research on Canadian Public Administration

The slow development of the study of public administration in Canada and the consequent dearth of research and writing in this field has obliged Canadians to rely primarily on American publications for teaching purposes. The absence of Canadian textbooks may be regrettable but the scholarly foundation of specialized studies on which adequate texts must be based has not yet been laid. Before 1960, very few books on Canadian public administration were published. The only general works were *The Civil Service of Canada*[1] and *The Canadian Bureaucracy.*[2] Notable studies of a more specialized nature included *Financing Canadian Government,*[3] *Pioneer Public Service*[4] and *Public Ownership and Accountability.*[5] Since 1960, three books of readings—*Canadian Public Administration,*[6] *Public Administration in Canada*[7] and *Bureaucracy in Canadian Government*[8] have been used as textbooks or as supplements to American texts. Another book, entitled *Public Administration,*[9] is a highly practical, descriptive-institutional work which utilizes Canadian, British and American illustrations and is aimed at the pre-university level. *The Structures of Policy Making In Canada,*[10] a book of essays focusing on executive-bureaucratic interaction in the policy process, signals greatly increased Canadian interest in public policy-making.

A number of recently published works examine in a policy context the structures and operations of particular government departments and agencies. These studies include the first two volumes in the Canadian Public Administration Series sponsored by the Institute of Public Administration, namely, *Canada and Immigration: Public Policy and Public Concern,*[11] and *The Biography of an Institution: The Civil Service Commission, 1908-1967.*[12]

---

[1] R. MacGregor Dawson (Toronto: Oxford University Press, 1929).

[2] R. Taylor Cole (Durham: Duke University Press, 1949).

[3] A.E. Buck (Chicago: Public Administration Service, 1949).

[4] J.E. Hodgetts (Toronto: University of Toronto Press, 1956).

[5] L. Musolf (Cambridge: Harvard University Press, 1959).

[6] J.E. Hodgetts and D.C. Corbett, eds. (Toronto: The Macmillan Co., 1960).

[7] W.D.K. Kernaghan and A.M. Willms, eds., 2nd ed. (Toronto: Methuen Publications, 1971).

[8] W.D.K. Kernaghan, ed., 2nd ed. (Toronto: Methuen Publications, 1973).

[9] J.S. Hodgson (Toronto: McGraw-Hill, 1969).

[10] G. Bruce Doern and Peter Aucoin, eds. (Toronto: The Macmillan Co., 1971).

[11] Freda Hawkins (Montreal: McGill-Queen's University Press, 1972).

[12] J.E. Hodgetts et al. (Montreal: McGill-Queen's University Press, 1972).

Other similar studies are *Science and Politics in Canada*[13] and *Policy, Politics and the Treasury Board in Canadian Government*.[14] The major periodical literature is found in two quarterly journals — *Canadian Public Administration* published since 1958 by the Institute of Public Administration, and *Optimum: A Forum for Management* published since 1970 by the Bureau of Management Consulting of the Department of Supply and Services. Finally, the reports and research studies of such royal commissions as those on *Government Organization,* on *Bilingualism and Biculturalism* and on *Security*[15] are a rich source of information and analysis on the structures and processes of Canadian public administration. Moreover, the vastly increased number of task forces appointed in recent years serve a similar purpose.[16]

Patterns of Organization

The so-called "crisis of identity" facing public administration is primarily the consequence of two distinct and largely countervailing developments. The first is the historical evolution of public administration under the parentage of *political science.* The second is the continuously expanding dimensions of the study and practice of public administration and the increasingly *interdisciplinary* approach to its study and teaching. The critical issue bearing upon the status of public administration is whether it should properly be considered a subdiscipline of political science or simply a part of the broader field of administration in general.

The opposing positions on the appropriate theoretical base for the organization of studies in public administration have been succinctly stated by Professors William Robson in Britain and Lynton Caldwell in the United States. Robson asserted that

any tendency for public administration to break away from the parent discipline must ultimately weaken both political science as a whole and the study of public administration. It will weaken political science by removing the part of it which brings the teacher into closest relationship with the practical business of government. It will weaken the study of public administration by divorcing it from political theory and the principles of government which underlie political and administrative institutions.[17]

---

[13]G. Bruce Doern (Montreal: McGill-Queen's University Press, 1972).

[14]W.L. White and J.C. Strick (Don Mills: Science Research Associates (Canada) Ltd., 1970).

[15]Canada, *Royal Commission on Government Organization* (Glassco Commission), 5 volumes (Ottawa: Queen's Printer, 1962-63); *Royal Commission on Bilingualism and Biculturalism,* especially Book 3A, *The Federal Administration* (Ottawa: Queen's Printer, 1969); and *Royal Commission on Security (Abridged)* (Ottawa: Queen's Printer, 1969).

[16]See, for example, Canada, *To Know and Be Known, Report of the Task Force on Government Information* (Ottawa: Queen's Printer, 1969), and *Canadian Agriculture in the Seventies, Report of the Task Force on Agriculture* (Ottawa: Queen's Printer, 1970).

[17]William Robson, *The University Teaching of Social Sciences: Political Science* (UNESCO, 1954), p. 47.

More recently, however, Caldwell argued that

the greatest promise for study of public administration in the universities will be in association with the growth of an integrative, organizing, generic concept of administration. From the nucleus of general administrative studies, it may be possible to interrelate more meaningfully the study of administration to the various disciplines and professions. In the modern world, no clear line separates administration in government from the administrative processes of the total society. The organization of administrative studies in the university must ultimately correspond to this reality.[18]

Both approaches are persuasive when viewed from different theoretical perspectives and in different national settings.

Public Administration as Administration

Those who view public administration as a generic process contend that the study of administration may be most fruitfully pursued by dividing the general field into public, business, hospital, educational, police, or other types of administration. To proponents of this view, the similarities between these various forms of administration are greater than their differences. This belief has led to the establishment of "professional" schools or faculties of administrative studies.

It appears also that a growing number of scholars are convinced that intellectual developments are moving inexorably in the direction of a rigorous *discipline* of administrative studies. This new discipline will be interdisciplinary and integrative in its subject content and teaching approach. Its programme will be characterized by a flowing together for mutual enrichment of the present "academic" and "professional" streams in administrative studies. Discussion of the distinctive nature of "public" administration will be founded on a solid base of knowledge about the concepts and techniques of administration generally. All students, regardless of the type of administration in which they are primarily interested, e.g. public, business, educational, will normally be required to take a group of "core subjects" in administration. The "core subjects" will normally include organizational behaviour, accounting, micro-economics, macro-economics and quantitative methods. Specialization in a particular type or problem of administration will be founded on this base of common knowledge.

Canadian universities have established faculties or schools of public administration which grant distinct degrees in public administration and provide specialized training for public service careers. At both the graduate and undergraduate levels, the programmes offered are integrative and interdisciplinary but vary greatly in content and purpose. Some are "professional" in orientation; others stress the "academic" approach. Some organize their programmes around the concept of public policy; others simply offer

---

[18] Lynton Caldwell, "Public Administration and the Universities: a Half Century of Development," *Public Administration Review,* vol. 25 (March, 1965), p. 60.

courses on various aspects of public policy. In several universities, mid-career programmes for administrative practitioners are an integral part of the course of study.

Clearly, a number of alternative structural arrangements for the teaching of public administration are possible — and available. The programmes lead to one- or two-year M.A. degrees, to B.A. degrees with Honours in public administration, to B.A. degrees in Administration with some subject emphasis on "public" administration, and to special certificates in public administration. One of the most difficult problems of designing public administration programmes at the undergraduate level is reconciling the desire for a high degree of specialization with the widely expressed need for a liberal education.

A different kind of education is required for teachers and scholars than for aspiring and practicing civil servants. A teacher of public administration holding a Ph.D. degree will likely continue to receive a substantial portion of his education in political science supplemented by courses in economics, sociology, psychology and research methods, and by some practical experience in the civil service. The graduate training of civil servants, however, may best be carried out in a school or faculty organized and staffed specifically for this purpose. Given the existing high demand for teachers of public administration and the projected demand for public employees at all levels of Canadian government during the next decade, there is an easily demonstrable need for both kinds of programmes.

Public Administration as Political Science

The emergence of alternative patterns of organization for the teaching of public administration has weakened the already tenuous links between public administration and political science. As these organizational bonds become more fragile, it is important to evaluate the pedagogical and intellectual implications of treating public administration as a sub-field of political science.

The political scientist teaching public administration, whether at the graduate or undergraduate level, is often suspect in the eyes of both his academic colleagues and practicing administrators. To his colleagues, he is too practically oriented in teaching and too policy oriented in research. To practitioners, he is too academically oriented and of little assistance in resolving policy issues. He has been aptly described as "the academic's practical man and the public administrator's academic."[19]

The ignorance of many political scientists about the content and purpose of the study of public administration is unfortunate. If public administration is to live comfortably as a subdiscipline of political science, even for teaching purposes, it is essential that those political scientists *not* teaching public ad-

---

[19] Dwight Waldo, "Public Administration", *The Journal of Politics,* vol. 30, no. 2 (May, 1968), p. 445.

ministration try to learn something about the field. It is a continuing source of amazement and dismay that some political scientists teaching the government and politics of particular nation-states make little or no reference to administrative structures or to the role of bureaucrats in the political system.

The major approaches to the study of the broad range of subjects in public administration may be classed as managerial, political and socio-psychological. The "politics" of public administration forms the core of most introductory courses in the field (i.e. focus on the interaction in a political system between administrators and other participants, both governmental and non-governmental, concerned with the determination of government objectives). The content of the "traditional" course supplements this "political" approach with examination of managerial functions whereas more recent emphasis in course design is on organization theory. The truly imaginative and knowledgeable teacher strives to utilize the contributions of all three approaches.

There are sound theoretical grounds for teaching public administration as part of political science. Knowledge of the administrative structures of government and of the political and legal environment in which the public administrator works is essential to understanding of the political system. In addition, the bureaucracy plays a central role on the output side of the political system through its active involvement in the making, enforcement and adjudication of laws and regulations. Less evident, but extremely significant, intellectual bonds between public administration and political science lie in their shared concern for inquiry into such key theoretical concepts as responsibility, authority and the public interest. Political theorists who fail to explore the meaning of these themes in the particular milieu of public administration omit a perspective essential to adequate analysis.[20] All these factors attest to the status of public administration as an integral part of the study of political science.

The most productive approach for political scientists may be to treat public administration as a *subdiscipline* both on the basis of existing organizational patterns and of theoretical links between public administration and political science. It seems probable also that theoretical developments in *public* administration are more likely to issue from the research efforts of political scientists than other disciplinary representatives. Political scientists may resolve the identity crisis, at least to their own satisfaction, by ceasing to agonize over the vast scope of public administration and by seeking agreement on achievements made toward a general theory of public administration.

---

[20] Glendon Schubert, for example, has acknowledged the valuable contributions of senior federal administrators in the United States in reformulating his thinking "about some aspects of the subject" of public-interest theory. *The Public Interest* (Glencoe, Illinois: The Free Press, 1960), p. ix.

Conclusions

Despite these organizational, pedagogical and theoretical problems, the future of public administrative studies in contemporary democratic states will be an exciting and challenging one. Civil servants participate actively in policy formulation and execution; government responsibilities in old and new policy fields grow steadily; and societal and technological change is increasingly turbulent and rapid. These developments will ensure a high demand for administrative practitioners, for teachers of public administration and for research to support and explain their activities. The future emphasis in education for public administration will be increasingly on the training of public officials for various levels of government. This trend will be accompanied by the continuing establishment of public administration programmes, whether "academically" or "professionally" oriented, on an interdisciplinary basis. Whatever success schools or faculties of public administration enjoy in promoting a professional education through more practically-oriented teaching, a large number of universities will continue to offer graduate and undergraduate programmes in public administration along traditional academic lines.

That even these "traditional" programmes will be more interdisciplinary in course content and interdepartmental in organization has significant implications for relations between public administration and political science. The interdepartmental programmes will include courses taught by faculty members attached to the established academic departments of Political Science, Economics, Sociology, Psychology and others. Through the development of interdepartmental cooperation in public administrative studies at both the graduate and undergraduate levels, students may benefit from a greater choice of courses in public administration within a coherent programme. The scope of public administration is now so broad and its subject matter so heterogeneous that it cannot realistically be considered *solely* as a subdiscipline of political science. It is clear that appropriate settings for education in public administration exist outside the structural framework of political science departments and that a variety of organizational patterns has evolved. Each of these forms of organization serves a different, but still important, purpose. Moreover, a diversity of arrangements for public administrative studies in Canada is essential to take account of the fact that most university courses in public administration are now taught within political science departments.

Readings

General

Dimock, M.E. and G.M. Dimock. *Public Administration.* 4th ed. New York: Holt, Rinehart and Winston, 1969.

Morstein Marx, F., ed. *Elements of Public Administration.* Englewood Cliffs, N.J.: Prentice-Hall, 1965.

Nigro, Felix A. *Modern Public Administration.* 2nd ed. New York: Harper and Row, 1970.

Pfiffner, J.M. and R. V. Presthus. *Public Administration.* 5th ed. New York: The Ronald Press Company, 1967.

Rowat, Donald C., ed. *Basic Issues in Public Administration.* New York: The Macmillan Company, 1961.

Sharkansky, Ira. *Public Administration.* 2nd ed. Chicago: Markham Publishing Company, 1972.

Simon, Herbert A., D. W. Smithburg, and V. A. Thompson. *Public Administration,* New York: Alfred A. Knopf, 1950.

Canadian

Brownstone, Meyer. "The Canadian System of Government in the Face of Modern Demands." *Canadian Public Administration,* vol. 11, no. 4 (Winter, 1968), pp. 428-39.

Cole, Taylor. *The Canadian Bureaucracy, 1939-1947.* Durham, N.C.: Duke University Press, 1949.

Cahoon, Allan R. "Towards a New Public Administration." *Optimum,* vol. 3, no. 1 (1972), pp. 19-27.

Carson, J.J. "The Changing Scope of the Public Servant." *Canadian Public Administration,* vol. 11, no. 4 (Winter, 1968), pp. 407-13.

Deutsch, J.J. "The Public Service in a Changing Society." *Canadian Public Administration,* vol. 11, no. 1 (Spring, 1968), pp. 1-8.

Gow, Donald. "Public Administration Training: For Whom? For What?" *Optimum,* vol. 1, no. 3 (1970), pp. 22-33.

Gow, James Iain, ed. *Administration publique québécoise.* Montreal: Librairie Beauchemin Limitée, 1970.

Hodgson, J.S. *Public Administration.* Toronto: McGraw-Hill, 1969.

Hodgetts, J.E. "Challenge and Response: A Restrospective View of the Public Service." *Canadian Public Administration,* vol. 7, no. 4 (December, 1964), pp. 409-21.

Hodgetts, J.E. *Pioneer Public Service: An Administrative History of the United Canadas, 1841-1867.* Toronto: University of Toronto Press, 1955.

Hodgetts, J.E. and D. C. Corbett, eds. *Canadian Public Administration: A Book of Readings.* Toronto: The Macmillan Company of Canada, 1960.

Johnson, A. W. "Education and the Development of Senior Executives." *Canadian Public Administration,* vol. 15, no. 4 (Winter, 1972), pp. 539-57.

Kernaghan, W.D.K. "An Overview of Public Administration in Canada Today." *Canadian Public Administration,* vol. 11, no. 3 (Fall, 1968), pp. 291-308.

Kernaghan, W.D.K. and A. M. Willms, eds. *Public Administration in Canada: Selected Readings.* 2nd ed. Toronto: Methuen Publications, 1971.

Parenteau, Roland. "Une nouvelle approche dans la formation des administrateurs publics: l'Ecole nationale d'administration publique." *Canadian Public Administration,* vol. 15, no. 3 (Fall, 1972), pp. 465-80.

Porter, John. *The Vertical Mosaic: An Analysis of Social Class and Power in Canada.* Chapter 14. Toronto: University of Toronto Press, 1965.

Rowat, Donald C. "The Study of Public Administration in Canada." *Public Administration (U.K.),* vol. 40 (Autumn, 1962), pp. 319-24.

Santos, C.R. "Public Administration: The Gap Between Theory and Practice." *Optimum,* vol. 2, no. 2 (1971), pp. 40-47.

Chapter Two

Organization,
Personnel and
Finance

During the past decade, revolutionary changes in the internal management of
the federal public service have resulted primarily from the implementation of the recommendations of the Royal Commission on Government
Organization (The Glassco Commission). Indeed, the pace of innovation has
been so rapid that some public servants have complained that they are devot-
ing more effort to introducing administrative reforms than serving the public.
Particularly notable changes have occurred in the areas of organization,
personnel and finance which are examined in this chapter. Important, related
— and controversial — developments in federal-provincial administrative
relations, bilingualism and biculturalism, and collective bargaining are discussed in Chapter Six.

The first two articles, by A.M. Willms, describe the executive functions
of Cabinet ministers, the organization of government departments, and the
functions and diversity of crown agencies. R.H. Dowdell sets personnel
management in its political context and touches on such significant personnel
matters as merit systems, career planning and training. Finally, H.R. Balls
provides a succinct but comprehensive summary of financial administration
in Canada, including an explanation of the budgetary process.

3

The Executive and the Departmental Structure*

A. M. Willms

The Executive

Cabinet ministers in Canada bear extremely heavy responsibilities both as members of Parliament and as the top executives of government departments. Although the legislative and executive roles of ministers overlap, attention will be focussed here on their executive functions as members of the Cabinet and heads of administrative departments.

The executive tasks of ministers have been well stated by the Glassco Commission:

> ... ministers need not be administrative experts; on the contrary, it is desirable save in the stress of emergencies, that they do not become deeply involved in the administrative process. As members of the Cabinet, their principal obligation is to reflect and give effect to the collective point of view — drawing together the public interests, attitudes and aspirations that find expression in the political process, and, by reconciling these, providing the basis for an essential unity of government in policy and action. As heads of departments, it is the task of ministers to define the ends to be pursued, and to instill their own sense of purpose and of urgency in the permanent officials.[1]

For each government department there is a Cabinet minister who takes full responsibility for its actions and who is credited with its achievements. Each minister is responsible to Parliament for the operation of his department and by convention the act of every public servant in the department is regarded as the act of the minister. The extent to which a minister can in fact be held accountable for the maladministration of his departmental subordinates is not clear. In practice, a minister's survival under such circumstances depends largely on his influence within his party and whether the party feels it can face criticism of its administration without being defeated in Parliament or at the next election.

The Canadian Cabinet tends to be excessively large in membership because the Prime Minister traditionally appoints ministers to meet the demands for representation of provinces and regions and of ethnic, linguistic, and religious groups. Clearly, the Prime Minister must take account of such a crucial political consideration despite possible adverse effects on the

---

* A.M. Willms, "Organization in Canadian Government Administration", unpublished manual (Ottawa: Carleton University, 1965). Revised and abridged by the editor.
[1] *Royal Commission on Government Organization*, vol. 5 (Ottawa: Queen's Printer, 1963), p. 33.

fulfillment of administrative needs. Canada now has twenty-five federal departments and about four times as many agencies. The number and diversity of these administrative units creates a span of control that is far too wide for a Cabinet which has onerous political and constitutional responsibilities. The Glassco Commission, however, recognized the primacy of political factors over administrative interests in organizing the executive structure of government.

Above all, the organization of government, no less than the policies it pursues, must reflect the order of importance, in the minds of the public, of the problems requiring attention. Unless there is, in rough form, this correlation between the content of ministerial posts and the degree of public concern, government policy and action will almost certainly fail to respond adequately to public wants.[2]

Indeed, new departments or agencies may have to be established to emphasize or point up a new government policy. It may not be sufficient merely to enunciate new functions and allot these to an existing department or agency. To give these government activities prominence in the public mind another administrative unit may have to be created. The establishment of Central Mortgage and Housing Corporation immediately after the war and of the Department of Consumer and Corporate Affairs in 1967 are striking examples of this need. Since it is very difficult to dissolve a governmental unit once it has been set up, the number of units tends to increase.

A good case can be made on administrative-managerial grounds for fewer, more uniform, and necessarily larger administrative units. The following comments pertain specifically to departments although they are generally applicable to government agencies also. The overhead cost for adequate departmental services in small units may be disproportionately large, and the provision of such services as organization and methods or research and development may not be warranted. In addition, the existence of larger departments permits much more coherent government planning. Central control agencies such as the Treasury Board and the Public Service Commission can more readily stay out of planning when the allocation of scarce resources can be thrashed out in a few large departments. For example, if all the labour functions, including unemployment insurance, were centred in one department, the Treasury Board would be less concerned with the proportion of funds that should go to each of the various governmental units in the labour field. Larger departments also provide a wider field of training, development and advancement for capable junior and intermediate staff. The advantages of specialization can best be realized in larger departments, whether in the line functions, the staff functions, or the departmental services. A substantial measure of decentralization is almost inevitable in larger departments and with fewer, but more comprehensive field offices, the government can expect

---

[2] *Royal Commission on Government Organization,* pp. 41-42.

greater effectiveness with smaller overhead costs. Moreover, in a federal state many government activities require consultation and coordination between provincial and federal administrators; fewer and larger departments would make such cooperation easier.

There are, however, persuasive arguments for a larger number of smaller departments. Individual ministers and deputy ministers can handle a small department more effectively than a large department. This is not so much a factor of size in manpower or budget as of political sensitivity and diversity of functions. The more sensitive the departmental functions in the political-social-economic atmosphere of the day, the more care must be given to policy decisions and the more skill must be employed in representing the department to the Cabinet, Parliament and the public. The more diverse the functions, the more overall policies must be coordinated by the man who must answer to Parliament for their implementation.

Instead of decreasing the size of any department, perhaps the functions of government could be redistributed so that similar functions would come under one responsibility and the diversity of some of the larger departments would be decreased. Such a reallocation could actually reduce the number of departments.

Departmental Structure

In general, the structure of departments resembles the normal scalar pyramid of private or corporate enterprise. At the top is the deputy minister who is the administrative head of the department and at the bottom are the numerous employees who actually carry out most of the functions of the department. In between are the various levels of supervision, management and specialization which make up the pyramidal structure. There is some uniformity in the terminology used to describe departmental organization at or near the pyramid's peak. The deputy minister or deputy head is at the pinnacle; below him there are assistant deputy ministers, or in a few instances, associate deputy ministers. Below the assistant deputy minister in the departmental pyramid are the branch heads who are usually called Directors or Directors-General. The branches are often further subdivided into divisions with Directors or Chiefs in charge. The divisions are subdivided in turn into what may be called sections, units, groups, services, staff, offices, or detachments and the head of each may carry any one of a great variety of titles.

The deputy minister often has a staff to assist him in his management of the department and he may also retain direct control of one or several of the branches or of the administrative services. Sometimes the deputy minister has a government agency reporting to him. Thus the Deputy Minister of Agriculture has the Agricultural Stabilization Board and the Board of Grain Commissioners reporting to him. The span of control of a deputy minister may cover anywhere from two or three to twelve or more subordinates. Most departments have only two or three assistant deputy ministers but as the size of the departments increases this number will grow.

The planning and organization of an individual department's internal structure requires a different approach from that which is taken in dividing up the functions of government between departments and agencies. The different approaches reflect the different objectives involved. In the division of the total functions of government among administrative units, the primary aim is to allot functions to a structure that satisfies political and public needs. Although the aim of the internal organization of a department or agency is to carry out the assigned functions as efficiently and effectively as possible, the minister's political and constitutional role remains an important determinant of the final structure. An organization plan should

1. Recognize the division of powers between the federal and provincial governments; in sensitive areas of jurisdiction even the appearance of federal overlapping into provincial fields must be avoided unless government policy on the subject is clear.

2. Recognize that the government exists to serve the people; recommendations that are administratively sound must also be acceptable to the segment of the population the agency has been set up to serve. In field organizations, in particular, it is sometimes necessary to modify organization principles to meet such a situation and to provide for local requirements.

3. Recognize that the minister concerned is one member of the Cabinet and that the functions of the agency, including the funds necessary for carrying them out, are often subject to balancing mechanisms within the Cabinet which supersede purely administrative considerations. Recommendations which propose the extension of an agency's functions into areas where other agencies have an interest, for instance, should be made only after the most careful exploration with the agencies concerned.[3]

In planning the department's structure, an initial decision must be made as to whether the parts of the department will be organized according to the criteria of purpose, process, clientele, or area. In the past, the factor of purpose (or function) has probably been given too much prominence in the building of branches, divisions and sections of departments. It is unwise to assume that if purpose is used to allocate the job to the department that it can also be used consistently in designing the whole departmental structure. It is often quite undesirable to emphasize the purpose factor within the department because

1. Design of departmental branches or divisions by purpose often results in too much emphasis in each branch or division on a small part of the department's overall functions; there may be too much concern for the parts and not enough for the final product.

2. Subdivision by purpose leaves little scope for competition between units which is an effective form of setting work standards and motivating units and employees.

---

[3] Civil Service Commission, *The Analysis of Organization in the Government of Canada* (Ottawa: Queen's Printer, 1964), pp. 13-14.

3. Specialization by purpose can lead to overspecialization with attendant difficulties in effective employee development.

There probably isn't a department or an agency that does not use all four organization factors in one way or another. It is the manager's responsibility to choose the factor or factors applicable and to decide to what extent each is necessary. In this decision consistency appears to have little virtue and the manager may combine the use of several or all of the factors as circumstances dictate.

4

Crown Agencies*

A.M. Willms

In the British political tradition Cabinet ministers take complete responsibility for the actions of government departments, but a great part of government administration is carried out by non-departmental units called agencies which have varying amounts of ministerial surveillance.

 Like many other governments the Canadian federal government has a wide range in the types of administrative units it uses to put its objectives and policies into practice. The Financial Administration Act of 1951, with subsequent amendments, divides these as follows:

Government departments 25
Departmental corporations 14
Agency corporations 16
Proprietary corporations 15
Designated as departments for purposes of this Act .... 46[1]

The Act classifies government units for the purpose of clarifying their budgetary relations with the Treasury Board and with Parliament, and it uses both financial practices and agency functions to effect the classification. The definitions which result leave a lot of gaps and a great deal of overlapping; neither the definition nor the classification is satisfactory for purposes other

*W.D.K. Kernaghan and A.M. Willms, eds., *Public Administration in Canada*, 2nd ed. (Toronto: Methuen Publications, 1971), pp. 102-109.
[1]Financial Administration Act, R.S. 1970, c. 116, schedules A, B, C and D.

than those of the Act. For instance, in the last category it leaves in one catch-all-class the commissions, royal commissions, boards, the Auditor General, the Chief Electoral Officer, the Privy Council Office, the National Library, and many others varying in structure, functions, methods and in almost every administrative feature. Nor is the list which the act presents exhaustive. It lists more than 100 units; the number varies from year to year; but this is not complete. It does not name agencies whose finances are regulated entirely by the creating statute such as the Bank of Canada, the Canadian Wheat Board or the Board of Grain Commissioners. Nor does it include those agencies which for budget purposes are closely affiliated to a government department such as the Dominion Bureau of Statistics, the Agricultural Prices Support Board or the Defence Research Board, or those agencies which have provincial as well as federal representation such as the Eastern Rockies Forest Conservation Board and the Canadian Council of Resource Ministers.

There are a great number of types of units in the governmental administrative net with a wide range of functions, of organization and of procedures, and no classification that is useful for purposes of discussion and study has been devised. But it is possible to distinguish departments from the assortment of corporations, boards, commissions and others which are generally labelled *agencies*. Some of the more obvious differences are:

1. Departments are answerable directly to a Cabinet minister and that minister takes responsibility for their actions. Agencies usually have a minister designated to them through whom they report to Parliament but the degree of supervision and accountability varies and is much smaller than that with departments. When questioned in Parliament on the activities or policies of an agency the minister who reports for that agency will frequently disclaim responsibility: "This is a matter involving an independent agency and I can answer only in so far as the agency sees fit to provide me with the information".[2]

2. Departments are all subject to the estimates system of budgeting, that is, revenues coming from the Crown must be spent exactly as directed by Parliament and Treasury Board, and receipts must be returned to the Receiver-General. Agencies vary widely in their budget practices.

3. The personnel of departments are generally recruited by the Public Service Commission and their promotion and transfer is closely supervised by the Commission. Only a few of the agencies recruit through the Public Service Commission. Generally speaking they are responsible for their own personnel matters.

4. Departments have deputy ministers as the administrative heads while agencies vary widely in the nature of their management. Some have boards of directors, others have chairmen, commissioners, or directors.

---

[2] J.E. Hodgetts and D.C. Corbett, eds., *Canadian Public Administration* (Toronto: Macmillan Company of Canada Limited, 1960), p. 199.

It is also commonly accepted that a short-term purpose is to be served by an agency while the long-term, continuing functions more often rate the creation of a department. Thus the numerous wartime enterprises of the government took the form of agencies while the long-term function of caring for veterans was incorporated in a department. Royal commissions are a group that is obviously set up on an ad hoc basis. But many agencies are set up for the long-term, such as the CNR and the CBC, and there have been departments such as Soldiers Civil Reestablishment created for a short-term function. It is also suggested that departments are set up to carry out functions that would not normally be tackled by private enterprise while agencies frequently compete with private business. This has a grain of truth but once again there are a number of exceptions; the Department of Public Works, the Department of Industry, Trade and Commerce, and other departments carry on activities commonly found in private business.

We have seen that departments can be distinguished from the agencies. The departments are a group that has some semblance of uniformity in its ranks, but this cannot be said of the agencies. They are just about as diverse as can be, but even so we can discern a few classes among them. One type of agency that has a title and has been treated as a genre is the Crown Corporation. This group is described fully in the Glassco Commission *Report*[3] and its members are readily distinguishable because they are identified in the Financial Administration Act. The Crown Corporation can be defined as an institution operating a service of an economic or social character on behalf of the government, but it possesses most of the legal and commercial attributes of private enterprise. Though largely autonomous in management it is still responsible to the public and subject to some direction by the government.[4]

Crown corporations are created in two ways — by special statute or by incorporation by order-in-council under the Companies Act. There are about a dozen of the latter and they form another distinguishable group known as Crown companies and carry the commercial designation "Limited" in their name. This little flourish is of course meaningless.

(The corporate device)...provides a means by which a group of individuals, the shareholders, can band together to create a legal personality, the corporation, the existence of which is unaffected by the withdrawal or even the death of individual shareholders, and toward which the financial obligations of the shareholders are limited to the share capital they have subscribed. None of these things is of any relevance to a government organization.... It is inconceivable that a corporation could survive the extinction of its sole shareholder, the Government of Canada. It is equally inconceivable, in terms

---

[3] *Royal Commission on Government Organization,* vol. 5 (Ottawa: Queen's Printer, 1963), pp. 58-75.

[4] W. Friedmann, *The Public Corporation* (Toronto: The Carswell Company Limited, 1954), p. 541.

of political realities, that the government would ever claim a limited liability and permit the organization to be forced into liquidation by its creditors.[5]

The parliamentary authority for the creation of Crown companies is found in any one of a number of acts which give ministers the power to procure the incorporation of bodies for carrying out the purposes of the act.

The Financial Administration Act has divided the Crown corporations into three classes. The departmental corporation "is a servant or agent of Her Majesty in right of Canada and is responsible for administrative, supervisory or regulatory services of a governmental nature".[6] Examples of this class are the National Research Council and the Unemployment Insurance Commission. The second class of Crown corporation is the agency corporation which is defined as "an agent of Her Majesty in right of Canada and is responsible for the management of trading or service operations on a quasi-commercial basis, or for the management of procurement, construction or disposal activities..."[7] Typical examples are the Crown Assets Disposal Corporation, Canadian Arsenals and the National Harbours Board. Lastly, there are the proprietary corporations, "any Crown corporation that (i) is responsible for the management of lending or financial operations, or for the management of commercial and industrial operations involving the production of or the dealing in goods and the supplying of services to the public, and (ii) is ordinarily required to conduct its operations without appropriations".[8] Examples are the CBC, Central Mortgage and Housing Corporation and Air Canada. The purpose of these definitions is to classify these agencies in their budgetary relations with Parliament and the government but there are also a few other distinguishing features in these groups. Thus, no departmental corporations are created under the Companies Act while there are about half-a-dozen Crown companies in each of the agency and proprietary classes. No agency or proprietary corporations are subject to the Public Service Employment Act while one third of the departmental corporations are. All departmental and agency corporations are audited by the Auditor General's staff while some proprietary corporations choose their own auditors. However, all Crown corporations are uniformly required to submit annual reports to their ministers.

Another form of government agency which can be distinguished is the royal commission. Royal commissions may be appointed by order-in-council under the authority of the Inquiries Act, and their function is usually to gather information on a specific topic which is of concern to the government.

Besides Crown corporations and royal commissions there is a whole host of other agencies ranging from the permanent quasi-judicial such as the Tax

---

[5] *Royal Commission on Government Organization,* p. 69.
[6] Financial Administration Act, par. 66.
[7] *Ibid.*
[8] *Ibid.*

Review Board, to the ad hoc administrative, for example, the Bureau of Government Organization. There is no common pattern in the organization, staffing or procedures of these bodies.

Questions inevitably arise: Why do these agencies exist? Does this diversity in government administration serve a purpose? Thomas McLeod has suggested that the agencies have been created because of popular misconceptions concerning the public service. These include the belief that senior public servants are more docile and less sensitive than their business counterparts, that departmental administration invariably attracts routine and red tape, and that political direction is interference motivated by ignorance, stupidity, venality, nepotism and graft.[9] There can be no doubt that one of the purposes in creating such agencies as the Canadian National Railways and the Canadian Broadcasting Corporation was to keep them from detailed political control and therefore from political interference. The history of the Inter-Colonial Railways suggested to the government of Sir Robert Borden that the newly acquired government railways would be much better off with a management that would feel truly independent in the appointment of staff, the location of railway stations and other similar matters which had hitherto been subject to political patronage.[10] Today the departments are more adequately shielded than the agencies from patronage in appointments and contracts by those watchdogs the Public Service Commission, the Treasury Board and the Auditor General, and following Sir Robert's logic the CNR should now become a department.

It is desirable to keep politically sensitive functions such as broadcasting, the redistribution of electoral seats, the investigations of commissions and quasi-judical actions from the detailed supervision of government and such activities can profit from the political aloofness of an agency. It is much more difficult to justify the difference between departments and agencies in controls over personnel and financial management. There appears to be a general consensus that the facility of expeditious hiring, firing and promotion, the privilege of fixing salaries and allocating budgets without the double check of the Public Service Commission and Treasury Board has made agencies generally more effective than many departments and that it would be undersirable to hedge them about with the restrictions which departments have to accept. This leaves the uncomfortable question: If these detailed management controls lessen effectiveness why must departments suffer them?

Some of the agencies, such as Air Canada, Canadian National Railways, Eldorado, St. Lawrence Seaway and several others, are organized to carry on activities in direct competition with private industry. Therefore, they feel that they must be free to copy commercial practices in such areas as trade secrecy,

---

[9] Institute of Public Administration of Canada, *Proceedings* (Toronto: University of Toronto Press, 1956), pp. 153 ff.

[10] *Debates* (Commons), May 15, 1918, p. 1,999; see also a statement of Sir Thomas White, p. 1,634.

legal accessibility, and investment without detailed justification before a board of civil servants, business decisions based on business considerations rather than government policy and so on. Moreover, these agencies find that their dealings with other enterprises, such as contractors and suppliers, are easier, and staff development and training is simpler when the organization resembles that of the other enterprises with which it is in daily contact.

Our federal constitution as interpreted by the courts does not permit the federal and provincial levels of government to share each others' functions or to delegate responsibilities one to the other. With ingenuity, the consequent inflexibility can be modified. Agencies can be staffed by personnel who are "coincidentally" acceptable to both governments. This would be difficult to do in a department. The National Battlefields Commission, the Halifax Relief Commission, the Eastern Rockies Forest Conservation Board and various marketing boards have proved efficacious in bridging this constitutional gap.

Agencies set up in the form of boards or commissions permit the representation of a diversity of interests as with the Canadian Radio-Television Commission or the representation of interested groups as in the labor and management representation in the Unemployment Insurance Commission.

Lastly, the agencies provide a device which helps to make distasteful political ideas acceptable to the Canadian public. Socialism or the nationalization of activities which are normally in the field of private enterprise is unpopular in Canada. The political parties advocating socialism have, as a rule, had fairly slim backing but our goverments have found it expedient to put into practice many socialist ideas and when the government takes over the operation of such functions as the manufacture and distribution of electricity or the retailing of liquor it does this with devices which have little connection in the public mind with public ownership of enterprise. The agencies are acceptable politically because they are different. They are not identified with the civil service in the public mind and therefore are considered quite proper competitors with private enterprise.

We have noted that in the conglomeration of government agencies there is this common pattern: a tendency to independence from detailed ministerial control and a freedom from the restraints of the Public Service Commission and Treasury Board. Does this mean that agencies can be independent of government policy, that they can act irresponsibly without regard to government or Parliamentary supervision? Far from it. Both Parliament and Cabinet have a number of ways in which they can control the functions and actions of these agencies. These controls have not always been exercised but they do exist.

The Cabinet appoints the directors or commissioners or board members who are the heads of the agencies. Usually it is the Cabinet collectively, the Governor-in-Council, which makes the appointments although sometimes individual ministers are charged with this responsibility. The heads may be appointed for a set period of time; three years, five years, seven years and ten years are popular periods, although "during pleasure" is used in almost one third of the statutes. Most statutes of incorporation state that heads may be reappointed and none bar further terms of office. Some heads may be "removed for cause" while in other statutes this is not explicit. The experience of the Diefenbaker government with the dismissal of James Coyne from the post of Governor of the Bank of Canada will probably lead other governments to hesitate before attempting similar measures, but it is established that the government can dismiss as well as appoint the heads of agencies.

Another measure of control is exercised by the appointment of those as heads of an agency who are already responsible to the minister in another capacity. Thus senior public servants, such as the deputy minister, the assistant deputy minister, or other senior men in a department may serve as directors or board members of an agency and in many agencies civil servants are members of the board.

In most cases the civil servants are drawn from departments having a particular interest in the operations of the agency concerned. They constitute, in effect, an interdepartmental committee advising the chief executive of the agency concerned. . . . It is one thing for ministers to disclaim responsibility for the affairs of undertakings having a board of management with independent status; but it would seem to be quite a different matter when the board consists of or is controlled by permanent officials, each of whom is answerable to his own minister for his actions. [11]

Some provinces have gone one step further in that they have appointed ministers to the directorates of agencies. This practice seems to have been forestalled in the federal government by the declaration of the father of many agencies, Hon. C.D. Howe, that "the board will function very much better if no minister of the Crown is a member of it." [12] Since political aloofness is one of the justifications for the existence of agencies it would be difficult to disagree with Howe.

In many agencies the power to make regulations is "subject to approval of the Governor-in-Council". This veto power of Cabinet is seldom used and, in fact, isolated incidents, such as the Coyne affair, indicate that neither the Cabinet nor the minister are always consulted or informed about the regulations that have been made even when the regulations are subject to approval of the Cabinet. But the control is available.

The minister through whom the agency reports to Parliament has a number of prerogatives in connection with that agency. Thus the Canadian Transport Commission may issue licenses subject to the approval of the Minister of Transport. "Subject to the directions of the Minister the Commission shall make investigations and surveys", and "the Board shall make recommendations to the Minister and advise the Minister". [13] With few excep-

---

[11] *Royal Commission on Government Organization*, p. 63.
[12] *Debates* (Commons) 1946, pp. 2,482-83 as quoted in Hodgetts and Corbett, *Canadian Public Administration*, p. 203.
[13] Aeronautics Act, R.S. 1970, chap. 2, pars. 12 and 13.

tions, all agencies report to Parliament through the minister and they are usually required by the founding statute to make an annual report to the minister who is required to table the report in the House.

Most agencies are subject to the provisions of the Financial Administration Act which invokes various financial controls. These controls vary from the whole gamut to which departments are subjected, as in departmental corporations, to the virtual financial autonomy of the proprietary corporations which must submit annual capital budgets but have full banking and borrowing freedom and, so long as no further revenue is required, can act independently except for the requirement to report to the minister as the shareholder. Agency corporations must submit both capital and operating budgets for ministerial approval. The extent of the minister's scrutiny will depend on the minister but is not likely to be in great depth. Most agencies are subject to audit by the Auditor General which involves more than a purely accounting audit.

As well as being subject to Cabinet controls, the agencies are also responsible to Parliament in varying degrees. Two agencies, the Public Service Commission and the Auditor General report directly to Parliament in their annual reports although in each case the responsible minister must table the report. The designation of each to a minister makes quite clear that these two agencies, contrary to popular opinion, are subject to some Cabinet supervision. In the main, however, these two agencies consider themselves responsible to Parliament and not to the government as incorporated in the Cabinet.

Members of Parliament may show their interest in the agencies by asking questions of the minister through whom the agency reports and they will normally get the answer to their questions. Parliament can discuss the affairs of any agency in the general debates such as those which precede the budget debates and if the agency has to ask for Parliamentary appropriations then it expects a discussion of its affairs. The review of agency affairs by Parliamentary committees could be an effective control and Parliament can institute such an investigation at any time. The best known reviews have taken place in the meetings of the Public Accounts Committee.

The government does not lack control devices to measure and regulate the conduct of agencies. These controls are not always used but even when exercised they affect the general tenor of policy making and not the details of management.

5

Personnel Management in the Federal Public Service*

R. H. Dowdell

The Influence of the Political Environment

Despite broad and growing similarities, personnel management in the public service is different in many ways from its counterpart in the private sector. One of the principal differences can be identified at the highest level in government organization. In the public service, the concept of management must include the political heads of departments — i.e. the ministers of the Crown. It is commonly thought that the deputy minister — the senior appointed official under the minister — is the top management official in the department, but reference to any of the Acts of Parliament establishing government departments will dispel this notion. For example, section 2(2) of the Government Organization Act (1969) reads as follows:

The Minister of Fisheries and Forestry holds office during pleasure and has the management and direction of the Department of Fisheries and Forestry.

If the Minister is a manager, he is also a politician. Indeed, perhaps first and foremost a politician, for he will not remain a minister for long unless he can get elected to Parliament, be re-elected whenever the occasion demands, and exercise considerable political skill in executing his portion of the government's programme.

In a commercial enterprise, the product or service must be produced at a profit. In the long run, there must be prospects of a reasonable rate of return on investment to bring the business into being and ensure its continued existence. The profit criterion is at once an important motive underlying plans, policies and decisions, and a yardstick against which their effectiveness can be assessed. Personnel directors in the private sector are in general agreement that one of their chief objectives is to contribute to their firms' profitability.

The pervasive characteristic of the public service is political rather than commercial. The administrator in the public service implements public policies and programmes which have been shaped by political forces. His superiors are politicians — leaders of a political party or coalition which obtained, if not a majority, at least the largest number of seats in the House of Commons because it convinced the electorate it had the best programme and

---

*R.H. Dowdel "Personnel Administration in the Federal Public Service," in *Public Administration in Canada,* 2nd ed., eds. W.D.K. Kernaghan and A.M. Willms (Toronto: Methuen Publications, 1971), pp. 276-304. Reprinted and abridged by permission of the author and publisher.

was best qualified to carry it out. These elected executives will tend to do the things likely to ensure their re-election and to avoid doing things which jeopardize it. The public service is subject to their direction and accountable to them. They in turn are accountable to Parliament for the conduct of the public service and not the least of the senior public servant's concerns is to avoid embarrassing his minister. Thus the political criterion is to the public service what the profit criterion is to industry — the thread which runs through the decision-making process, and the standard against which these decisions must ultimately be weighed. That is not to say that every action must be calculated for the political advantage of the party in power any more than every action in business must be calculated to maximize profit. Short-run disadvantages must sometimes be borne and there are many actions whose political consequences are too remote to affect decisions significantly. But in the long-run, top management of the public service must on balance redound to the credit of the party in power and in the short-run, actions which may produce adverse political consequences must be avoided as much as possible.

If these considerations are true of management generally in the public service, they are equally true of personnel management in particular. In a commercial organization, personnel policies and actions are evaluated by the profit criterion. The political criterion, however, is a nebulous thing at best and less susceptible to objective estimate. It is more likely to be applied by evaluating the sum of immediate consequences arising out of policies and actions. There is a temptation to regard each personnel action as an opportunity to secure a return of political advantage and to avoid those which are politically dangerous. For example, before the reform of the Canadian public service it was generally accepted that the party in power would use its power of appointment to secure or reward political support and the opponents of reform argued that a government must be able to depend on the loyalty of those who administer its policies.

Whatever may be said in theory for personnel practices based on short or long-term political advantage, the results were generally unfortunate. Although political appointees were sometimes people of great ability (Mackenzie King got his start in the public service as a patronage appointee), it was generally true that their qualifications for the job in question were a secondary consideration and frequently even minimum standards of ability were disregarded altogether. Security of tenure was uncertain and few political appointees tended to regard the public service as a career. The inevitable result was a low standard of competence and a poor quality of service to the public. At a time when government activity was highly circumscribed by today's standards, this situation could be tolerated. However, as the activities of the government began to expand, it became more and more necessary to employ people with the highest possible level of technical and administrative ability. To achieve this, methods of appointment and conditions of employment had to be changed.

The Merit Principle and Merit Systems

The merit principle which has replaced the patronage system as one of the cornerstones of personnel policy in the public service is an attempt to abandon political considerations altogether in managing the human resources of the public service. The significance of this policy may not be readily appreciated. To take politics out of public personnel management is to run counter to the very nature of the public service as an organization established to pursue political objectives. However necessary such a course may be, it generates stresses which are comparable to the psychological effects of repression. The political character of the public service which is denied outward expression in personnel management is nonetheless at the root of many of its problems, and accounts for many of its inconsistencies and shortcomings. One of the criteria by which public personnel management must be judged is its ability to cope with this dualism in its own character.

The merit principle is really two interrelated principles:

1. Canadian citizens should have a reasonable opportunity to be considered for employment in the public service.

2. Selections must be based exclusively on merit, or fitness to do the job.

These principles are among the most important goals of policy in public personnel management. The merit *system* is the mechanism in use at any given time by which these goals are achieved. The merit principle has become, and should remain, a relatively stable part of our public ethic, although like all ethical tenets it may suffer somewhat in practice. A merit system is an administrative device which can and should be adapted to changing circumstances.

Some Aspects of Organization

The relationships involved in the development and implementation of personnel policy in the Canadian public service have been compared to a triangle, comprising the Treasury Board, the departments and the Public Service Commission. The first two are part of the management structure whereas the third is not. Yet the Commission has had a prominent — indeed until recently the pre-eminent — role in this three-way partnership. In 1966, Parliament passed three pieces of legislation which were proclaimed in force in March, 1967:

1. The Public Service Employment Act (replacing the Civil Service Act).

2. Amendments to the Financial Administration Act.

3. The Public Service Staff Relations Act.

All three had a bearing on the future role of the Commission. The first established a Public Service Commission to regulate staffing in the portion of the public service over which the former Civil Service Commission had jurisdiction. In addition, prevailing rate employees and ships' crews, previously exempt, were brought under the Act and provision was made to extend it by Order-in-Council to other parts of the service. The amendments to the Financial Administration Act transferred responsibility for position classification to the Treasury Board. The Public Service Staff Relations Act included terms which made the new Public Service Staff Relations Board responsible for pay research and for hearing grievances on disciplinary matters which were previously the subject of appeals to the Commission.

Improvements in Career Planning

Through Data Stream, a manpower inventory has been set up to include the four senior occupational groups, namely Executive, Scientific and Professional, Administrative and Foreign Service, and Technical. Techniques of this kind can facilitate staff development and career planning, but other important measures must also be taken. Some of these have been incorporated in recent legislative and procedural changes in the public service.

1. The right of employees to appeal the lateral movement of another employee from one position to another at the same salary level was eliminated in the Public Service Employment Act of 1967. This removed a formidable barrier to the mobility of the work force.

2. In certain occupations, notably personnel and financial administration, it is now accepted that the stage on which an employee's career role will be played is service-wide and the tendency to limit careers to a single department is being overcome.

3. Career-planning guidelines are being established on a trial basis for certain occupations and the lessons learned will enable improvements to be made when similar guidelines are developed for other occupations. These guidelines endeavour to balance management and employee interests under a rational staffing policy which permits planned assignments, varied experience, periodical consideration for promotion, and a reduction of raiding between departments.

4. Manpower planning and development is now recognized as a sub-specialization of the personnel function and provision for its exercise is being made in the organization of the Treasury Board and departments. This function includes organization planning, the analysis of manpower requirements, employee evaluation, and training and development.

5. Long-term staff development programmes such as the Career Assignment Programme have been introduced. These include formal training and planned work assignments lasting several years, requiring the assumption of responsibility and the achievment of results fully commensurate with the employee's salary level. They are primarily a departmental responsibility within policy guidelines set by central management. And they use the facilities of the Public Service Commission to supplement departmental training resources and to effect interdepartmental assignments.

6. Financial barriers to interregional mobility are being reduced by compensating employees for some of the cost of buying and selling homes, and

for incidental expenses which were not previously admissible under the travel and removal regulations.

7. Rules governing in-grade salary increases have been altered in a number of classes to permit more appropriate recognition of superior performance. Instead of the one-increase-a-year which became virtually automatic, deputy ministers can now grant increases of varying amounts, depending on the calibre of an officer's work in relation to that of his peers. Performance pay budgets have been designed in such a way that larger increases for the best performers must be balanced by smaller increases or none at all for others. Varying forms of performance pay are now applicable in the senior Executive category, the upper two or three levels of the Administrative and Foreign Service category, and in the Research Scientist class. Similar plans will probably be instituted for other scientific and professional classes, and perhaps also for lower levels in the Administrative and Foreign Service category.

Training

Training is the process through which an employee acquires the knowledge, skills and attitudes required to make him fully effective in doing his job. Along with other techniques, such as planned work assignments, it is one of the elements in his development toward positions of greater responsibility. The public service has a particularly great demand for training of all kinds. It employs a greater variety of occupational skills than any other organization, including many that are unique to government. Like all employers, it must cope with rapid technological change. And the service it provides to the public is subject to frequent change, sometimes on short notice, because of the introduction of new government programmes.

Training activities in the public service are so extensive and varied that a book could be devoted to their cataloguing. For example, in addition to the induction, skill, supervisory and management training found in all larger organizations, government must train *ab initio* in a number of highly complex fields such as air traffic control and meteorology. It must adapt basic professional skills in engineering and accounting to unique job requirements in purchasing and contract administration. As the largest employer of physical, biological and social scientists in the country, it sponsors post-graduate education for several hundred employees each year. In recent years it has undertaken the massive task of training thousands of employees to serve the public in both official languages.

The Treasury Board is responsible for training policy in the public service and for determining the resources to be allocated for this purpose. Most training programmes are administered by the departments. The Public Service Commission interprets its mandate in staffing to include all measures required to meet the needs of the service for qualified personnel. Its Training and Development Branch conducts courses in administrative and managerial skills which are common to all departments and will assist them in developing training programmes of their own.

6

Financial Administration in Canada*

H.R. Balls

The financial affairs of the Government of Canada are administered and controlled under the fundamental principles that no tax shall be imposed and no money shall be spent without the authority of Parliament and that expenditures shall be made only for the purposes authorized by Parliament. The most important constitutional provisions relating to Parliament's control of finances are contained in the British North America Act; this Act provides that all federal taxing and appropriating measures must originate in the House of Commons and all requests for grants must come from the Crown through responsible Ministers, and for such requests the Government is solely responsible. In practice, financial control is exercised through a budgetary system based on the principle that all the financial needs of the Government for each fiscal year be considered at one time so that both the current condition and the prospective condition of the public treasury are clearly in evidence.

Estimates and Appropriations

The co-ordination of the Estimates process is carried out by the Treasury Board. This Board is a separate department of government, its Minister having the designation of President of the Treasury Board. In addition to the President, the Board consists of the Minister of Finance and four other Privy Councillors. Under the Financial Administration Act, the Board may act for the Privy Council in all matters relating to financial management including estimates, expenditures, financial commitments, establishments, revenues, accounts, terms and conditions of employment of persons in the public service and general administrative policy in the public service.

The Estimates for any one fiscal year are determined as a result of a two-phased review by the Treasury Board of departmental proposals for expenditure. In the spring of each year, at the request of the Secretary of the Treasury Board, each department submits to the Treasury Board a forecast of expenditures for the current and following four fiscal years. During the summer, a review of the programmes giving rise to these expenditures forecasts is carried out by the Treasury Board, as a result of which tentative expenditures figures are determined for each department for the coming fiscal year. The Board reviews each departmental programme submission in the light of probable

*H.R. Balls, "Financial Administration in Canada," in *Canada Year Book 1970-71* (Ottawa: Information Canada, 1971), pp. 132-37. Reprinted by permission of the author and publisher.

revenues and governmental policy generally, usually consulting the appropriate Minister and officials. Each department, using the figure resulting from this review as a guideline, develops in detail its manpower and other resource requirements and submits them to the Treasury Board late in October in the form of Main Estimates for the fiscal year beginning the following April 1. These Estimates are analysed by the Treasury Board staff and compared with the guidelines determined during the spring programme review. The Board reviews each departmental submission in the light of the current budgetary outlook. The Estimates may be rejected or reduced and unresolved differences of opinion may be referred to the Cabinet for decision. When the Board is satisfied with their substance and form, the Main Estimates are submitted to the Cabinet and later to the Governor-in-Council for approval and are then laid before the House of Commons.

On the motion of the President of the Privy Council, the Estimates of each department are initially referred for consideration to the appropriate standing committee of the House on or before March 1. Under the Standing Orders, the House is deemed to have reported by May 31. The Government House Leader must give forty-eight hours notice of a motion for the House to concur in the Estimates that have been considered by the committee. The consideration of the Estimates usually extends over a period of several months and under the Standing Orders, the Speaker is required to put every question necessary to dispose of any item of business relating to supply not later than the last sitting day in the period ending June 30 of each year. Each vote is the subject of a separate resolution and Members of the House may question the Minister on any item but no private member or Minister on his own responsibility can introduce any new expenditure proposal or any amendment to an Estimates item that would result in an increased expenditure. When the examination of the individual items has been completed, a resolution approving the granting of moneys is referred to a committee of the whole House. When such resolutions are passed, an appropriation Bill is introduced which, when approved by the House of Commons and the Senate, is given Royal Assent and becomes law. Grants in the Appropriation Acts are grants to the Crown and funds cannot be disbursed until the supply voted by Parliament to the Crown is released by a warrant prepared on an Order of the Governor-in-Council and signed by the Governor General.

As weeks or months may elapse after the commencement of the fiscal year before the main Appropriation Act is passed, funds are made available for the conduct of government functions by the passage of an interim supply Bill granting one or more twelfths of the total of each item in the Estimates. Additional interim supply Bills may be introduced if required, awaiting Parliament's detailed consideration of the Estimates. In addition, to cover any new and unforeseen requirements that might arise during the year, Supplementary Estimates may be introduced, and just prior to the end of the fiscal year further Supplementary Estimates are laid before the House. These Supplementary Estimates are dealt with in the same manner as the Main Estimates.

In addition to the expenditure items included in the annual Appropriation Acts, there are a number of items such as interest on the public debt, family allowances, and old age assistance payments, which have been authorized under the provisions of other statutes. Although it is not necessary for Parliament to pass annually on these items, they are included in the Main Estimates for purposes of information. Statutory provision also exists for the expenditure of public money in emergencies where no parliamentary appropriation is available. Under the Financial Administration Act, the Governor-in-Council, upon the report of the President of the Treasury Board that there is no appropriation for the expenditure, and upon the report of the appropriate Minister that the expenditure is urgently required, may order the issuance of a special warrant authorizing disbursement of the amount required. Such warrants may be issued only when Parliament is not in session, and every warrant must be published in the *Canada Gazette* within thirty days of issue and reported to Parliament within fifteen days of assembly. The Fire Losses Replacement Account Act also provides for emergency expenditures for the urgent repair or replacement of property destroyed or damaged by fire, where there is not sufficient money available in the appropriation for the service suffering loss. Such amounts must be charged subsequently to an appropriation or included in the Estimates for the department or agency concerned.

In addition, disbursements are made for purposes not reflected in the budgetary accounts but recorded in the Government's statement of assets and liabilities, such as loans to and investments in Crown corporations, loans to international organizations and to national, provincial and municipal governments, and loans to veterans. There are also disbursements in connection with deposit and trust accounts and annuity, insurance and pension accounts which the Government holds or administers, including the old age security fund and the Canada Pension Plan fund which are operated as separate entities. Although these disbursements are excluded from the calculation of the annual budgetary surplus or deficit, they are all subject to appropriation by Parliament either in the annual Appropriation Acts or in other legislation.

The Budget

Some time after the Main Estimates have been introduced, the Minister of Finance presents his annual Budget Speech in the House of Commons. Budget papers, tabled for the information of Parliament at least one day prior to the presentation of the Budget, include a general review of economic conditions and a preliminary review of the Government's accounts for the fiscal year then ending. The Budget Speech itself reviews the state of the national economy and the financial operations of the Government for the previous fiscal year and gives a forecast of the probable financial requirements for the year ahead, taking into account the Main Estimates and making allowances for Supplementary Estimates and probable lapsings. At the close of his address, the

Minister tables the formal resolutions for changes in the existing tax rates and customs tariff which, in accordance with parliamentary procedure, must precede the introduction of any money Bills. These resolutions give notice of the amendments which the government intends to ask Parliament to make in the taxation statutes. However, if a change is proposed in a commodity tax, such as a sales tax or excise duty on a particular item, it is usually made effective immediately; the legislation, when passed, is made retroactive to the date of the Speech.

The Budget Speech is delivered in support of a motion that the House go into committee, the debate on which may take up six sitting days. With the passage of the motion, the way is clear for the consideration of the Budget resolutions and, when these have been approved by the Committee, a report to this effect is made to the House and the tax Bills are introduced and thereafter dealt with in the same manner as all other government financial legislation.

Revenues and Expenditures

The administrative procedures whereby revenues are collected and expenditures are made are, for the most part, contained in the Financial Administration Act.

With respect to revenues, the basic requirement is that all public money shall be paid into the Consolidated Revenue Fund, which is defined as the aggregate of all public money on deposit to the credit of the Receiver General. (Under the Government Organization Act of 1969, the Minister of Supply and Services is the Receiver General of Canada). The Treasury Board has prescribed detailed regulations governing the receipt and deposit of such money. For the actual custody of public money, use is made of the Bank of Canada and the chartered banks. Balances are allocated to the various chartered banks on the basis of a percentage allocation established by agreement among all the banks and communicated to the Department of Finance by the Canadian Bankers' Association. The daily operating account is maintained with the Bank of Canada and the division of funds between it and the chartered banks takes into account the immediate cash requirements of the Government and consideration of monetary policy. The Minister of Finance may purchase and hold securities of, or guaranteed by, Canada and pay for them out of the Consolidated Revenue Fund or may sell such securities and pay the proceeds into the Fund. Thus, if cash balances in the Fund are in excess of requirements for the immediate future they may be invested in interest-earning assets. In addition, the Minister of Finance has established a purchase fund to assist in the orderly retirement of the public debt.

The Treasury Board exercises central control over the budgets, programmes and staffs of departments and over financial and administrative matters generally. Although the most important part of this control function is exercised during the annual consideration of departmental long-range plans and the Estimates, the Board has the right to maintain continuous control over certain types of expenditure to ensure that the scale of activities and commitments for the future is held within approved policies, that departments follow uniform, efficient and economical practices, and that the Government is informed of and approves any major development of policy or significant transaction that might give rise to public or parliamentary criticism.

To ensure that the decisions of Parliament, the Government, and Ministers — in regard to expenditures — are enforced, the Financial Administration Act provides that no payment shall be made out of the Consolidated Revenue Fund without the authority of Parliament, and no charge shall be made against an appropriation except upon the requisition of the appropriate Minister or a person authorized by him in writing. These requisitions, and certificates that the work has been performed, the material has been supplied or the services have been rendered, and that the price charged is reasonable or according to contract, together with such documents as may be required, are presented to the Receiver General who makes the payment.

At the beginning of each fiscal year or at such other time as the Treasury Board may direct, each department, unless otherwise directed by the Board, submits to the Treasury Board a division into allotments of each vote included in its Estimates. Once approved by the Board, these allotments cannot be varied or amended without the approval of the Board and expenditures charged to appropriations are limited to such allotments. To avoid over-expenditures within a fiscal year, commitments coming in course of payment within the year for which Parliament has provided or has been asked to provide appropriations are recorded and controlled by the departments concerned. (The Minister of Supply and Services may perform these services on behalf of departments). Records are maintained of commitments made under contract that will fall due in succeeding years, since the Government must be prepared in future to ask Parliament for appropriations to cover them. Any unexpended amounts in the annual appropriations lapse at the end of the year for which they are granted, but for thirty days subsequent to March 31 payments may be made and charged to the previous year's appropriations for debts payable prior to the end of that fiscal year.

Under the Financial Administration Act, every payment pursuant to an appropriation is made under the control and direction of the Receiver General by cheque or other instrument in such form and authenticated in such manner as the Treasury Board may direct. In practice, such cheques or instruments are cleared daily by the chartered banks through the Bank of Canada to the Cheque Adjustment Division of the Receiver General's office, and reimbursement is made by means of a cheque drawn on the Receiver General's account with the Bank of Canada.

Public Debt

In addition to the collection and disbursement of public money for budgetary and non-budgetary purposes, the Government receives and disburses substantial sums in connection with its public debt operations. The Minister of

Finance is authorized to borrow money by the issue and sale of securities at such rate of interest and subject to such terms and conditions as the Governor-in-Council may approve. Although the specific authority of Parliament is required for new borrowings, the Financial Administration Act authorizes the Governor-in-Council to approve the borrowing of such sums of money as are required for the redemption of maturing or called securities and, to ensure that the Consolidated Revenue Fund will be sufficient to meet lawfully authorized disbursements, he may also approve the temporary borrowing of such sums as are necessary for periods not exceeding six months. The Bank of Canada acts as the fiscal agent of the Government in the management of the public debt.

Accounts and Financial Statements

Under the Financial Administration Act, and subject to regulations of the Treasury Board, the Receiver General requires accounts to be kept to show the revenues of Canada, the expenditures made under each appropriation, other payments into and out of the Consolidated Revenue Fund, and such of the assets and direct and contingent liabilities as the Minister of Finance believes are required to give a true and fair view of the financial position of Canada. The statement of assets and liabilities is designed to disclose the amount of the net debt, which is determined by offsetting against the gross liabilities only those assets regarded currently as readily realizable or interest-or revenue-producing. Fixed capital assets, such as government buildings and public works are charged to budgetary expenditures at the time of acquisition or construction and are shown on the statement of assets and liabilities at a nominal value of $1.

Annually, on or before December 31, or, if Parliament is not then sitting, within any of the first fifteen days next thereafter that Parliament is sitting, the Public Accounts, prepared by the Receiver General, are laid before the House of Commons by the Minister of Finance. The Public Accounts contain a survey of the financial transactions of the fiscal year ended the previous March 31, statements of the revenues and expenditures for that year and of the assets and direct and contingent liabilities as at the end of that year, together with such other accounts and information as are necessary to show the financial transactions and financial position of Canada or which are required by law to be reported in the Public Accounts. Monthly financial statements are also published in the *Canada Gazette*.

The Auditor General

The Government's accounts are subject to an independent examination by the Auditor General who is an officer of Parliament. With respect to expenditures, this examination is a post-audit for the purposes of reporting whether the accounts have been faithfully and properly kept, whether the money has been expended for the purposes for which it was appropriated by Parliament and whether the expenditures have been made as authorized. With respect to revenues, the Auditor General is required to ascertain that all public money is fully accounted for and that the rules and procedures applied are sufficient to ensure an effective check on the assessment, collection and proper allocation of the revenue. With respect to public property, he is required to satisfy himself that essential records are maintained and that the rules and procedures applied are sufficient to safeguard and control such property. The Auditor General reports to Parliament the results of his examination, calling attention to any case which he considers should be brought to the notice of the House. He also reports to Ministers, the Treasury Board or the Government any matter which in his opinion calls for attention so that remedial action may be taken promptly.

Public Accounts Committee
It is the usual practice to refer the Public Accounts and the Auditor General's Report to the Public Accounts Committee of the House of Commons, which may review them and report its findings and recommendations to the House of Commons.

Readings

Organization

Ashley, C.A. and Smails, R.G.H. *Canadian Crown Corporations.* Toronto: The Macmillan Company of Canada, 1965.

Bowland, J.G. "Geographical Decentralization in the Canadian Federal Public Service." *Canadian Public Administration,* vol. 10, no. 3 (September, 1967) pp. 323-61.

Bridges, The Right Hon. Lord. "The Relationships between Governments and Government-Controlled Corporations." *Canadian Public Administration,* vol. 7, no. 3 (September, 1964), pp. 295-308.

Caldwell, G.H. "Unity of Command: A Comparison of the Top Level Organization Structures of the Government of Canada and of Large Scale Private Enterprises." *Canadian Public Administration,* vol. 7, no. 4 (December, 1964), pp. 510-45.

Canada. *Royal Commission on Government Organization* (Glassco Commission) *Report.* Vol. 1, *Management of the Public Service,* reports 1-4. Vol. 2, *Supporting Services for Government,* reports 5-11. Vol. 3, *Supporting Services for Government,* reports 12-13 and *Services for the Public,* reports 14-18. Vol. 4, *Special Areas of Administration,* reports 19-23. Vol. 5, *The Organization of the Government of Canada.* Ottawa: Queen's Printer, 1962-1963.

Des Roches, J.M. "The Evolution of the Organization of the Federal Government in Canada." *Canadian Public Administration,* vol. 5, no. 4 (December, 1962), pp. 408-27.

Gelinas, André. Trois modes d'approche à la détermination de l'opportunité de la décentralisation de l'organisation politique principalement en système fédéral." *Canadian Public Administration,* vol. 9, no. 1 (March, 1966), pp. 1-26.

Hanson, E.H. *Public Enterprise.* Brussels: International Institute of Administrative Sciences, 1956.

Irvine, A.G. "The Delegation of Authority to Crown Corporations." *Canadian Public Administration,* vol. 14, no. 4 (Winter, 1971), pp. 556-79.

Laframboise, H.L., "Administrative Reform in the Federal Public Service: Signs of a Saturation Psychosis." *Canadian Public Administration,* vol. 14, no. 3 (Fall, 1971), pp. 303-25.

Laframboise, H.L. "Portfolio Structure and a Ministry System: A Model for the Canadian Federal Service." *Optimum,* vol. 1, no. 1 (1970), pp. 29-46.

McLeod, T.H. "Glassco Commission Report." *Canadian Public Administration,* vol. 6, no. 4 (December, 1963), pp. 386-406.

Musolf, Lloyd D. *Public Ownership and Accountability: the Canadian Experience.* Cambridge, Mass: Harvard University Press, 1959.

Taylor, K.W. "Co-ordination in Administration." *Proceedings of the Ninth Annual Conference.* Toronto: Institute of Public Administration of Canada, 1957, pp. 253-73.

Yeomans, D.R. "Decentralization of Authority." *Canadian Public Administration,* vol. 12, no. 1 (Spring, 1969), pp. 9-25.

Personnel

Archibald, Kathleen. *Sex and the Public Service.* Ottawa: Queen's Printer, 1970.

Callard, K.B. *Advanced Administrative Training in the Public Service.* Toronto: University of Toronto Press, 1958.

Canada, Civil Service Commission. *Personnel Administration in the Civil Service: a Review of Civil Service Legislation.* Ottawa: Queen's Printer, 1958.

Carson, J. J. "New Trends in Canadian Public Personnel Administration." *Public Administration (Sydney),* vol. 31, no. 3 (September, 1972), pp. 193-201.

Dowdell, R.H. "Personnel Administration in the Federal Public Service." In *Public Administration in Canada,* eds. W.D.K. Kernaghan and A.M. Willms. 2nd ed. Toronto: Methuen Publications, 1971, pp. 276-304.

Frankel, S. J. *Staff Relations in the Civil Service: the Canadian Experience.* Montreal: McGill University Press, 1962.

Gow, James Iain. "La modernisation de la fonction publique du Québec." *International Review of Administrative Sciences,* vol. 36, no. 3 (1970), pp. 234-42.

Hodgetts, J.E. and O.P. Dwivedi. "The Growth of Government Employment in Canada". *Canadian Public Administration,* vol. 12, no. 2 (Summer, 1969), pp. 224-38.
Hodgetts, J.E., William McCloskey, Reginald Whitaker, and V. Seymour Wilson. *The Biography of an Institution: The Civil Service Commission, 1908-1967.* Montreal: McGill-Queen's University Press, 1972.
Johnson, A.W. "Productivity, People and the Public Service." *Optimum,* vol. 2, no. 1 (1971), pp. 8-22.
Morley, D. "The Career Assignment Program." *Canadian Public Administration,* vol. 14, no. 1 (Spring, 1971), pp. 100-111.
Swettenham, John and David Kealy. *Serving the State: A History of the Professional Institute of the Public Service of Canada, 1920-1970.* Ottawa: Le Droit, 1970.

Finance

Balls, H.R. "The Budget and its Function." *Cost and Management,* vol. 41 (October, 1967), pp. 25-28.
Balls, H.R. "The Budget and the National Accounts." *Cost and Management,* vol. 41 (November, 1967), pp. 28-31.
Balls, H.R. "Improving Performance of Public Enterprises through Financial Management." *Canadian Public Administration,* vol. 13, no. 1 (Spring, 1970), pp. 100-23.
Balls, H.R. "Planning, Programming and Budgeting in Canada." *Public Administration (U.K.),* vol. 48 (Autumn, 1970), pp. 289-306.
Bird, Richard M. *The Growth of Government Spending in Canada.* Toronto: Canadian Tax Foundation, 1970.
Buck, A.E. *Financing Canadian Government.* Chicago: Public Administration Service, 1949.
Canada. *Report of the Auditor General.* Ottawa: Queen's Printer, annual.
Fowke, Donald V. "PPB for Provinces." *Canadian Public Administration,* vol. 12, no. 1 (Spring, 1969), pp. 72-77.
Johnson, A.W. "Efficiency in Government and Business." *Canadian Public Administration,* vol. 6, no. 3 (September, 1963), pp. 245-60.
Little, P.L. and C.L. Mitchell. "The Program Budget: Planning and Control for the Public Sector." *Cost and Management,* vol. 41 (September, 1967), pp. 22-26.
MacLean, R.D. "An Examination of the Role of the Comptroller of the Treasury." *Canadian Public Administration,* vol. 7 no. 1 (March, 1964), pp. 1-133.
Sterns, A.A. "The Functions of the Treasury Board." In *Public Administration in Canada,* eds. A.M. Willms and W.D.K. Kernaghan. Toronto: Methuen Publications, 1968.
Strick, J.C. "Conditional Grants and Provincial Government Budgeting." *Canadian Public Administration,* vol. 14, no. 2 (Summer, 1971), pp. 217-35.
Strick, J.C. "Recent Developments in Canadian Financial Administration." *Public Administration (U.K.),* vol. 48 (Spring, 1970), pp. 69-85.
Ward, N. *The Public Purse: a Study in Canadian Democracy.* Toronto: University of Toronto Press, 1962.
White, W.L. and Strick, J.C. *Policy, Politics and the Treasury Board in Canadian Government.* Don Mills: Science Research Associates (Canada) Limited, 1970.
White, W.L. and Strick, J.C. "The Treasury Board and Parliament." *Canadian Public Administration,* vol. 10, no. 2 (June, 1967), pp. 209-22.

Chapter Three

Politicians
and Bureaucrats

Before 1945, the separation of politics from administration was generally accepted as the existing and desirable state of affairs in government. The functions of public servants were ostensibly limited to the implementation of policy decisions taken by elected representatives.

In the immediate post-war period, a number of political scientists, particularly those who had gained practical administrative experience during the war years, launched a successful assault on the validity of this traditional politics-administration dichotomy. The power of bureaucrats in the policy-making process has been clearly recognized and documented. Moreover, the interaction of bureaucrats with legislators, with the general public, and with representatives of the mass media and of interest groups manifests the prominent position of the bureaucracy in the political system. This interaction enables public servants to provide policy advice to elected representatives that is both better informed and more "politically sensitive".

The selections in this chapter focus on relations between senior public servants and political executives. Gordon Robertson draws on first-hand experience to explain the changing nature of policy-making structures involving the Prime Minister, Cabinet ministers and the bureaucratic elite. Bruce Thordarson complements this account with his description of one Prime Minister's efforts to utilize bureaucratic experience and expertise to achieve *politically* determined government objectives. Then, Mitchell Sharp, a former member of the bureaucratic elite, reminisces about the participation of senior officials in policy formation and politics.

7

The Prime Minister, the Cabinet and the Privy Council Office*

Gordon Robertson

The Cabinet Committee System

On January 20, 1964, former Prime Minister Pearson announced that

since September, the use of Cabinet committees has been developed to a greater extent than in the past. This development will now be carried farther in order that the Cabinet form of administration may be efficiently adapted to the needs of modern government in Canada. Greater use of committees is the best way to obtain, under the Prime Minister's leadership, thorough consideration of policies, co-ordination of government action, and timely decisions in a manner consistent with ministerial and Cabinet responsibility.[1]

Nine Cabinet committees were established. Rather than being oriented toward specific ad hoc problems or operations, they were for the first time directed toward defined areas of the total governmental process.

A change in procedure was also initiated. Previously things had gone to the Cabinet first and had been referred by it to Cabinet committees when special consideration and report were required. The new procedure provided that matters requiring Cabinet decision in most cases be first brought to the appropriate standing committee by the minister concerned. The committee thus became a normal and formal part of the decision-making process: a stage before consideration in the Cabinet itself. In addition to the nine committees listed in Mr. Pearson's announcement, there was a tenth — the Treasury Board — which has functioned since 1867. It was established by statute. At that time it was regarded as a committee to aid the Minister of Finance and was scarcely recognized as a committee of Cabinet at all. It continued its powerful and quasi-independent existence; setting administrative standards in departments, improving management in the public service, dealing with contracts, departmental programmes and estimates and the expenditures of government in general.

The system established by Mr. Pearson in 1964 lasted throughout his regime. The only important change was the addition in January, 1968 of a Cabinet Committee on Priorities and Planning. The government found itself in recurring financial difficulties and crises and it became apparent that there

---

*Gordon Robertson, "The Changing Role of the Privy Council Office", *Canadian Public Administration,* vol. 14, no. 4 (Winter, 1971), pp. 487-508. Reprinted and abridged by permission of the author and publisher.
[1] Press release, Office of the Prime Minister, January 20, 1964.

was serious need of a systematic assessment of over-all priorities of expenditure with a view to better long-term planning. It is true that programme priorities were set implicitly in the annual estimates, the annual expenditure plans, but this was done by the Treasury Board in the absence of any broad direction from Cabinet as to over-all objectives or priorities.

When Mr. Trudeau became Prime Minister, one of his earliest actions, announced on April 30, 1968, was a modification of the Cabinet committee system. He said:

This system has worked well for the past five years and greatly improved the efficiency of government. It has, however, become apparent that further changes are now required to permit a greater centralization of functions and the delegation of certain powers of decisions to the committees. To meet these difficulties, I have revised the system of Cabinet committees to reduce the number of committees and to provide for a regularity in their meetings.[2]

The establishment of regular times each week for the meeting of each of the standing committees of the Cabinet produced the major improvement that it was designed to achieve. Ministers are overwhelmed by the obligations, engagements and pressures that throng upon them. Time is committed weeks and even months in advance. With no regular schedule for the meetings of their committees, attendance was poor and spasmodic. Continuing attention to areas of policy by the committee members was impossible. With regular meetings over the entire year, it became possible to have systematic and orderly consideration of problems for submission to the Cabinet.

The second important change in 1968 was to give the committees the power, not simply to recommend courses of action to the Cabinet, but to take specific decisions. The main object was to remove as many questions as possible from the over-burdened Cabinet. It was recognized, however, that there would have to be some means by which ministers who were not on a Cabinet committee, or who did not attend a meeting, could re-open discussion or could register a view that differed from the decision of the committee. Without such a capacity, they could not reasonably be expected to assume their share of collective responsibility for policy. Two provisions were made: one was that all ministers, whether members of a committee or not, would receive agendas and documents. They would then know the questions to be discussed and decide whether they had an important interest or view. They could attend any meeting they wished to attend, with the exception of the Cabinet Committee on Priorities and Planning which the Prime Minister wanted to keep relatively small. The second provision was that decisions of the committees would not become effective simply by reason of such decision. They would be listed on an annex to the Cabinet agenda for its next meeting. Any minister could notify the deputy secretary to the Cabinet before the meeting of the Cabinet that he wished to have any particular committee decision

---

[2] Press release, Office of the Prime Minister, "Statement by the Prime Minister on Cabinet committee structure," April 30, 1968.

discussed. However, if no such notice were given, items on the annex were to be taken as approved by the Cabinet and became its own decisions. At that point they were operative and became part of government policy.

Of the standing Cabinet committees that now exist, five deal with areas of government activity: External Policy and Defence, Economic Policy, Social Policy, Science, Culture and Information, Government Operations. Four are co-ordinating committees: Priorities and Planning, Treasury Board, Legislation and House Planning, Federal-Provincial Relations. In addition, the Special Committee of the Cabinet handles regulations and other proposed orders-in-council that do not require the attention of the full Cabinet. Other special committees deal, at irregular intervals as required, with questions relating to security and intelligence, the public service, and a few other matters. From time to time special problems assume an importance that require ad hoc committees that are abandoned when a satisfactory solution is reached.

One result of the changes introduced in 1968 was to increase greatly the number of Cabinet committee meetings. The other was to reduce equally sharply the number of meetings of the Cabinet. As compared with the situation before the revisions in the system were made in 1968, Cabinet is dealing with a larger volume of business but taking only half as many Cabinet meetings to do it. The number of Cabinet committee meetings has more than doubled and, according to calculations in the Privy Council Office, the number of "minister-hours" devoted to the total executive function has remained about the same as in 1966-7. The difference is in the more probing, searching and formative nature of discussion that the committees permit, with both Ministers and officials present.

Organization of the Privy Council Office

Making the Cabinet and Cabinet committee system work effectively has involved a substantial development of the Cabinet secretariat begun in 1910. In 1945 there were ten officers in the Cabinet secretariat. In 1971, there are 55 officers engaged in work relating to the secretariat proper, and there are 13 officers providing the key services in relation to Cabinet documents, orders-in-council and administrative and financial services. There is, of course, in addition, the normal complement of clerical and secretarial staff. But it is not a large office to attempt the tasks that are involved in relation to the entire range of government activities.

The Privy Council Office is divided into three main divisions: the Operations Division, a Plans Division and a Federal-Provincial Affairs Division, each headed by a deputy secretary to the Cabinet. The Operations Division has five secretariats, each under an assistant secretary to the Cabinet and each responsible for the work of one of the standing committees which, together, are designed to cover all the fields of government operations. Each secretariat is responsible for moving forward, to and through the Cabinet, the proposals that must be considered and decided in relation to the "operations" of government coming within its area of responsibility. The division also services a number of other special and ad hoc Cabinet committees with assistance from the other divisions, and has the primary responsibility of providing service to the Cabinet itself.

The other main divisions of the Office are responsible for the coordinating committees of the Cabinet other than the Treasury Board, which continues to be served by a separate department of government under its own minister, the president of the Treasury Board. The secretary and deputy secretaries of the Board maintain close collaboration with the secretary of the Cabinet and the several deputy and assistant secretaries. In the Privy Council Office the Plans Division services the Cabinet Committee on Priorities and Planning as well as the Cabinet Committee on Legislation and House Planning. The Federal-Provincial Affairs Division has a general responsibility for federal relations with the provinces, including constitutional questions, and serves the coordinating committee where policies on matters affecting the provinces are considered. It is, significantly, two of these coordinating committees that are chaired by the Prime Minister: the Cabinet Committee on Priorities and Planning and the Cabinet Committee on Federal-Provincial Relations. All other standing committees are chaired by designated ministers and are not attended by the Prime Minister unless some quite unusual circumstance makes it desirable.

The scope of the Cabinet Committee on Priorities and Planning is now more inclusive than the mainly financial aspects of policy toward which it was directed in 1968. It gives special attention to the broad objectives of the government and to major questions of policy having long-term implications. It is in that committee that the basic decisions on objectives and strategies are taken, for recommendation to the Cabinet. A very important aspect of these is, of course, deciding the general priorities of the government for the allocation of financial resources, and in the policy discussion of other Cabinet committees the determination of such priorities is obviously related to and conditioned by the decisions as to policies and strategies. The priorities are set in broad terms: objectives to be achieved, the amount of effort and resources to be directed toward each, the increase or decrease in the emphasis to be accorded to general areas of government action. It is on the basis of such broad decisions that the Treasury Board determines in detail the funds to be made available for specific programmes administered by the various departments and fixes the personnel establishment to be allocated to them.

Despite its key role, it is quite wrong, as some have done, to call the present Cabinet Committee on Priorities and Planning an "inner cabinet." Like other committees, its decisions or recommendations go to the Cabinet for confirmation or for debate and final decision. They have no status without that confirmation. Moreover the committee is intended to deal with matters of long-term and broad scope. It is not a committee intended to cover any and all areas of government action or to take quick decisions on urgent matters.

Federal-Provincial Relations

The Federal-Provincial Affairs Division, in developing a uniform and consistent policy in relations with the provinces, maintains liaison with government departments and tries, within the limits of its resources, to keep contact with the provinces as well. It coordinates preparations for major federal-provincial conferences and for constitutional review meetings.

It has become a common theme of public comment that federal-provincial relations should be more constant and intimate, and that this would remove the disagreements that have been, and continue to be, a feature of our national life. I must confess to a certain scepticism. At times one could be led to wonder whether it is not the very plethora of meetings that has provided the occasions for the disagreements and for the wide reporting of them. A Canadian Parkinson could probably demonstrate that the number of federal-provincial disputes in any one year varies in direct proportion to the number of federal-provincial meetings multiplied by the cube of the number of federal-provincial coordinating agencies in the respective governments. The following list indicates the number of formal committees as of June, 1970 that meet at the ministerial or deputy ministerial level: federal and all provinces, 28; federal and all provinces plus outside groups, 9; federal-provincial-municipal, 2; interprovincial, federal representatives as observers, 12; federal and provincial-regional representatives, 6; total, 57. On the same date the total number of multilateral committees and sub-committees involving officials was 260. There were another 150 bilateral committees of the same type. Whatever the source of problems may be, it is not the lack of meetings to talk about them.

Cabinet Government — Some Modern Aspects

The organization and the activities of Cabinet committees and of the Cabinet secretariat are directed to one essential purpose: the more effective operation of our Cabinet system, in which a collective executive decides the objectives, policies and programmes of government and in which its members take a joint responsibility for the result. From the nature of our executive, so different from that in countries like the United States where it is a single person, there flow a number of implications and consequences. The first and most obvious is that each member of the executive must know what is involved in the policy and programme decisions for which he shares responsibility, whether they are his direct concern or that of a colleague. The second is that each must have an opportunity to participate in those decisions. Participation is at its most rudimentary if it is simply to approve or disapprove a fully developed proposal. To be real and substantial it should involve awareness of problems and relevant consideration and discussion of lines of solution at a stage early enough that a minister can share in shaping the final result. Either to accept or to reject a finished product may be totally unsatisfactory and, indeed, the wrong decision so far as the government as a whole is concerned; some unknown and unconsidered alternative might have been the preferred and much better course if participation could have been effected at an earlier stage.

The changes of 1964 brought a greater measure of real consideration beyond departmental boundaries than in the past, but the situation was still one of discussing the end result rather than of participating in its production. The 1968 reforms brought that further stage. Discussions now on broad policy and general priorities mean that all ministers have an opportunity to share in giving shape to government in general and to the areas of policy for which others of their colleagues are directly responsible.

The second feature of today's system has already been pointed out. In all but the most exceptional circumstances, matters go to a Cabinet committee *first* before coming to the Cabinet. The essential officials of all interested departments are normally present. There can be, and is, probing of the information by any minister, as well as reasoning and views expressed by officials serving the minister putting forward the proposal. Ministers talk to other deputies than their own, and deputies to other ministers. Advice is less monolithic and discussions much more real. Frequently the result is to refer a matter back to officials or to the originating department for further work or for development of a different proposal. At the very least, significant modifications may be suggested in the report to the Cabinet for further discussion and final decision.

The positive results of the new system are many. Ministers have the opportunity to learn more of what their colleagues are doing and to be better informed about all aspects of government activities than under the previous methods. Policies and programmes are related more consciously and more constantly to the totality of problems and less to partial or sectional aspects. Ministers have more influence on the shape of policy as a whole, and on its development, and officials have proportionately less than they used to. This judgement is at variance with the conventional wisdom but, after thirty years in the operation of government, more than half of it at the centre, I feel confident that it is correct. Finally, there is a more planned attempt to assess in advance the probable nature of developments of broad national and social moment before they arrive as immediate problems for urgent action. Such things rarely fall within the boundaries established for administrative convenience, and, when plans were confined within these tidy limits, some quite major questions remained neglected. Obviously the success of such efforts is only partial, but they do constitute important gains. They have, however, had their price.

One price is in ministerial time: the rarest of government commodities. Better understanding and analysis of complex interrelated problems and policies take time. Discussion that leads to mature decision-making takes time. All this time, and the energy that is expended in the decision-making process, is subtracted from the finite capacity and endurance of the minister. If a minister works a five-day week of eleven hours a day, plus a good part of each week-end, what competition is there for those hours? There is attendance in the House, executive work in his department, constituency business, general work for the party, general work for the government; consultation with businessmen, representatives of public organizations and others to keep him informed and to learn their views; ceremonial duties, travel to and from the constituency, travel to and from departmental assisgnments away from Ottawa; personal business; and finally, as part of the collective executive, reading Cabinet documents, attending Cabinet committees and attending Cabinet. To do these last three thoroughly in the face of all the other demands is almost impossible. Something must suffer if more time goes into the process of executive decision. It is quite possible that the improvements in the cabinet system may have been too high a cost in the time ministers can devote to the total political role that they fill. The right balance will never be final or certain: it will change with prime ministers, governments and the stages in their four- or five-year life cycles.

I have mentioned that the old days of fiefdom are passing. To work efficiently, a complex system requires some elements to give something to other elements to maintain a balance. Ministers now, in many cases, have to give up some share of their authority and control to other ministers if the totality of policies is to be coordinated. This is unpleasant, frustrating and can cause natural resentment when the minister thinks he sees clearly what is needed, wants to make a success of his particular portfolio and is anxious to fulfil perfectly natural ambitions. Understandably, some ministers feel their new share in the policies and programmes of others to be unequal compensation for the subtraction they suffer in their individual capacity to decide and to act. Speed of action is certainly less in the new system, and ministers have less chance to appear in roles of clear and firm decision.

Another resentment which ministers must feel is that caused by the ubiquity of officials, including Privy Council officers. This, too, is a part of the price for a system that in total gives broader and more real ministerial participation in policy as a whole. Without the documents, reports and interaction between ministers and officials, it could not work as well — if it could work at all.

The relationships between ministers and officials are seen in interesting and sensitive focus at Cabinet committee meetings. Ministers in general carry the discussion, but officials participate actively, especially on factual and operational aspects. They are conscious that policy decision, and therefore the main aspects of policy assessment, are for ministers. There are, however, occasions when a deputy must objectively review the full policy and public implications of proposed action. There are times when the responsible minister lets the deputy explain: there are equally times when the deputy remains silent while the minister explains. Both normally participate in active discussion. It is a blending of roles that requires mutual confidence and an awareness of their differences. The seasoned public servant will recognize that what are at issue are the policies of the government, to be decided by the judgement of the ministers, even though this means accepting gracefully decisions that may be personally distasteful. The advantages in decision-making are clear. There are, equally, advantages in administration. The exposure of senior officials to the thinking and policy concerns of ministers helps them to explain to their departments the logic of decisions that might otherwise seem wrong, incomprehensible or "petty politics".

During policy discussion there comes a time when the ministers must be alone. Candour is required. There must be no restraints on frank talk. This occurs at Cabinet where the ultimate decision is taken. The ministers are responsible. It is their government. There must be no inhibition caused by the presence of an advocate official. He advises, he has full opportunity to be heard in the appropriate forum, but the Cabinet decides, not the senior officials or any group of them.

Governing Canada has some special complications: the fact of our bilingual national character, our multicultural nature, or sheer size, the regional differences in economic growth and prosperity, the geographic, economic and cultural bonds that fuse us to the United States of America while we struggle to be different. All of these social, economic, physical, psychic and systemic factors and forces produce stress. Much of the task of regulating these stresses and strains, assuaging the pain and balancing the growth, falls upon the federal government.

With this increasing complexity, and partly as a result of it, comes the new scale of operation for those who must decide. The problems involved in tax reform, foreign ownership, the respective powers of the provinces and the federal government, the balance between environmental protection and resource development, inflation and unemployment, to name only a few that have been with us in recent months, come at a speed and with a level of expectation as to results that create a governmental load quite new in our history. For ministers to know the factors, the possible courses of action and the implications of alternative policies with respect to a single problem — or even to one part of a single problem — requires a thorough presentation of all the issues, time to weigh and analyse them, and adequate opportunity to discuss and to decide. Ministers today have a load that tries the limits of physical and intellectual powers.

On Planning

The principal *planning* objective of the past three years has been to increase the time available between the perception of a problem by ministers and the necessity of action with regard to it. An effort has been made to identify ministerial responsibility for the problem as clearly and as soon as possible and to marshal whatever is required to examine and prepare a plan to try to manage it, and finally, to allow time to organize for action.

What is urgent will always clamour for attention and probably get it. What is important must receive attention well in advance and be given lots of time for organization for action. If this does not happen — and if it is not insisted on whatever the pressures may be — the urgent pushes out the important. The consequence is to be overtaken by crises and to let events, rather than choice, determine the direction we take.

A good deal is being written about "normative planning" and what is taken by some to be the converse, "incrementalism."[3] Considerable improvement has been made in the Privy Council Office in the last four years in methods of analysis, using general systems theory and to some extent general communications theory. Understanding the governmental system and the social system better, due to the insights of these theories, is one thing, but successful application of the theories by the central executive in a rational, creative way is another. The policy sciences taken together constitute a frontier field, and applying policy science to cabinet government is still a frontier effort. From our experience it might be said that "top down" policy determination works part of the time, "bottom up" policy determination works much of the time, and that, despite all efforts, many governmental decisions will continue to be in response to problems arriving at a different time and in a different form from what was anticipated. The process of integrated planning has, however, made great strides in the last few years at all levels of the government.

Cabinet, Prime Minister and Departments

In the complex operation of the cabinet system, with ministers together deciding the policies and the strategies of government, it is obvious that the role of the Prime Minister is crucial. He alone of the Cabinet is responsible for no one aspect of government. He alone looks constantly at the total picture. He it is who has chosen his colleagues; he is recognized by the country and by Parliament as the person generally responsible for the success or failure of government in meeting the problems of the state. Within the Cabinet he must be the master of his administration but he must recognize its collective nature and avoid autocracy. Where necessary he must change the functions of his colleagues and, when necessary, invite or require a departure. He is the only one with the authority to police and to change the boundaries between them. The many-sided role of the Prime Minister is nowhere more difficult or more demanding of a sensitive balance of intellectual and human qualities than when he is chairman of the collective executive. Assisting the Prime Minister in ensuring a coherence of policy and giving support in the total process of decision-making are two of the main functions of the Privy Council Office.

As a department provides its ministers with analysis, advice and recommendations on the objectives of the department, so the Privy Council Office gives the Prime Minister information, analysis and advice on the totality of policies. The probability of a coherence of policy is thus enhanced.

It will be readily apparent that the information, analysis and advice for the Prime Minister ties in completely with the broader function of the Privy Council Office in servicing the entire system of Cabinet and Cabinet committees which I have described. Programmes and policy proposals

---

[3] Malcolm Rowan, "A Conceptual Framework for Government Policy Making", *Canadian Public Administration,* vol. 13, no. 3 (Fall 1970), p. 279; A. Etzioni, "Mixed Scanning: A 'Third' Approach to Decision Making", *Public Administration Review* (1967), vol. 27, pp. 385-92.

come to the Office as submissions to the Cabinet and are immediately circulated to all ministers. At the same time they are allocated to one or another of the Cabinet committees. The appropriate secretariat picks it up at that point. If more information is needed, that is secured. If it has aspects that relate to another committee or secretariat, there is consultation to see how best to cover all aspects of consideration. When the matter goes to the committee, the secretariat records the discussion, prepares the minutes and draws up the report of decision, or recommendation to go on to the Cabinet. All of this provides the information for a briefing document to the Prime Minister covering all essential aspects of every question on each Cabinet agenda. It provides too the basis for the information system of the office on the operations of government as a whole.

When decisions are taken by the Cabinet, or when committee recommendations or decisions are confirmed, the next stage in the Privy Council Office function is to inform departments and agencies with speed and precision so that action may follow. This may be done orally if the need for speed is great, but the standard procedure is communication by a "Record of Decision" within twenty-four hours. Orders-in-council may or may not be involved; usually not. It is only when a formal, legal instrument is required that they enter the picture.

This, in essence, is the role of the Privy Council Office: one of information, coordination, follow-up and support provided to the Prime Minister and the Cabinet as a whole with, as a vital aspect, constant relations with all departments of the government.

One other matter that must be referred to is the relationship between the Privy Council Office and the Prime Minister's Office. It is one that calls for the greatest harmony. Given the Prime Minister's functions as leader of a political party, leader of the government in the House of Commons, and chairman of the Cabinet, the Prime Minister's own staff are constantly securing information, analysing and recommending on matters that relate to policies and objectives of the government. The Prime Minister's Office is partisan, politically oriented, yet operationally sensitive. The Privy Council Office is non-partisan, operationally oriented yet politically sensitive. It has been established between the principal secretary to the Prime Minister and his senior staff on the one hand, and the clerk of the Privy Council and his senior staff on the other, that they share the same fact base but keep out of each other's affairs. What is known in each office is provided freely and openly to the other if it is relevant or needed for its work, but each acts from a perspective and in a role quite different from the other.

Obviously each office requires a knowledge of the areas of action of the other and the actions of the two must, to the extent that they affect the total policy or action of the government, be consistent. To aid in information and coherence two sets of meetings with the Prime Minister, involving both offices, have been established. The first, a daily meeting with two officers from the Privy Council Office and two from the Prime Minister's office has been a constant base for coordination for many years. It started with one officer from each place and, as life became more complex and difficult, became the two from each that now attend. It deals with the day-to-day flow of affairs that the Prime Minister must know, consider, prepare for or decide. The second meeting is on planning, and occurs once a week with an additional person from each office who has responsibility in the longer term development and direction of policy.

It goes without saying that mutual confidence and mutual respect — and mutual understanding of the basic difference between the two roles — are the foundations of cooperation between the Prime Minister's Office and the Privy Council Office. All have been present, in my experience, and without them the operation of government under the stresses of today would be difficult indeed.

Of politics and public service

Finally, a word about politics and liberty. The popular will is expressed through politics. Ideology, technology and bureaucracy have to be restrained so that politics may rule; otherwise theories, inventions and organizations would smother life. The elected representative of the people, who makes a trade of politics, but who makes no claim to total knowledge or wisdom, must be provided with optimum liberty to decide what set of relationships ought to prevail, stabilized at a chosen level, to constitute the goals of government. Providing this liberty to the politicians is exceedingly difficult. From the standpoint of the Cabinet Minister, the complications start with the catalogue of complexities of existing policies, programmes and activities. To ensure that responsible politicians and not civil servants have the final say, the Cabinet has the responsibility of decision. For what it does, it is responsible to Parliament. It would be entirely unrealistic to expect the larger body of politicians to be quiescent and, in fact, our democratic system would be failing if they were. Thus the desired freedom of ministers to consider and to decide is conditioned by a torrent of observations, questions, and advice all proclaimed publicly from committees of the House of Commons and Senate, backbenchers of all parties and from party conventions.

Further constraints on freedom of decision come from the fact of instant communications. Opinions and reactions, relevant or irrelevant, tumble in without ceasing. The speed with which society moves has conditioned the public to expect instantaneous decision and action on matters of public policy. Unrealistic expectations clamour for action at once. The final complication is the most serious of all. There is an unrecognized inconsistency in the demand for both speed and participation in difficult decisions on complex issues.

Conscious of the catalogue of complexities in the society which they have been elected to regulate, surrounded by the reality of the existing amalgam of policy programmes and activities, sensitive to the clamour of friendly and unfriendly voices and often urged to act boldly but with due regard, in the light of all considerations but at once, Cabinet ministers can only feel more captive than free. The staff of the Privy Council Office has, as its duty, to provide whatever aid and assistance it can to permit individual and collective judgement to prevail in the Cabinet chamber and, through its wise application, sound policy to emerge to meet the problems of the present and the future. To assist government in this way is demanding employment, but for sheer interest and intellectual challenge it would be hard to match. The agenda of Cabinet, week by week, reflects the problems, interests and aspirations of the Canadian people. To understand, to inform, to advise and to share in the discussion of such meetings is a reward in itself. For an official to feel that he has contributed, however modestly, to constructive decisions for a better country in a better world brings no glory, but a great sense of participation in events that count.

8

The Prime Minister and the Bureaucratic Elite*

Bruce Thordarson

As Minister of Justice in the Pearson government, Pierre Elliott Trudeau realized that the federal civil service had a great deal of power and at least the potential to make effective use of it, but that it lacked centralized political leadership. It was his desire to establish co-ordinated control and guidance when he became Prime Minister that led him to take such an active personal part in policy formulation that he was soon labelled a "crypto-president". It was his desire to organize around him a group of advisers upon whom he relied so much that they became known by some disgruntled civil servants as "the supergroup", and to bring order and discipline to the operations of the Cabinet.

One of Mr. Trudeau's first steps after the 1968 election was to re-organize and expand the Prime Minister's Office (PMO) and the Privy Council Office (PCO). Unaffected by the budgetary freezes imposed on most government organizations, the two increased in size by forty per cent

*Bruce Thordarson, *Trudeau and Foreign Policy: A Study in Decision-Making* (Toronto: Oxford University Press, 1972), pp. 85-93. Reprinted and abridged by permission of the publisher. Published in conjunction with the Canadian Institute of International Affairs.

during the first year of Trudeau's administration. According to Marc Lalonde, Trudeau's Principal Secretary, the Prime Minister was determined to achieve two major objectives: to enable the government to respond more effectively to the increased demands being placed upon it, and to ensure a greater political control over the entire government apparatus.[1] It was Trudeau's belief that power had slipped in the past to civil servants and was not sufficiently in the hands of the country's elected representatives, who alone were responsible to the public. Mr. Trudeau also believed that there was a need to co-ordinate more effectively the activities of various departments so that they complemented, rather than conflicted with, one another. "In order to have this team effect", he said in 1969, "we must make sure that every ministerial recommendation is meshed in with what is happening in the other departments . . . and in order to plan we must have a strong planning control body."[2]

The Privy Council Office was responsible for co-ordinating government planning, and its role in this field was increased by Mr. Trudeau. In February 1969, he announced that it was being split into two divisions, one for operations and one for plans, in accordance with his government's desire to give "added emphasis to planning and priorities".[3] The increase in the planning duties of the Prime Minister's Office was largely a response to his desire to inject a greater "political input" into policy planning. Its members—specially chosen by the Prime Minister and, unlike those of the PCO, not civil servants—are responsible for injecting Mr. Trudeau's "own input" into a few selected areas that require the personal involvement of the Prime Minister. Gordon Robertson, the head of the PCO, has summarized the differences between the two organizations in the following way: the PMO is "partisan, politically oriented, yet operationally sensitive", while the PCO is "non-partisan, operationally oriented yet politically sensitive".[4] In other words both advise the Prime Minister, but the first concern of the PMO is the effect the policies it recommends will have on the Liberal Party's electoral fortunes, while the PCO thinks in terms of the effective operation of the Canadian government. There is undoubtedly some overlapping between the two, for the distinction between "partisan" and "political" cannot always be maintained; however, both are intended to improve the government's ability to plan effectively and to avoid as much as possible the need for ad hoc decisions.

This noticeable expansion in the size and duties of the PMO and PCO has been cited as evidence by critics who accuse Mr. Trudeau of wielding "in-

---

[1] Marc Lalonde, "The Changing Role of the Prime Minister's Office". A paper presented to the 23rd Annual Meeting of the Institute of Public Administration of Canada, September 8, 1971, p. 22.

[2] Marc Lalonde, "The Changing Role of the Prime Minister's Office," p. 23.

[3] Globe and Mail, February 3, 1970, p. 7.

[4] Gordon Robertson, "The Changing Role of the Privy Council Office". A paper presented to the 23rd Annual Meeting of the Institute of Public Administration of Canada, September 8, 1971, p. 20. Reproduced in this book on pp. 52-63.

creasing and arbitrary power" at the expense of Cabinet, Parliament, and the civil service.[5] But Trudeau is not the first Prime Minister to recognize the importance of the PMO and PCO, for both grew in size and importance in previous administrations in response to the proliferation of government's responsibilities in the post-war period. Moreover, there are technical considerations that partly explain the rapid growth of both offices under Mr. Trudeau. In the past many of their members were not officially attached to the PMO or PCO but were merely seconded from the civil service, with the result that the official size of both offices remained relatively small. Part of the staff increase is also due to the rapid growth of service, as distinct from planning duties; for instance, the number of letters sent to the Prime Minister has soared since Mr. Trudeau took office, and all must be answered by the PMO's correspondence section (by far its largest branch). Furthermore, it is not correct to assume that the increase of the power of the Prime Minister since 1968 has necessarily decreased the important roles played by the Cabinet, Parliament, or the civil service. The responsibilities of government grow almost daily, and even when some are assumed by the Prime Minister and his assistants, the workload of other government bodies continues to increase as well. There is no doubt that Mr. Trudeau has attempted to ensure that he maintains control over the most important decisions — especially those dealing with the establishment of overall priorities, which require a great deal of interdepartmental co-ordination—and that he has assembled a large and capable staff to provide him with the best advice possible. But it is surely an exaggeration to say that he has done so with the ulterior motive of gaining "arbitrary" power for its own sake, or to imply that he has left other arms of government virtually powerless.

One of the dangers of building up such a highly specialized body of advisers is that this might lead to a deterioration in relations between the political leaders and the civil service. This is particularly likely if the Prime Minister's advisers go beyond their role of co-ordinating the policies of several departments and begin participating in the formulation or implementation of policies for which one department is particularly responsible — as they did, for instance, in determining the NATO decision of 1969. The official government view is that relations between the Prime Minster's staff and the civil service are excellent; indeed there is little present evidence of conflict, especially since the roles of the PMO and PCO have recently been publicized in speeches by their respective heads and thereby made less mysterious and less likely to arouse suspicion. But during the first two years of the Trudeau administration, such was not always the case. Senior civil servants may not have understood the functions of the expanding PMO and PCO, and the officers of these two organizations may not have realized the dangers of becoming involved in issues that civil servants had long regarded as their own responsibility.

---

[5] Walter Stewart, *Shrug: Trudeau in Power* (Toronto: New Press, 1971), p. 175.

Some members of the Department of External Affairs, for example, resented the important role played by two former foreign-service officers: Ivan Head, then the Prime Minister's legislative assistant and later his special assistant; and Marshall Crowe, responsible until 1971 for the operations side of the Privy Council Office. The greater political responsibilities of the PMO led to Mr. Head's becoming Trudeau's chief adviser in matters of foreign policy. In 1969 he made two trips to Nigeria as the Prime Minister's personal representative in an attempt to facilitate the flow of Canadian aid, and in the following year he visited Washington and Moscow in connection with Canada's Arctic activities. The important part he played in the 1969 NATO decision also contributed to his reputation as the Prime Minister's number one foreign-policy adviser. One External Affairs official, decrying what he saw as a shift of the centre of policy formulation from his department, remarked: "One of our most astonishing diplomatic failures was our failure to establish a link with Ivan Head." This consternation in the ranks of senior bureaucrats was clearly not unwelcome to either the Prime Minister or his assistants. Ivan Head commented: "I don't think it hurts the mandarins to know that the Prime Minister has people in his office with both experience and ability to challenge what comes up".[6]

Mr. Trudeau also set out to reform the working of his Cabinet. From his predecessor he inherited twenty-seven Cabinet committees whose task had been to make policy recommendations and leave the final decision to the whole Cabinet. Aware of the duplication of effort that such a procedure created, Trudeau slashed this number to nine and gave them the responsibility for making many of the final policy decisions.[7] The most important of these standing committees is the Priorities and Planning Committee, sometimes referred to as the "Inner Cabinet", which is concerned with establishing the government's overall priorities and integrating the policies of the various departments to fit these priorities. It is chaired by the Prime Minister himself, as is the Committee on Federal-Provincial Relations. There are four functional committees dealing with external policy, economic policy, social policy, and culture and information, as well as a statutory committee for science policy and technology. The normal procedure is for the decisions made in these committees to be given routine approval by the full Cabinet; only if there is a division of opinion in the committee, or if the committee's decision is challenged by another minister, does the policy in question become a matter for debate in Cabinet. The intention is clearly to minimize the number of issues requiring examination by the Cabinet as a whole, for the committees speed up decision-making only when they themselves make the final decisions.

---

[6] *Globe and Mail,* January 15, 1969, p. 9.

[7] For an excellent description of the organization of Cabinet committees in the Trudeau administration, see Fred Schindeler, "The Prime Minister and the Cabinet: History and Development", in *Apex of Power: The Prime Minister and Political Leadership in Canada,* ed. Thomas Hockin (Toronto: Prentice-Hall, 1971), and Gordon Robertson, "The Changing Role of the Privy Council Office".

Prime Minister Trudeau has also altered the way in which Cabinet ministers participate in the formulation of policy. According to a senior civil servant, the administration has created a "consensual" system of Cabinet decision-making in which every interested minister is given the opportunity to voice his opinion even when the issue under discussion does not come under his ministry. The system means that ministers act "less on their own" than in the past. The extent to which a Prime Minister allows members of his Cabinet to determine foreign policy, for example, is largely a matter of individual temperament and style. It is Trudeau's style to invite the participation of as many ministers as are interested. His temperament, however, does not allow him to be influenced on issues of major importance by any but a few key ministers — most importantly Jean Marchand, Gérard Pelletier, and Donald Macdonald.

In a paper presented to the 1971 Commonwealth Prime Ministers' Conference at Singapore, Mr. Trudeau discussed the role of the civil service in a modern government. He said there was a need for new techniques of administration to do away with the sluggishness and resistance to change of entrenched bureaucracies. "To overcome this inertia and to redirect the momentum requires all the energy a government has, and frequently even this is not enough".[8] Disparaging remarks about the civil service were nothing new for the Prime Minister. On February 28, 1968 he said that the government could not find answers to problems if it had to depend on the advice of bureaucrats looking for the best theoretical or abstract solution.[9] Peter Newman reports that much of Trudeau's hesitancy to run for the leadership of the Liberal Party was due to his distrust of the growing power of the inherently conservative federal bureaucracy. "Before I make my decision", he quotes Trudeau as confiding to a few friends, "I've got to find out whether it's really possible to do anything once you get into the prime minister's office."[10] As early as 1951 Trudeau wrote that it was a tendency of the federal civil servant "de se croire omniscient et omnipotent", and to bring to modern government a stifling "fonctionarisme" that constitutes "un danger très sérieux pour le régime de la liberté".[11] Mr. Trudeau's disapproval of the policy-making role of the civil service may well have increased during the Pearson administration. In 1968 even R. G. Robertson, Clerk of the Privy Council, Secretary to the Cabinet, and the government's highest-ranking civil servant, was writing that

without changes from present methods, there is a real risk of a steady reduction in the efficiency of government in coping with growing needs, together with a shift of effective decision-making from the ministers, where it ought to be, into the hands of civil servants.[12]

---

[8] *Ottawa Citizen,* January 21, 1971, p. 15.
[9] Quoted in Donald Peacock, *Journey to Power* (Toronto: Ryerson, 1968), p. 255.
[10] Peter Newman, *The Distemper of Our Times* (Toronto: McClelland and Stewart, 1968), p. 447.
[11] Pierre Elliott Trudeau, "Politique fonctionelle II", Cité Libre, février 1951, pp. 24, 26.
[12] R.G. Robertson, "The Canadian Parliament and Cabinet in the Face of Modern Demands", *Canadian Public Administration,* vol. 11, no. 3 (Fall, 1968), p. 276.

When financial problems necessitated the imposition of spending guidelines on the civil service, Mr. Trudeau's views of the relative importance of the various departments became more apparent. Policies to promote bilingualism and regional economic expansion dominated the first tier of spending priorities and were allowed to expand; international-development assistance and health and welfare were among the "medium-growth" functions in the second tier of priorities; while military and foreign expenditures were assigned to the bottom tier and designated "low-growth" functions.

Another result of Mr. Trudeau's attitude to the civil service has been an alteration in the way policy recommendations are made to Cabinet.[13] In the past, departments tended to suggest to ministers the approach they favoured, while under Trudeau they present not recommendations but a list of all the available policy options relating to the matter under consideration. If the department has a strong preference for one point of view, this can be made obvious in its presentation. It must still, however, inform the Cabinet of the alternative courses available and provide an analysis of the pros and cons of each. Failure to do so lessens the department's credibility within Cabinet. This approach is consistent with the Trudeau administration's desire to relieve the civil service, to a greater degree than in previous administrations, of responsibility for policy formulation. If Cabinet is to have a greater role in this area it must be aware of all the policy alternatives. When these options are received from the department, they are examined by the Cabinet Secretariat and then by Cabinet committees in the light of information obtained from a variety of sources — other departments and their ministers, parliamentary committees, public opinion, and, of course, the PMO and PCO. With this multiplicity of inputs — a characteristic of the Trudeau administration — the Cabinet has succeeded in increasing political control over policy formulation.

---

[13]This paragraph is based primarily on interviews with a Cabinet Minister in the Trudeau government and with a senior civil servant.

9

The Bureaucratic Elite
and Policy Formation*

Mitchell Sharp

What I wish to convey to you are personal impressions of what it is like to be a senior civil servant and comments on the role of civil servants in the formulation of policy in Canada.

First, contrary to what I had expected and contrary to the common opinion, I found a civil service career to be far from dull and humdrum. Those 16 years were full of stimulating experiences and highly exciting activities. Like so many others, I was called to Ottawa early in the war to do a wartime job in the Department of Finance. But when the time came to return to private business, I made the choice to remain in Ottawa and I have never regretted it.

The main reason for that decision was one man — the late Clifford Clark, Deputy Minister of Finance. The contribution of this man to the Canadian nation will never be fully appreciated, because the story can never be fully told of his influence upon the course of events. Being a civil servant, he worked anonymously, in the background, his views and his actions finding their expression in official utterances of Ministers and in the statutes approved by Parliament. Nor would he have wished it otherwise, and he inculcated into all of us his ideal of the good civil servant.

To a greater degree than at any time before or since, the Department of Finance, during Dr. Clark's tenure as Deputy Minister, was the central idea-generating department of government. Under any circumstances, the Treasury, through control of the purse strings, has a key position in the Ottawa hierarchy. But Dr. Clark was not content that the Treasury should merely control. His curiosity and his energy found expression in the advocacy of policies touching every aspect of Canada's economic life. Price control, housing, family allowances, veterans' benefits, export credits insurance, and agricultural price supports are only a few subjects of the many, apart from those of a purely financial character, on which he had imaginative views — and to which he made significant contributions.

I was fortunate, too, in working under three excellent Ministers. The first was J. L. Ilsley. He is a man of great intelligence and broad human understanding. If he had a fault as Minister, it was his over-conscientiousness. He spent

*Mitchell Sharp, "Reflections of a Former Civil Servant". Reprinted by permission of author from notes used in an informal talk to a group of Toronto businessmen, November 14, 1958, and reproduced by the Civil Service Commission, Ottawa. The author, now Secretary of State for External Affairs, was formerly Deputy Minister of the Department of Trade and Commerce.

hours debating difficult problems. And after he had made his decision, he spent hours debating whether he had made the right decision. It was strenuous to work under him but at least one had the satisfaction of knowing that the opposition was not likely to succeed in raising an argument he had not thoroughly considered. One of the most important jobs of a senior civil servant is guessing what questions or arguments the Opposition is likely to raise in Parliament and providing the answers in advance.

D. C. Abbott was a different kind of Minister. He had the characteristics of the good corporation lawyer, one of which is to be able to master a brief in short order. His mind was extraordinarily quick. It was a pleasure to sit before him on the floor of the Commons when the House was in Committee. It required only two or three whispered words of advice for him to get to his feet and in reply to a question give an answer lasting 5 minutes. It seemed to me that of the Ministers I had the privilege to know, he understood best the political art of the possible. On occasion he could show remarkable courage, but he selected the issues on which to fight with great care and a sure instinct.

C. D. Howe, of course, was unique. It is most improbable that we shall see his like in Canadian politics in our time. His intuition on economic matters was little short of miraculous and his fund of knowledge the despair of his advisers. I tried my best, when his Deputy, to keep myself well-informed about economic developments in Canada. Yet I can say truthfully that seldon was I able to tell Mr. Howe anything about which he had not already heard or surmised. His wide acquaintanceship was one of the reasons. He knew every important businessman in Canada and they seemed to have made a practice of talking to "C.D." whether they wanted anything from the government or not. Most of all, they seemed to want his opinion.

Interplay of personalities and the constant exchange of views among the leading public servants that formed such a characteristic and stimulating feature of the Ottawa scene when I was there also explain why I got so much satisfaction out of working in Ottawa.

Some observers have referred disparagingly to the Ottawa "brains trust". Those who use this term, of course, do not think that those who are supposed to comprise this mythical body either have brains or can be trusted. Needless to say, there is no "brains trust" that pretends to know all the answers and there never has been. Indeed, on many matters it was considered undesirable to try to reach common views for presentation to Ministers. To have attempted to do so might have given a quite unjustified authority to the resulting piece of paper or have glossed over differences of interpretation that Ministers should have been aware of.

Fortunately, however, the leading advisers of the Government do not work in water-tight compartments within their Departments jealously guarding their prerogatives; they make a practice of consultation. They do this partly in formally constituted committees created by Cabinet and partly, and even more importantly, in informal gatherings at lunch, at dinner, at receptions, at evening parties and at the fishing club. It is taken for granted at most Ottawa social gatherings that the wives gravitate to one end of the room while their husbands collect at the other for that infinitely fascinating occuaption of "talking shop".

From observation and from conversation with civil servants in other countries, I have come to the conclusion that this close contact and constant exchange of views among leading civil servants in Ottawa is in many respects unique. In Washington inter-departmental consultation hardly exists except in formally constituted committees. In London, there is greater informality during working hours than in Washington, but after hours civil servants depart for their homes in widely separated suburbs of the city and have relatively few social contacts.

It was therefore something of an intellectual adventure to be a senior public servant in Ottawa during my time and I am sure it continues to be so. One's horizon was always being broadened by contact with a variety of first class minds working on a variety of matters of national interest. And I might add, one's pet ideas had to be supported by more than mere enthusiasm to survive the abundant doses of cold water that were politely poured on them by fellow civil servants. I can assure you that it is much more difficult to be an acknowledged authority on fiscal and monetary policy, foreign affairs, full employment, trade and like matters in the civil service community of Ottawa than it is in the business community of Toronto.

From time to time someone refers disparagingly to "ivory tower" thinking in Ottawa. I suppose there is always some of that kind of thinking everywhere, including Ottawa, and I, for one, believe that it has its place. To suggest, however, that the thinking that goes on behind the scenes in Ottawa is highly theoretical and divorced from the everyday world, is to misjudge the intellectual atmosphere in the senior public service. The touchstone for every idea is and has to be, "will it work?" Moreover, this test of practicality is applied more rigorously in Ottawa than elsewhere because political as well as economic considerations have to be given due weight.

In one sense, of course, public servants do not concern themselves with "politics". That is, they do not concern themselves with party politics. All my senior public servant colleagues were selected on the basis of their qualifications and most of them had come up through the ranks. There were virtually no what-might-be-called political appointments. Indeed, with one or two exceptions, I hadn't the slightest idea of my colleagues' political persuasions, or if they had any. Clifford Clark, himself, had been appointed by Bennett and became one of the most trusted advisers of the Liberal regime. Graham Towers, too, was appointed Governor of the Bank of Canada by Bennett and was re-appointed by King and St. Laurent.

In another sense, however, the senior advisers to the Ministers must be interested in "politics". If they are to be any good at all, they should give advice to their Ministers on all the implications of proposals under consideration, including political implications. The Ministers themselves, of course, are the final authorities on political acceptability. They make the decisions and take the consequences, good or bad.

Although the permanent senior public servant has no political axe to grind, it is his duty to support his Minister by giving him the best advice of which he is capable and by ensuring that the decisions ultimately reached are put into proper effect. To put it more shortly, the good public servant tries to keep his Minister out of trouble. This is not only the tradition of Canadian public service, but it rests upon the very practical consideration that the Department cannot be divorced from the Minister. If the Minister is successful, the Department officials bask in the reflected glory. If the Minister blunders, the Department has often the unenviable job of helping to straighten out the mess. If the public servant does his job properly and the Minister knows how to use him, a close relationship of mutual respect, even friendship, is bound to arise between them, which has nothing to do with party politics. It may even happen that the best "political" advice a Minister receives, in the sense of adding to his public reputation, comes from his non-political advisers.

I have often thought that this is really one of the most effective arguments for the merit system in public service appointments. The Minister who appoints political supporters to jobs at the top level in his Department is cutting himself off from good advice. The political appointee, being dependent upon the Minister for his job, is likely to tell the Minister what he thinks the Minister would like to hear, not what he should hear. A civil servant, appointed on merit and having security of tenure, gives disinterested advice, without fear or favour. The Minister does not have to accept that advice but at least he knows it has no ulterior motive, which cannot be said of much of the advice freely available to those in positions of authority.

I overheard a conversation one day between a Minister of the Crown and one of his constituency friends. This friend was asking the Minister how he ran his Department. "I suppose", he said, "you call in your Deputy Minister, tell him what you want done, and he goes and does it." The Minister, who was an honest man, replied: "No, that is not at all how it happens. I call in the Deputy Minister, tell him what the problem is and he brings forward a number of possible solutions. Then I make the decision and he carries it out." That Minister was not only honest; he knew how to use his advisers to best advantage. He left himself free for the major political tasks of decision making, leadership in Parliament and getting re-elected.

Civil servants do not make policy, all rumours to the contrary notwithstanding; that is the prerogative of the elected representatives of the people. But in this day and age, civil servants do have a profound influence upon the making of policy. In the first place, someone must assemble the relevant facts and analyze their significance. The Ministers simply do not have time to do so regardless of how many hours they work. Nor can Ministers depend entirely upon non-governmental advisers for the facts and their analysis, however useful this kind of contribution may be from time to time. When decisions are to be made, the Ministers have to be sure that the facts are really facts and the analysis unbiased.

This function of fact gathering and analysis is an important facet of the policy-making functions of the public service. But it is by no means the whole story. Senior public servants are and should be the source of ideas. Their job is to present to Ministers well considered plans of action, not only in response to requests for advice, but even before Ministers have even thought that anything needed to be done.

This should be obvious but I don't think it is . The typical senior civil servant seems to be thought of as a quite intelligent but passive agent of government, waiting to be set in motion by his Minister and producing in time a memorandum of well-balanced pros and cons. There are occasions, of course, when the senior adviser has to perform exactly that function. But when I think back over my experience, I remember more occasions when civil servants by fruitful initiatives led the Government to adopt lines of policy which would never have occurred to them otherwise.

Perhaps you have heard the story about Winston Churchill's first Ministerial appointment. Someone is said to have overheard a conversation between Mr. Churchill, as he then was, and his permanent secretary — corresponding to our Deputy Minister — who had been Head of the Department for some years. Mr. Churchill is speaking: "I know, Sir Edward, that you are the Permanent Secretary, and I am only the Minister, but at least I think that you should give some consideration to my views."

This is probably an apocryphal story and could never happen in Canada. It most certainly does not represent the attitude of the present permanent heads of Departments in Ottawa, who from my observation, behaved in a most exemplary manner when the change of Government occurred in 1957. For the sake of good government in Canada, however, there should be a better appreciation of the important role of senior civil servants. We are more dependent upon them that most of us realize. Fortunately the standard at Ottawa is, on the whole, excellent, largely because of the high ideals and strong personalities of those who laid the foundations of the present structure.

It will take continuing effort to maintain that standard. The Civil Service Act [now the Public Service Employment Act] does not, by itself, assure a competent service. It is essentially a protection against politics in the civil service. Positive recruitment must be carried on and a career in the civil service must be made to appeal as an opportunity and a challenge to the best brains among our young people.

Readings

Bellamy, David, J. "Policy-Making in the 1970's." *Canadian Public Administration,* vol. 15, no. 3 (Fall, 1972) pp. 490-95.

Bieler, J.H. "The Role of the Deputy Minister: I." *Canadian Public Administration,* vol. 4, no. 4 (December, 1961), pp. 352-56.

Black, Edwin R. "Opposition Research: Some Theories and Practice." *Canadian Public Administration,* vol. 15, no. 1 (Spring, 1972), pp. 24-41.

Blakeney, Allan. "The Relationship Between Provincial Ministers and Their Deputy Ministers." *Canadian Public Administration,* vol. 15, no. 1 (Spring, 1972), pp. 42-45.

Bridges, the Right Hon. Lord. "The Relationships between Ministers and the Permanent Departmental Head." *Canadian Public Administration,* vol. 7, no. 3 (September, 1964), pp. 269-81.

Burns, R.M. "The Role of the Deputy Minister: II." *Canadian Public Administration,* vol. 4, no. 4 (December, 1961), pp. 357-62.

Close, Lawrence J. and Ronald M. Burns. *The Municipal Winter Works Incentive Program: A Study of Government Expenditure Decision-Making.* Toronto: Canadian Tax Foundation, 1971.

Doern, G. Bruce. "The Budgetary Process and the Policy Role of the Federal Bureaucracy." In *Structures of Policy-Making in Canada,* eds. G. Bruce Doern and Peter Aucoin. Toronto: Macmillan, 1971, pp. 79-112.

Doern, G. Bruce, "The Development of Policy Organizations in the Executive Arena." In *Structures of Policy-Making in Canada,* eds., G. Bruce Doern and Peter Aucoin. Toronto: Macmillan, 1971, pp. 39-78.

Doern, G. Bruce. "Recent Changes in the Philosophy of Policy-Making in Canada." *Canadian Journal of Political Science,* vol. 4, no. 2 (June, 1971), pp. 243-64.

Doern, G. Bruce. *Science and Politics in Canada.* Montreal: McGill-Queen's University Press, 1972.

Hicks, H.D. "Civil Servants and Politicians: a Defence of Politicians." *Canadian Public Administration,* vol. 6, no. 3 (September, 1963), pp. 261-73.

Hodgetts, J.E. "The Civil Service and Policy Formation." *Canadian Journal of Economics and Political Science,* vol. 23, no. 4 (November, 1957), pp. 467-79.

Hoffman, David, "Liaison Officers and Ombudsmen: Canadian MP's and their Relations with the Federal Bureaucracy and Executive." In *Apex of Power,* ed. Thomas A. Hockin. Toronto: Prentice-Hall, 1971, pp. 146-62.

Jewett, Pauline. "The Political and Administrative Aspects of Policy Formation." In *Canadian Economic Policy,* ed. T. Brewis et al. 2nd ed. Toronto: The Macmillan Co. of Canada, 1965, pp. 305-57.

Johnson, A.W. "Management Theory and Cabinet Government." *Canadian Public Administration,* vol. 14, no. 1 (Spring, 1971), pp. 73-81.

Johnson, A.W. "The Role of the Deputy Minister: III." *Canadian Public Administration,* vol. 4, no. 4 (December, 1961), pp. 363-73.

Lalonde, Marc. "The Changing Role of the Prime Minister's Office." *Canadian Public Administration,* vol. 14, no. 4 (Winter, 1971), pp. 509-37.

Mallory, J.R. "The Minister's Office Staff: an Unreformed Part of the Public Service." *Canadian Public Administration,* vol. 10, no. 1 (March 1967), pp. 25-34.

Mallory, J.R. and B. A. Smith. "The Legislative Role of Parliamentary Committees in Canada: the Case of the Joint Committee on the Public Service Bills." *Canadian Public Administration,* vol. 15, no. 1 (Spring, 1972), pp. 1-23.

Matheson, William A. "The Cabinet and the Canadian Bureaucracy." In *Public Administration in Canada,* eds. W.D.K. Kernaghan and A.M. Willms. 2nd ed. Toronto: Methuen Publications, 1971, pp. 339-47.

McKeough, W. Darcy, "The Relations of Ministers and Civil Servants." *Canadian Public Administration,* vol. 12, no. 1 (Spring, 1969), pp. 1-8.

Pickersgill, J.W. "Bureaucrats and Politicians." *Canadian Public Administration,* vol. 15, no. 3 (Fall, 1972), pp. 418-27.

Porter, J. "The Bureaucratic Elite: a Reply to Professor Rowat." *Canadian Journal of Economics and Political Science,* vol. 25, no. 2 (May, 1959), pp. 205-7.

Porter, J. "Higher Public Servants and the Bureaucratic Elite in Canada." *Canadian Journal of Economics and Political Science,* vol. 24, no. 4 (November, 1958), pp. 483-501.

Robertson, R.G. "The Canadian Parliament and Cabinet in the Face of Modern Demands." *Canadian Public Administration,* vol. 11, no. 3 (Fall, 1968), pp. 272-79.
Robertson, Gordon. "The Changing Role of the Privy Council Office." *Canadian Public Administration,* vol. 14, no. 4 (Winter, 1971), pp. 487-508, and Ottawa: Information Canada, 1971.
Rowan, Malcolm. "A Conceptual Framework for Government Policy-Making." *Canadian Public Administration,* vol. 13, no. 3 (Fall, 1970), pp. 277-96.
Rowat, Donald C. "On John Porter's Bureaucratic Elite in Canada." *Canadian Journal of Economics and Political Science,* vol. 25, no. 2 (May, 1959), pp. 205-7.
Szablowski, George. "The Optimal Policy-Making System: Implications for the Canadian Political Process." In *Apex of Power,* ed. Thomas A. Hockin. Toronto: Prentice-Hall, 1971, pp. 135-45.

Chapter Four

Sources of Public Policy
Influence and Advice

Public policies are the outputs and outcomes of interaction among a multiplicity of actors in the political system. The counsel which politicians receive from bureaucrats may be either buttressed or challenged by the information, recommendations, claims and grievances originating from alternative sources of influence and advice. These sources include, among others, the mass media, pressure groups, the university community, royal commissions, task forces and advisory councils. The influence of these individuals, groups, and institutions on public policy formation and implementation depends to a large extent on the quality of advice they bring to bear on public policy issues. It depends also on their potential impact on the government's political fortunes.

Maurice Lamontagne begins this chapter by challenging those who point to the enormous influence of the bureaucracy on policy determination. He contends that "the twilight of the civil servants" is at hand and that new and competing power centres are emerging in the Canadian political system. Ronald Ritchie analyzes the virtues and limitations of various sources of policy advice and sets forth the arguments and recommendations accepted by the federal government as a basis for the founding of the Institute for Research on Public Policy. Then, the Economic Council of Canada calls for the more effective distribution to Canadians of information about existing and proposed public policies. The Council contends further that all actors in the political system must become more knowledgeable about both the process of government decision making and the actual content of public policies. In the final selection, J.E. Anderson describes the influence of pressure groups on government decisions, with particular reference to relations between bureaucrats and pressure group representatives.

10

New Centres of
Policy-Making Influence*

Maurice Lamontagne

I shall devote my remarks mainly to the influence being felt by the politican, particularly by ministers since they are the most important and the most successful politicians. But first, le us see how the rise and fall of ministers came about. To describe this most interesting evolution, I wish to rely on an article published by the *Economist* in 1947 and entitled "The Twilight of Ministers." Those of you who have already read that article will undoubtedly remember its opening paragraph:

The principle of complete royal subjection to ministerial control was firmly embedded in the British Constitution in the course of the nineteenth century. Though theoretically all powerful the Monarch had, by the end of Queen Victoria's reign, completely accepted the position that he could do nothing without ministerial advice and, indeed, that he could not refuse to do anything that his Ministers advised him to do.

In Canada, a similar evolution took place at about the same time. It started in 1791 and reached a very important moment in 1848 when the principle of responsible government was recognized. The Byng incident in 1926 merely served to formalize what was already implicit. But this rise of ministers to a position of great influence was not to last very long.

The correspondent of the *Economist* goes on to say:

But there is no such thing as finality in human development. The cabinet had no sooner removed the last formal checks on its power than it, too, began to be something of an outward show and the reality of power began to move elsewhere. Ministers, in the middle of the twentieth century, were subject to three pressures which together made it impossible for them to fulfil the role that the Constitution, as then understood, assigned to them. In the first place, with the advent of Socialism, the subject-matter of state action was enormously extended. Secondly, the subject-matter of public affairs became much more technical and difficult and this, coinciding with the growth of the belief that it was a positive advantage for a politican to have spent his formative years in the mine or at the bench, made it a rarity for a Minister to be able to understand the papers that were put before him, even if he had time to read them. Thirdly, the number of personal appearances required of a Minister—in Parliament, at conferences, and at luncheons, dinners and meetings of all kinds—increased so greatly that

---

* Maurice Lamontagne, "The Influence of the Politician", *Canadian Public Administration*, vol. 11, no. 3 (Fall, 1968), pp. 263-71. Reprinted and slightly abridged by permission of author and publisher.

even these activities, hitherto pre-eminently those of the Minister himself, came to be beyond the powers of a single man, except with the assistance of a Public Relations officer. Under these pressures, the Minister gradually became a figure-head... only those Ministers who combined the most forceful personalities with a willingness to work cruelly long hours could really be said to be responsible for their own words and actions, let alone those of the Department they nominally controlled.

But this gradual change was not apparent for many years. The permanent civil servants, while engrossing more and more of the reality of power, studiously preserved the outward forms of Ministerial supremacy —as, indeed, Ministers in their turn did [as regards] the King. Just as laws were still enacted "by the King's Most Excellent Majesty", and Ministers spoke of their "loyal duty" to the Crown, so also the most eminent and powerful civil servant would still refer to his Minister as "my master", and would begin his letters, "I am directed by the Secretary of State...".

This long quotation sums up very well also what happened in Canada. I need here to recall just a few landmarks which illustrate the fall of ministers and the rise of civil servants. The civil service began to emerge as a new force with the recognition of the merit system and the creation of the Civil Service Commission in 1917. Fifty years later, the peak of its rise was reached when, a few months ago, full bargaining rights were granted by Parliament to the staff associations. Some objections were raised before the adoption of this important piece of legislation. Her Majesty the Queen could not bargain with her subjects. The supremacy of Parliament could not be encroached upon by collective agreements. The fact that these arguments were not even considered seriously shows how removed our political symbolism has become from the new reality.

Meanwhile, especially after 1935, the Establishment emerged and gradually became the centre of power within the federal administration. Generally speaking, at least until recently, when the Establishment was united behind or against a certain policy, its advice was accepted by the Cabinet; when there was a division of opinion between the officials of a particular department and those of the Department of Finance, including the Treasury Board, then the views of the latter would prevail at the Cabinet table. I have seen situations when two important groups of the Establishment had not been able to reconcile their views on vital policy issues; in those circumstances, the Cabinet failed to act.

The supremacy of the Establishment may have reached its peak recently when, as a result of the implementation of the Glassco report, deputy ministers have been given important managerial responsibilities which had been viewed before as being too sensitive to be exercised by ministers and had been transferred to the Civil Service Commission. The special position of influence of the Establishment was underlined again not long ago when a minister was asked to resign by the Opposition for having consulted outside experts and when another minister had to resign for having reached a decision without proper consultation with his civil servants.

A story, which is supposed to be true, illustrates the fall of ministers and the rise of civil servants. It is reported that a Liberal backbencher who had ambitions and also a sense of humour decided one day to write to Mr. King and ask to be appointed to the Cabinet. In his reply, Mr. King, who could then afford to be straightforward, told the daring backbencher that he did not have the competence and the high intellectual qualifications required for such an important assignment. The persistent member, who was obviously not satisfied with this answer, wrote back to Mr. King and said: "My dear Prime Minister, I believe that you have misunderstood the nature of my request; high as my ambition can aspire, I do not expect to become a deputy minister, I merely want to be a minister!" Whether it is true or not, this story symbolizes very succinctly "the twilight of ministers" in Canada.

Nous ne devrions pas conclure, cependant, que le pouvoir des hauts fonctionnaires s'est toujours manifesté dans le même sens et qu'il n'a jamais connu de limites. A mon avis, l'apogée de leur influence positive coincida avec les dernières années du régime St. Laurent. Sous l'administration Diefenbaker, leur rôle fut surtout négatif selon le témoignage souvent répété de l'honorable Alvin Hamilton. A l'en croire, les projets du gouvernement conservateur étaient systématiquement bloqués par les hauts fonctionnaires. Cet aveu en dit long sur l'impuissance des ministres de cette période. Par contre, au cours de fameux 60 premiers jours du gouvernement Pearson, l'influence des hauts fonctionnaires fut presque nulle. Cette indépendance retrouvée conduisit à des erreurs qui ne seront pas facilement oubliées et le déséquilibre traditionnel des forces en présence fut rapidement rétabli.

J'ai la conviction, toutefois, que nous franchissons déjà les premières étapes d'une nouvelle période. Le parti libéral, dans l'opposition et avec l'aide de conseillers qui n'appartennient évidemment pas à la fonction publique, avait préparé un programme précis et détaillé. L'erreur qui fut faite en arrivant au pouvoir de le mettre à exécution trop rapidement et dans l'isolement n'aura d'importance à long terme. Seule en aura le méthode suivie par les libéraux dans l'élaboration de leur programme et qui s'inspirait d'ailleurs de celle que l'équipe de Jean Lesage avait utilisée avant 1960. J'ai l'impression que l'expérience faite par le parti libéral dans l'opposition sera dorénavant répétée par tous les principaux partis politiques, même ceux qui sont parvenus au pouvoir. C'est là l'un des facteurs qui me portent à croire qu'une ère nouvelle quant aux sources de l'influence politique est déjà commencée au Canada.

Thus, a new period is emerging in our country. I would describe it as the "twilight of civil servants." I do not mean by this that the fall of the civil servant will be as dramatic as that of the politician many years ago or that it will correspond to the rise of ministers to a new position of influence. I mean, however, that the Establishment will play a more limited role than in the past 25 years and that it will have to share its privileged position near ministers with new sources of political influence.

In the first place, I believe that civil servants will have less and less to do with the development of new policies. Conversely, the intellectual community outside the civil service will play an increasing role in the determination of new policy objectives and proposals. The rising number of royal commissions, task forces, advisory boards, and councils is an obvious sign of the shift which is taking place. But it is only part of the new story.

In the past, political parties could win elections by making vague promises, by relying on their record, or merely by attacking the opposition. When they assumed office, they were not committed to an over-all political programme and they were free to accept the advice of civil servants even in connection with the formulation of policy. This situation is changing rapidly. The public and the press now expect political parties to be identified with a concrete, detailed, and co-ordinated set of policy proposals, especially during electoral campaigns. Moreover, this identification has become almost inevitable since political parties have decided to hold national conventions every two years. Their public image would greatly suffer if such meetings were not devoted to serious thinking and discussions. But such an identification means that when a given party is newly elected or even is returned to office, it will be committed to a detailed set of policies which will have been developed with little, if any, consultation with civil servants.

The politician, however, will not be more responsible for the formulation of policy than he was before. But he will have new masters. The new pattern for the preparation of political platforms is already set. It involves the consultation of the public by taking polls and conducting motivation surveys in order to know the priorities of its needs and pre-occupations and also, more and more frequently, the calling of a thinkers' conference to determine how those priorities can best be met. Resolutions based on this preliminary work will then be adopted in a more or less modified form by national conventions and become the official platform of our political parties. Thus, the public without really knowing it and the intellectual community will become new sources of political influence and will play an increasing role in the selection and the formulation of policies.

There is another new pattern which is emerging and which will tend also to reduce the influence of civil servants while not contributing to increase the importance of ministers. It has to do with the working of Parliament. In the immediate past, Parliament had really very little to do with legislation. The legislative programme originated mainly from the Establishment which also prepared the ministerial speeches required for its presentation to the House of Commons. It was expected that once a bill had been accepted by Cabinet on the advice of the Establishment it would also be approved without modification by Parliament. In the House of Commons, the opposition could speak as long as it wished but it would have been a great sign of weakness on the part of a minister to accept any of its suggestions. As to the government backbenchers, they were expected to be seen when votes were called but not to be heard.

That situation is changing rapidly. We can even speak of a quiet revolution in Parliament. The private member, after having lost his administrative influence, which is a disguised definition of patronage, is now acquiring a legislative role which he should have had all along.

Several factors account for this change: the improvement in the quality of members, the succession of minority governments, and the length of sessions. It is fair to say that the evolution really originated from the government side. Competent backbenchers became tired of having to sit in the House with very little to do. They began to present their grievances at party caucuses and to press for more and better organized parliamentary committees. Ministers were not in a very good position to resist those pressures. It is indeed interesting to note that, with the minority situation and the length of sessions, ministers have never been more exposed to the influence of their own backbenchers. This is even more so when they have long-term political ambitions. In certain cases, it is not an exaggeration to say that they meet private members more often than their own officials. As a result, parliamentary committees have never been more influential than during the present sessions. They have proposed new legislation which the government will have to bring forward and they have substantially modified several important bills. Such an intrusion of Parliament in the legislative process would not have been tolerated just a few years ago.

Parliamentary reform has been long overdue. It has now become inevitable. When it comes, you will see that a lot of frivolities which the House of Commons is now engaged in will be removed, that Parliament will be more interested in the substance and less in the detail of legislative proposals, and that greater emphasis will be placed on parliamentary committees.

We are moving towards a compromise between the British and the American political institutions. As we reach it, the influence of civil servants in the legislative process will be less important. At least one type of politician will become more influential since the legislative role of the private member will be expanding.

Finally, I would like to mention a third and undoubtedly the most important new force which is competing with civil servants to influence ministers. I mean the press, broadly speaking, or the so-called mass media. If the correspondent of the *Economist* quoted at the beginning of my remarks is right when he says that the Cabinet has become "something of an outward show," then the main objective of a minister who wants to be successful and remain in the show ought to be to develop and maintain a good public image. Save the surface and you save all. Hence, the growing importance for a minister to be friendly with reporters and to have an efficient executive assistant or public relations officer.

Here again, substantial changes have taken place. In the past, the relationship between ministers and the means of communication was quite different. Television and even radio did not establish themselves as influential image-makers before the mid 50's. The press had a partisan approach to politics. Its owners, generally speaking, were closely identified with a political party and they made sure that their newspapers and their reporters would faithfully reflect their political views. In that context, the public image of the politician was largely determined by the good or bad relationship which existed between himself or, more precisely, his political party and individual publishers. Once that relationship had been defined, ministers could do very little about their image, especially on a day-to-day basis. It was not, therefore, one of their main daily preoccupations.

The philosophy of the mass media has changed drastically in the last decades. They have become businesses, and competition among them is acute. Party affiliation has disappeared or barely survives in the editorial page. The number of readers or audience rating has become the golden rule. In addition, there is the cynical assumption that the public has a strong preference for sensation.

This approach leads to a new role of ethics for reporters. From now on, they do not have to reflect the political views of their employers; thus, they can transmit their own in their articles. The thing they cannot afford is to be dull. But straight and objective information is not supposed to be interesting. So, the reporter who wants to be successful looks for rumours, scoops, and leaks. He writes today on the news of tomorrow. He puts the emphasis on personalities rather than on events. He appraises rather than informs. He is interested in the surface rather than in performance. He has few real friends but he is grateful to those who enable him to produce his daily article or his news broadcast "every hour on the hour". In previous days, he used to work hard to find an official source for his information; nowadays it is easier for him to rely on Cabinet leaks originating from ministers' offices.

Je ne crois pas avoir grandement caricaturé la réalité. J'ai vu des ministres portés aux nues par les journalistes avant même qu'ils aient pu faire quoi que ce soit et se faire détruire ensuite pour s'être montrés tout simplement humains. J'ai connu des ministres qui continuaient à avoir une bonne presse sans rien accomplir de valable. J'ai enfin entendu des journalistes me dire qu'ils avaient laissé la profession parce que, pendant la période des soi-disant scandales, ils avaient l'impression tous les soirs d'avoir du sang jusqu'aux coudes.

This general situation was always tempered by noble exceptions and has improved recently. It remains, however, that the minister who is preoccupied by his public image, as projected by the mass media, faces a difficult challenge. But, if he is not worried by it, he cannot continue for long to be a successful politician. There is, here, a paradoxical situation which I would like to explore more fully.

My contention is — and I could substantiate it by an impressive set of facts — that the mass media do not have a decisive impact on public opinion, at least in so far as politics is concerned. It would take too long for me to outline the factors which account for this situation. I will add, however, that most politicians share my view and recognize, in theory, that the mass media do not effectively guide or faithfully reflect public opinion. Ministers could, therefore, afford to ignore them, at least up to a point. Some successful politicians have done just that. In fact, however, most politicians are "newsworms". They are as fond of rumours, scoops, and personal stories as most reporters. Both groups live in the same isolated world, although they usually despise each other. This cohabitation produces strange results. In most cases, the politician is almost unconsciously mystified by the reporter. Thus, while the mass media have little impact on the public, they have a great deal of influence on the politician. There lies the secret of the rising power of the press. It is in this restricted context that a minister cannot ignore the mass media with impunity. If he enjoys a good press, he will be envied and respected or feared by his colleagues. If he has no press, he has no future. And, if he has a bad press, he is in serious trouble, because he will be viewed even by his own associates as a political liability, in spite of the qualities he may have.

That is why it has become almost essential for a successful minister to have a dual personality, to smile even if he does not feel like it, to talk when he should remain silent, to say the "right" thing in spite of his own convictions. That is why also ministers have two ears; one for the press and one for their policy advisers. What they hear from both ears may often be incompatible. The danger is that the desire to preserve the public image may prevail over the requirements of the public interest. In any case, it should be obvious by now that civil servants must be prepared to share with the press the monopolistic influence they used to have on ministers. From now on, ministers have to live in the limelight. This new position also contributes to the twilight of civil servants.

My general thesis can be summed up very briefly. To begin with, I make the distinction between the symbol of power and the reality of power or the real source of political influence. Then I contend that we have gone through different phases of a long evolution. It started with absolute monarchy which coincided, broadly speaking, with the colonial period. Then, with the development of our democratic institutions and the granting of responsible government, the Cabinet was recognized as the supreme political authority. Since World War II, gradually and for a variety of reasons, the Civil Service Establishment became identified with the reality of power. Although ministers could still do wrong and continued to be held responsible for their departments, they merely represented, in most cases, the authentic symbol of power. As to the Monarch, he could do no wrong and therefore could do nothing. He had become a very remote and almost undefinable political entity.

A new phase of this long evolution is now emerging. I have described it as the twilight of civil servants. I do not mean by this expression that the Establishment is following the same pattern as the Cabinet and tends to become another symbol of power. What I do mean is that it will have to share the monopolistic influence it had in the past on ministers with others, namely the public, the intellectual community, the private member of Parliament, and the press. In other words, the reality of power will be less concentrated in one group; it will be more diffuse.

What will happen to ministers in this complex new world? Generally speaking, a dependent becomes more independent when he has several masters instead of one. But I am inclined to think that this will not be true in this case.

Ministers will have to devote a growing portion of their time to their symbolic role. They will find it harder to reconcile their different loyalties. In the process of reaching a compromise which will make their masters at least equally dissatisfied, their true personality will be weakened and their convictions will become blurred. Their diverse activities will affect their health and their private lives. In the outward show which will be theirs as symbols of power, they will try to wear a mask to hide their tiredness and their boredom.

One might ask who will want to become a minister under such dismal conditions. My answer would be that we do not need to worry: to many people and to a great number of politicians, the symbols of power are more attractive than the reality of power.

11

Sources of Policy Advice: Royal Commissions, Task Forces, Advisory Councils and the Research Institute*

Ronald S. Ritchie

The questions of policy which face the public and governments in Canada are as involved, as difficult, as changing, and as continuing as those facing any other modern society. Both decision-makers and the public at large, therefore, stand in need of the kinds of skilled analysis in depth that clarify the problems, make the range of their implications clear, and illumine the alternatives for choice.

A traditional source of research-based advice on public policy in Canada has been the Royal Commission. The last dozen years have seen very frequent resort to this mechanism by the federal and by provincial governments. Such large questions as education policy, taxation policy, transporation policy,

---

*Ronald S. Ritchie, *An Institute for Research on Public Policy* (Ottawa: Information Canada, 1971), pp. 7-16, 42-3, 51. Reprinted and abridged by permission of the author and publisher.

monetary policy, linguistic and cultural policy, health care policy, and broadcasting policy have been turned over to Royal commissions for assessment and proposal. Task forces, which in many cases are Royal commissions under another name, have bloomed in similar profusion, frequently tackling equally difficult and complicated questions of public policy. The task forces which have recently completed their assignments in the fields of labour relations and government information services are good examples, as is the Special Study Group on Maritime Union which is supported by Nova Scotia, New Brunswick, and Prince Edward Island.

Royal commissions and task forces have usually been directed to inquire into some specified area of public policy concern and to produce recommended courses of action for the government concerned. Irreverent critics have suggested that the real purposes of Royal commissions have sometimes been to evade decisions rather than to prepare for them, to take the heat off a politically touchy problem rather than to seek a more adequate understanding of it. Even where such comment has been perceptive, its implied criticism may still have been misplaced. Institutionalized delay may have its merits where no adequate consensus for action exists. Grasping a nettle firmly is a fairly reliable formula for experiencing pain, but not necessarily for making progress. In any event, it is clear that in the case of a large majority of Royal commissions and task forces of recent years the object has been enlightenment, not evasion. Their aim has been to achieve more widespread public understanding of questions at issue and a more informed basis for policy choices by the decision-makers.

Public policy research is central to the role of Royal commissions and task forces. It frequently takes two forms. Royal commissions usually, and task forces occasionally, seek the views of the public, inviting submissions from interested individuals, groups, and organizations. They hold public hearings at which such submissions are supported and examined and they take testimony from various experts. Both types of bodies usually undertake programmes of directed and commissioned research. They create their own ad hoc research staffs and supplement these resources by contracts for particular studies by outside academics and other experts.

The directed and commissioned research programmes of Royal commissions and task forces are sometimes very large. This was true, for instance, in the cases of the Rowell-Sirois Commission, the Royal Commission on Canada's Economic Prospects, the Royal Commission on Banking and Finance, and the recent Task Force on Labour Relations. The results are undoubtedly useful. They help to clarify the problems and to identify their implications. They provide a basis for the conclusions reached and the recommendations made. They are usually available to the government concerned and frequently also to the public at large, thereby improving the basis for assessment of the proposals. In rare cases, some or all of the research product may not be made available to the general public. In fact, governments are not legally bound to release the reports of Royal commissions, although it is usually expedient politically for them to do so. One of the distinctions made between Royal commissions and task forces may be that it should be easier for a government to withhold the report of a task force than the report of a Royal commission.

The extensive resort by governments to Royal commissions and task forces in recent years for the illumination of important and complex public policy issues is highly significant. It must be seen as a response to a need for research and analysis not being adequately provided from other sources. There can be little debate about the need. The methods for meeting it do need assessment. Royal commissions and task forces are not cheap. It is a safe estimate that their cost to the federal and the provincial governments of Canada has averaged several million dollars annually over the past decade. The important question is not whether such sums should be spent, but whether spending so much on Royal commissions and task forces is the most productive way of applying them. There are compelling reasons for believing that it is not.

The research efforts of Royal commissions and task forces suffer the defects of the situation which creates them. Almost always, the appointment of a Royal commission or task force is an ad hoc response to a situation which is already urgent, if not critical. The whole research process is, therefore, under stringent, perhaps unreasonable, time pressures. The members of the commission or task force are likely to be under pressure from the government, from opposition politicians, or from the public at large to produce recommendations in the minimum possible time. They may be tempted to arrive at conclusions before all of the research evidence is in or, in any event, before there has been time for adequate objective identification and evaluation of major policy alternatives. For proper policy research results to be achieved, it is almost always evident that the research should have been undertaken much earlier and in circumstances where the pressure for policy answers was less acute.

Another defect of the situation is the ad hoc character of the organization. Public policy research depends to an important degree for its success on a combination of organizational and planning skills, on an appropriate mix of expertises, and on policy-oriented attitudes on the part of the researchers. The research effort of Royal commissions and task forces is likely to be less than optimum on each of these counts. The director of the research programme is usually a scholar of high professional standing, but he is unlikely to have had much experience in organizing and directing an integrated, multidisciplinary research team. He may, in fact, not be persuaded of the merits of a multidisciplinary approach to complicated questions of public policy. The members of his research staff, whether full-time or part-time, may also be highly competent scholars individually, but in their normal setting, often a university, they are unlikely to have had much opportunity to participate in centrally directed, team research projects. Their more normal experience will have been as individual entrepreneurs in research. In some cases, they may even have little interest in policy-oriented research itself. For some academics, these assignments represent welcome opportunities for additional income and guaranteed publication. With the recent profusion of Royal commissions and task forces, such opportunities, particularly for economists, have been so numerous that recruiting the desired level of talent and insisting on desired levels of performance have been equally difficult on occasion.

By any measure, impressive contributions to the making of public policy have come from the research programmes of Royal commissions and task forces. It is clear, however, that regardless of the individual merits of those engaged in such research under the conditions provided by a Royal commission or a task force, the odds are that the end result will suffer somewhat from the defects inherent in the situation. Those who say, therefore, that Canada has not had good results for its money from the wide profusion of policy research efforts of its recent Royal commissions and task forces undoubtedly have some justification. Whatever their merits for other public purposes, Royal commissions and task forces are only imperfect vechicles for public policy research and, therefore, in this respect, are for occasional rather than regular use.

Governments in Canada have established certain permanent bodies whose purpose is to study public policy questions and to give advice on them. Two examples at the federal level are the Economic Council of Canada and the Science Council of Canada. It is worth considering the present and potential contributions which these two examples can make to the general needs of governments and electors for public policy research and analysis.

The Economic Council of Canada is a Crown corporation created by Act of Parliament in 1963. It is charged basically with advising and recommending to the government "how Canada can achieve the highest possible levels of employment and efficient production in order that the country may enjoy a high and consistent rate of economic growth and that all Canadians may share in rising living standards; . . . ."

Its interests are specifically directed towards the medium-term and long-term prospects of the economy. It is specifically directed to publish an annual report on these prospects and on economic problems it foresees for the country in the medium and longer term. From time to time, the Council may be requested by the government to make special studies, one example in the period to date having been on combines, mergers, monopolies, and restraint of trade policy.

To discharge its responsibilities, the Council must engage in economic and social research. The chairman and the other two full-time members of the Council are well equipped professionally to do so. In addition, the Council has a staff of approximately 120, of whom half are professionals. It is empowered, as well, to commission outside scholars and specialists to undertake particular studies on its behalf. The area of public policy in which its mandate runs encompasses a wide range of public policy questions for both the present and the future. Its resources for tackling them are substantial. It has done much valuable work to date. What can one say in broad terms about its likely research contribution to the inputs required for effective public policy formation over the longer term?

First, it should be said that the Economic Council stands in an anomalous position. It is a part of Government and yet may find itself at any given time opposed to government policy. When it is so opposed, its position may be much more resented at both official and political levels than if it were not a part of Government. Great care was taken in its organization and its prerogatives to give it independence which would permit it to make objective judgements. Yet, this independence is, in the final analysis, vulnerable to its yearly financial dependence on the Treasury Board and to the appointment of its members by the Cabinet.

A number of features are intended to protect the independence of the Council. The chairman and its two directors are appointed for terms of seven years. Its other members, who serve part-time, are appointed from the public at large after consultation with "appropriate representative organizations." Most of them are unlikely to be particularly beholden to the government. The Council has full freedom to undertake studies of its own choice in the wide field of policy concern to which it has been assigned. It has unrestricted freedom to publish as it wishes. On the other hand, as a practical matter, the Council must be concerned about any excessively strained relations between it and the government and between it and those individuals and agencies in the public service whose good will and co-operation can be important to its daily work.

In the circumstances, the effectiveness of the Economic Council must depend to a significant degree both on the independence of mind and the wisdom of its chairman and on the understanding and the wisdom of the government at the political and at certain official levels. There can be no long-term guarantee that these requisite qualities will at all times exist to an adequate degree on both sides.

A number of other factors bear on the extent of the prospective public policy research contribution of the Economic Council. The first is the Council's obligation to produce an annual report on economic prospects and problems. From the beginning the annual report has been a sizable undertaking and the Council's chief product. It would appear to require throughout most of the year much of the time and much of the best talent of both the full-time members of the Council and its staff. The obligation to produce the annual report may make it difficult for the Council to bring balanced attention and resources to research on other important questions of economic policy.

The evidence to date suggests, too, that the annual report, even though it is intended to be directed to the relatively "safe" area of medium- and longer-term questions, is likely on occasion to catapult the Council into the midst of heated debates about current government policy. This seems unavoidable for at least two reasons. In the first place, economic prospects for the medium and longer term must depend on decisions and actions taken in the short term. The Council, therefore, cannot ignore them. In the second, the Council's duties call on it not only to make the kinds of assessment required as inputs for policy decisions, but also to make policy recommendations.

The representative character of Canada's Economic Council membership also has a bearing on the prospects for its research activities. Its 25 public members reflect a wide spectrum of interests from the private sector of the economy and the various regions of the country. They provide roughly equal representation for labour unions, manufacturing industry, commerce and finance, the primary industries and the general public. Such sector and sectional representation may be entirely appropriate to the processes of policy choice and policy recommendations. It is of doubtful value for the approval and direction of a research programme on public policy questions, for which a highly desirable ingredient is the opportunity and the desire to identify and assess not only all of the significant elements of the problem but also all of the worthwhile alternatives for its solution. It would seem likely that a consensus body, many of whose members have established positions to protect, would frequently find reasons to discourage avenues of research which, on broader grounds of national and regional interest, might be well worth undertaking.

Still another aspect of the Economic Council's position should be raised because of its significance for any public policy research programme in Canada. This is its relation, or lack of it, to the provincial governments. While there may be times when the federal government will take no great satisfaction in claiming title, it is clear that for the provincial governments the Economic Council is both a federal creation and a federal creature. The record of independence it has established so far would have to continue for a much longer period before a number of provincial governments would be prepared to alter this view. In fact, the basis for its appointment and financing might have to change. Such provincial government doubts would be an important limitation to the overall contribution which any research body can make to public policy formation in Canada.

The Science Council of Canada was established by Act of Parliament in 1966. Three years later it was given formal status as a Crown corporation by the *Government Reorganization Act.* At about the same time, it ceased to depend on the Science Secretariat of the Privy Council Office for staff support and began to create its own small but separate staff.

The duties of the Science Council parallel in many respects those of the Economic Council. It is directed to "assess in a comprehensive manner Canada's scientific and technological resources, requirements and potentialities and to make recommendations thereon to the Minister." It is free to initiate studies in the wide field allocated to it, and may from time to time receive requests from the Minister to undertake particular studies on his behalf. There has been some debate about the boundaries of the word "science." The Chairman of the Council takes it to mean "man's accumulated and organized knowledge about himself and his world", a definition which would evidently include the social sciences as well as the natural sciences. It seems clear that the Government's original intention was to limit the Council's concern to the natural sciences and technology — a conclusion substantially borne out by the type of university, industry, and official representation in the present membership of the Council.

The Science Council is not, its Chairman has stressed, a research body. Its task is to evaluate the adequacy and directions of scientific research and technological development in Canada, to draw conclusions about appropriate priorities, and to make recommendations to the federal government accordingly. The question is largely one of definition. The Science Council does not undertake laboratory research, but it does support its policy recommendations by surveys, analyses, and evaluations which include what this report would call public policy research. As the Council itself is very much aware, it continuously comes up against a need for defined national goals and priorities — questions which are basically political in nature but which can be at least partially illuminated by appropriate economic and social analyses. It is doubtless partly for this reason that the Chairman of the Science Council has indicated that he would welcome extension of the Council's field of interest to include the social sciences and, at the same time, of course, would welcome appropriate representation of social scientists in the Council's membership. It is doubtless partly for the same reason that the Social Science Research Council of Canada has proposed that it might fill a role somewhat similar to that of the Science Council as an advisory body to the federal government.

Both the Economic Council of Canada and the Science Council of Canada are designed in part to contribute to public policy research needs of the country. A serious attempt has been made in each case to provide enough genuine independence to permit objectivity in the assessment of problems and the proposing of policy. Yet, both bodies seem likely to encounter certain constraints occasioned by their somewhat anomalous position as parts of the federal government structure which are obligated from time to time to be critical of government policies. Also, despite their nominally wide areas of assigned interest, each is likely to feel some limitation on the subjects it can tackle. In the case of the Economic Council, one such limitation is that imposed by its obligation to produce an extensive annual review in an assigned area. In the case of the Science Council, there is the fact that recommendations on science and technology policy must be based in large part on economic and social assessments while the Council has been provided with no assured access to competence in these fields. Both councils suffer the probable handicap from a policy research point of view that they are policy advisory bodies, with the likelihood, therefore, that their policy proposals may from time to time become the subject of public controversy with, in turn, possible detrimental effects upon their policy research activities as such. In the special circumstances of Canada, too, they may suffer somewhat in overall effectiveness because of their exclusive identification with the federal government in the eyes of the provincial governments. All in all, therefore, these two bodies, much as they may contribute otherwise, can scarcely be relied upon as substantial long-term centres of research on broad ranges of public policy questions.

There are in the private sector in Canada a number of organizations which, in some degree, undertake planned programmes of public policy research. These include the Canadian Tax Foundation, the Private Planning Association of Canada, the Agricultural Economics Research Council of Canada and the Canadian Institute of International Affairs. Each of these organizations has its own special area of interest and in most cases research on public policy questions is not the sole objective. Their staffs and budgets for policy research purposes are small and usually much of their output is in the form of sponsored projects undertaken by individual academics. Collectively and separately they add measurably to the quantity of knowledge, analysis, and evaluation of alternatives open to policy makers and the public at large. In no case is their work the product of multidisciplinary research teams.

In Canada's universities there are scattered evidences of increasing interest in research on public policy questions and some attempts at special organization to work on such projects. The Institute on Inter-Governmental Relations at Queen's University is one example, but perhaps the one which seeks most ambitiously to emulate some of the policy research institutes to be found in the United States is the Institute for Quantitative Analysis of Social and Economic Policy at the University of Toronto.

The recent Report of the Science Council of Canada and the Canada Council on "The Role of the Federal Government in Support of Research in Canadian Universities" advocates more involvement by universities in research projects funded by government to aid in public policy formation. It notes, however, that

those wishing to use the university need to be reminded constantly that teaching and research are the primary responsibilities of the university. Service is secondary. The talent is available in the first instance for the internal purposes of the university and only if proposals are consistent with the university's primary responsibilities should they be considered by the university. Government departments should look upon the possibility of making use of the university as a privilege, not a right.

In light of the urgent and expanding need of both governments and electors for more knowledge, more thorough analysis and more objective identification and evaluation of alternatives as a basis for public policy choices, it is clear that the resources available in Canada are adequate neither in quantity nor in type to the requirements of the future. The stage is set, then, for an assessment of the public policy research institute as a supplement and, perhaps, as a partial replacement for what now exists.

It is as a contributor to better informed and better assessed choices in problem areas of these kinds that a public policy research institute must find its justification. Almost without exception the major questions which face Canadian makers of public policy at the federal, provincial, regional, and local levels cry out for multidisciplinary systems analysis, for studies which attempt to identify desired "futures" and to chart the paths to them. They call for orderly study by skilled professionals in an effort which is oriented towards providing ingredients for policy appraisal and decision. They call for study in an environment which is free from the distractions of immediate operational responsibilities and from the constraints on thinking imposed by present commitments to policies, programmes, and machinery. The evidence is that, properly organized and manned, a public policy research institute can contribute in just these ways; that it can consistently fill needs which are unlikely to be sufficiently met by the public policy research output of either universities or government departments and agencies.

Proposals

It is, therefore, proposed that:

1. There should be established in Canada an institute, which will have as its mission, research and analysis designed to improve the basis for informed choice and decision by the public of Canada and its leaders on questions of public policy.

2. The institute should dedicate itself to impartial service of the national cultures, the various regions and the various governments of the people of Canada in its research and analysis on public policy questions.

3. The Prime Minister of Canada ask a small number of distinguished citizens, whose competence and disinterested desire to serve the public good are widely accepted, to seek incorporation of the proposed institute as a non-profit corporation under the Canada Corporations Act, *to serve on its first permanent board of directors, to select and employ a president who should be its chief executive officer, and, with his help, to establish the institute as a functioning organization.*

4. The Government of Canada commit not less than $10 million in the form of a capital grant to the institute; that the directors of the institute seek additional grant support for the early years of the institute's life from the various Provincial Governments; that they seek to add to the capital endowment of the institute from the private sector; and that, once fully established, the institute rely for up to 50 per cent of its annual operating budgets on contracts from governments, such revenues to be supplemented by foundation, corporation, and individual grants and contributions, revenues from its own capital, conference fees, sales of its publications, and similar sources.

Response

On August 11, 1971, Prime Minister Trudeau announced that the federal government had in large part accepted these recommendations. He noted also that as a consequence of the establishment of the Institute, "governments will benefit from research identifying emerging policy issues; revealing new approaches to long standing problems; or suggesting new modes of government. Public officials — both elected and appointed, academics, and Canadians at large will benefit from the availability of new information on complex issues of public policy hitherto not available."[1]

---

[1] Based on Press Release, Office of the Prime Minister, August 11, 1971.

12

The Distribution of Knowledge
and Information on Public Policy*

Economic Council of Canada

The fact that there are many links in the chain of public decision-making greatly increases its complexity, but also provides an opportunity for effecting improvements in the process *simultaneously* at a number of strategic points. This essay explores some avenues for improved decision-making by focusing on the need for a wider distribution of knowledge and information among *all* the participants in the decision process.

Training

Strengthening of the critical and evaluative capacity of individuals and groups who contribute to policy formulation is basic to better decision-making. There is a variety of participants or "actors" in this process: politicans, public servants, policy analysts and advisers, the media, and the general public including the range of interest groups that represent them. There are many ways in which these participants could be encouraged and helped to broaden their knowledge about the *process* of government decision-making and the *content* of public policies. This would raise the level of debate about public decisions. The potentials for this kind of educational activity are large. Only a few examples can be covered here.

"The idea of improving politicians is regarded as quite taboo in Western Democratic societies, but this is not justified."[1] In recent years Canadian parliamentarians have frequently asked for wider participation, for increased powers of policy design by parliamentary committees, and for improved research facilities. This clearly indicates a desire for more active involvement at strategic points in the policy-making process. In this context, we believe that representatives would welcome "learning opportunities" to increase their individual effectiveness, and that special arrangements should be made to enlarge the analytical perspectives and increase the policy-making knowledge of elected officials at all levels of government.

The most sophisticated policy analysis techniques will not improve policy unless they are available to, understood and used by, senior advisers. Many of

*Economic Council of Canada, *Design for Decision-Making: Eighth Annual Review of the Economic Council of Canada* (Ottawa: Information Canada, 1971), pp. 82-86. Reprinted by permission of the publisher.
[1] Yehezkel Dror, "Some Normative Implications of a Systems View of Policy-Making", P-3,991-1 (Santa Monica, California: The Rand Corporation, February 1969), mimeo., p. 13.

these advisers have not had the background or opportunity to make the best use of the analytical tools that are available. The introduction of policy analysis into the decision system may, initially at least, tend to concentrate analytical know-how, and the power and authority associated with it, in a central agency rather than throughout the government in individual departments and agencies. We are inclined to believe that a high degree of centralization is not in the long-run interest of any level of government, and that senior advisers in all departments and agencies should participate actively in the development and evaluation of policy.

There are a number of points at which the existing education system could be used to give the growing professional establishment, the media and the general public, knowledge and information about public policy issues. Education is currently under fire for its lack of relevance. For education to reinforce a democratic society based on responsibility and involvement, we urge the inclusion of much more "policy content" in teaching and greater accessibility to these courses for people outside the formal schooling system.

In the United States, The Rand Corporation, a pioneer in the development of systematic approaches to decision-making, has established courses for policy training in all sectors — in business, and at all levels of government and the public service. Some universities are now teaching policy science and others are extending schools of business administration into this area. A considerable expansion of training facilities, both public and private, will be required if Canada is to achieve and maintain a momentum of knowledge about the processes and structures of public policy-making systems.[2]

In other countries there is a good deal more interchange of personnel among governments, universities, business enterprises, trade unions, the communications media, and other private organizations. Considerably greater mobility of this kind would, we believe, be highly desirable in Canada, and we urge governments to consider effective methods for facilitating such exchanges.

Information and the Public

The strengthening and extension of "policy training" for policy advisers and decision-makers represent only one part of the contribution that knowledge must make to the political process. The acquisition of more information by the public is equally, if not more, important. In a democratic system the views of the electorate are transmitted through representatives or by lobbies or special-interest groups. These latter groups reflect partial views and therefore the particular concerns of labour, business, regions or sections of the economy, and organized citizens' groups.

---

[2] One aspect of the processes of policy-making is being covered at the federal level by a training course for analysts in key policy-advisory units of government.

The evidence, admittedly impressionistic, suggests that involvement of the general public in policy issues is on the increase in Canada. This is undoubtedly associated with the evolution towards a more highly educated population and the development of a more urbanized society in which the production, distribution, and application of knowledge are growing rapidly. In the past few years, many new initiatives have arisen — native people's organizations, consumers' associations, environmental organizations, women's rights movements, and student groups. These organizations, based on some area of common interest or concern, could provide the rudiments of an expanded system of interest groups, reflecting elements of public opinion.

Public policy will be improved by this increase in vocal organized opinion if all these groups are enabled to inform themselves about the issues and to evaluate policy in a critically constructive fashion. At present, public involvement in policy-making suffers under a large handicap. By and large, the general public does not know, even after the fact, the arguments and evaluations on which public decisions are based. Public comment, which cannot be based on information and analysis, may be ill-informed and irrelevant. At worst, it may be a dangerous advocacy of simplistic solutions to complex human problems.

The increased use of "White Papers" by the federal government in recent years has most certainly stimulated a great deal more public discussion on various complex subjects. The federal government's expressed wish for participation must be matched by a high degree of openness at all levels of government about policy-making. One of the central requirements for developing a well-informed electorate is that there must be an increasing willingness and competence on the part of officials and politicans to discuss basic policy issues in the public arena.

A wider dissemination of information and knowledge about public policy issues should provide for: a discussion of policy objectives, and alternative strategies and programmes, *before* policy is determined; the rationale for selecting particular objectives and strategies *at the time* policies are announced; and *subsequent* periodic reports on the progress of operating programmes.

There are number of ways for governments to stimulate more meaningful discussion of public policy issues and bring information and knowledge into the public domain — by a more extensive use of the communications media, official publications,[3] and publicly available working papers.

The information flow between governments and the general public must, of course, be a two-way street. The more systematic use of new policy design and evaluation techniques will generate a demand for more information from

---

[3] In addition to the traditional use of "White Papers", the British government employs what it calls "Green Papers", which "set out for public discussion major Ministerial proposals while they are still at the formative stage". See *Information and the Public Interest,* Cmnd. 4,089 (London: Her Majesty's Stationery Office, 1969), p.5.

the general public. To meet this demand will in turn require the co-operation of the general public in providing information. The emphasis is shifting from simple modes of data collection in censuses and surveys to model-building and systems exploration, with an emphasis on behavioural and anticipatory responses. The public will increasingly be asked to participate in "social experimentation" and sophisticated data-collecting activities. One of the essential elements in moving towards more rational and more informed policy-making is the co-operation of the general public in reasonable attempts by government statistical agencies to collect more and better information.[4]

A more open, systematic and forward-looking approach to policy-making would provide for a broader and deeper exchange of views on objectives and policies between governments and the general public. Such a development may pose problems of many kinds, and may give rise to various strains and conflicts. However, it is our judgement—and ultimately it *is* a value judgement—that the potential benefits are more than sufficient to warrant the undertaking.

13

Pressure Groups and the Canadian Bureaucracy*

J. E. Anderson

"When I see members of Parliament being lobbied, it's a sure sign to me that the lobby lost its fight in the civil service and the Cabinet."
"It's the deputy minister, not ministers, who are courted by most lobbyists, which suggests where the real power in Ottawa lies."
"The actual rate of fiscal protection (tariffs) has become, in effect, a matter of departmental rather than parliamentary politics.... Thus, emphasis has tended to shift to influencing the policies and activities of government boards, commissions and departmental officials...."

---

[4] The public must, however, insist on the protection of its interest and privacy by proper systems and controls for the mass of personal and individual data which governments increasingly collect and integrate.

* W.D.K. Kernaghan and A.M. Willms, eds., *Public Administration in Canada,* 2nd ed. (Toronto: Methuen Publications, 1971), pp. 370-79. Reprinted and abridged by permission of the author and publisher.

These views of pressure group activity in Canada span a period of more than thirty years and carry the authority of an Ottawa lobbyist, a journalist for one of Canada's leading newspapers and a distinguished Canadian sociologist.[1] The significance of interaction between civil servants and pressure groups is widely, although many times only implicitly, recognized in studies of Canadian pressure groups. With very few notable exceptions, these studies allude almost incidentally to civil service-pressure group relations through description of the organization or general activities of pressure groups.[2] The topic of this essay then, like many other subjects touching Canadian public administration, remains in that rough and preliminary stage of study that requires reliance on scattered references in scholarly writing , the rare statements of various actors in the political process and informed speculation based on the literature of comparative politics.

More detailed study has been difficult and rare, simply because the activities of pressure groups and civil servants occur so close to the core of government and politics. Much information is kept secret or is unavailable because consultation between civil servants and pressure group officials is often informal rather than formal or institutionalized. Moreover, the interaction process may be very complex. Any one civil servant or pressure group official moves in a web of relationships between people, parties, pressure groups, political leaders and civil servants. The individual is probably aware to some extent of these inter-relationships and acts in part at least in anticipation of the reaction of others; in part too, he may have very private and even idiosyncratic motives. We may assume, however, that the extent, variety and content of the interaction between administrators and pressure groups depend largely on the government leaders' perception of the proper role of civil servants. The range of civil service activities considered appropriate may include the initiation and evaluation of policy proposals, the administration and adaptation of existing policies, advice on the likely public acceptability of policies, the explanation or defence of policies before the public, and the education of public opinion for the acceptance of new policies. Civil servants may in turn consult with pressure group representatives on one or all of these aspects of the policy process.

The increasingly complex and demanding nature of modern society has obliged governments to utilize available sources of special knowledge and experience outside the public service. This need for expertise explains the development of bureaucratically organized pressure groups which accompanied the growth of public bureaucracies in this century. It also

---

[1] Respectively, an anonymous lobbyist cited in F.C. Englemann and M.A. Schwartz, *Political Parties and the Canadian Social Structure* (Scarborough: Prentice-Hall, 1967), p. 105; Hugh Winsor, "A Primer for Innocents on the Art of Lobbying", *The Globe Magazine* (Toronto, February 27, 1971), p. 7; and S.D. Clarke, "The Canadian Manufacturers' Association: A Political Pressure Group", *The Canadian Journal of Economics and Political Science*, vol. 4 (1938), p. 251.

[2] Most of the published literature on Canadian pressure groups is identified in the bibliographies in F.C. Englemann and M.A. Schwartz, *Political Parties and the Canadian Social Structure;* and W.D.K. Kernaghan and A.M. Willms, eds., *Public Administration in Canada,* 2nd ed. (Toronto: Methuen Publications, 1971).

predetermined the close relations now existing between civil servants and informed pressure groups. Under a Cabinet system with a reliable legislative majority, and particularly in the case of one-party dominance, the civil servants best promote their own interests by serving and defending their ministers and the government. Civil servants will calculate the effect on voting behaviour of widely beneficial social and economic policies on the one hand and the impact of campaign contributions from disadvantaged interest groups on the other. These considerations constitute at least part of what is meant by "political" advice to the government. It is difficult to appraise the political costs and benefits of pursuing widely beneficial policies, since governments can fail by cumulatively disaffecting small minorities. A Canadian Cabinet Minister, perhaps conscious of the difficulty of assessing the relative effects of choosing between general and particular interests, and perhaps hoping to escape the dilemma, has suggested to pressure groups that "the strategy area where the interests of the politician, or bureaucrat, and the lobbyist effectively overlap is that which concerns itself with the sensitivity to the common good".[3] In Canada, it appears probable that the long dominance of the Liberal Party and its peculiar independence of specific economic interests because of the reliability of its support from Quebec has encouraged civil servants to emphasize "the public interest". They have, therefore, recommended generally beneficial policies even when these policies affect specific pressure groups adversely. These considerations also suggest that in Canada the relations between civil servants and pressure groups are usually dominated by civil servants.

Recognition of Pressure Groups

Allen Potter defines recognition as a prescriptive right to receive "a response which is more than an acknowledgment," one which is an agreement, an argument or a request for additional information. He notes also that "governmental [and other] requests for information from an organized group are a measure of its standing".[4] Where a pressure group already exists, recognition is manifested by the extensiveness of civil service replies or the frequency of their requests for information. In reference to the Canadian Better Business Bureaus' attempt to assume a leading role in consumer education, the Bureaus' president recognized that first

the bureaus must achieve rapport with the government agencies working in the area of consumer protection and, more particularly, with the Consumer Affairs Department. . . . Recently, however, it [Consumer Affairs] has asked the BBB to distribute a circular dealing with misleading ads for hearing aids and

---

[3] The Honourable Donald S. Macdonald, "Notes for Remarks to the Twenty-Third Session of the Canadian Institute for Organization Management", President of the Privy Council Press Release, June 19, 1969.

[4] Allen Potter, *Organized Groups in British National Politics* (London: Faber and Faber, 1961), pp. 190, 203.

department officials have been requesting information from the bureaus increasingly often ("I don't know if Mr. Basford knows how often") and it is possible that, as Mr. Dollard says, they will "come to depend on each other for exchange of information".[5]

It appears that civil servants grant recognition to interest groups primarily because these groups possess valuable knowledge and experience. One of the consequences of this emphasis on expertise is that civil servants will interact most frequently with those interests which must themselves be most diligent in producing and acquiring information in the ordinary pursuit of their own affairs, that is, with management more than with labour, with trading companies more than with farmers or consumers, and with self-governing doctors more than with salaried teachers. This bias in favour of relations with particular kinds of pressure groups may be corrected by the recognition of less expert groups. The purpose of this recognition may be a self-conscious pursuit of the public interest, an acknowledgement of the voting power of these groups or simply the creation of an illusion of countervailing powers. Whatever the purpose for their recognition, however, these less expert groups tend to remain of low status, to be prestige conscious and to be fearful of manipulation by government and civil servants. The recognition of pressure groups, then, is based most securely on expertise and the communication of this expertise to civil servants.

In granting recognition to a pressure group, public officials support it politically or, in some cases, maintain its sheer viability. This is one aspect of pressure group politics which has been relatively well studied in Canada. Accounts of the Canadian Federation of Agriculture and the Canadian Labour Congress emphasize the importance these groups attach to their annual presentation to Cabinet and to other formal relations with the government. It is probable that these presentations are most directly related to the need for status.[6] The Consumers' Association of Canada actually needs a direct governmental financial subsidy to survive.[7] These are examples of the *government's* decision to grant essential political support to pressure groups.

Much of this kind of political support, however, is channelled through *civil servants* who may go so far as to encourage the formation of pressure groups from unorganized but potentially useful interests. Long before the dramatic confrontation with a Cabinet minister which led to the Canadian

[5] Glenn Somerville, "Better Business Bureaus' president questions government techniques in handling consumer complaints", *The Globe and Mail,* Toronto, October 13, 1970, p. B3. (The article is from the *Globe's* "Man in the News" series, a particularly good newspaper source of current material on pressure group activities.)

[6] See Helen Jones Dawson, "Relations between Farm Organizations and the Civil Service in Canada and Great Britain", *Canadian Public Administration,* vol. 10 (1967), pp. 565-573; David Kwavnick, "Pressure Group Demands and the Struggle for Organizational Status; The Case of Organized Labour in Canada", *Canadian Journal of Political Science,* vol. 3 (1970), pp. 56-72. For recognition of the same phenomenon in the United States see David Truman, *The Governmental Process* (New York: Alfred A. Knopf, 1951), esp. pp. 459-60.

[7] Helen Jones Dawson, "Consumers' Association of Canada", *Canadian Public Administration,* vol. 2 (1969), pp. 103-117.

Federation of Agriculture's regular annual presentation, a civil servant appears to have been helpful in establishing the organization. H. H. Hannam, its first president, has related how the late Clifford Clark, then Deputy Minister of Finance, informally suggested the establishment of a national farm organization and how Hannam used Clark's prestige to enlist support for the organization of the Federation.[8] The viability of the Canadian Manufacturers' Association in its early days was very much aided by the decision of the Department of Railways and Canals to solicit the Association's views on rail rate changes.[9] Doubtless, many more instances of such bureaucratic initiative are unrecorded and civil servants rather than politicians made the supportive decision. Indeed, it may be inevitable that the public administrator be the agent most involved in the government's political support of pressure groups since that support is in large part just the obverse of the consultative, administrative relationship.

The importance of a pressure group's status with government also enables civil servants to exert counter pressure on a group. By looking elsewhere for information or for administrative assistance, civil servants can threaten pressure group officials and so achieve more compliance than the group might otherwise be inclined to grant. Moreover, by means of a cool response or a disinclination to communicate with a particular group representative, civil servants may sow discontent and discord among the group's leadership or even encourage part of the leadership to act as a more compliant influence within the group. If a group resists such pressure, civil servants may try to dilute its public influence. The Canadian Drug Manufacturers' Association was organized upon the suggestion of a civil servant and acted as a rival to the long established Pharmaceutical Manufacturers Association of Canada.[10]

Policy Making

Pressure groups gain recognition more easily and more rapidly if they are frequently invited to provide expertise to civil servants. The provision of this special knowledge also gives pressure groups an opportunity to participate in policy formulation. By supplying information used in the creation of policy, a pressure group contributes to policy making in a "passive" sense. The government may ask a pressure group for comments on the potential effects of a proposed policy in such areas as future investment, employment, costs and prices. The government may also make a general request for suggestions as to how it might assist a group to contribute to economic development or the general welfare. Evidence that government invites groups to participate in policy making as a matter of course and that the main arena of such

---

[8] H.H. Hannam, "The Interest Group and Its Activities", Institute of Public Administration of Canada, *Proceedings of the Fifth Annual Conference* (1953), pp. 172-73.

[9] S.D. Clarke, *The Canadian Manufacturers' Association* (Toronto: University of Toronto, 1939), pp. 48-9.

[10] An interview conducted by the author.

participation is civil service-pressure group interaction is provided by this statement of a Canadian Cabinet minister.

In the process of preparing legislation and also in considering general policy changes, the government requires as much information as possible about the areas to be affected and the possible implications of any proposed changes. In addition to all the other reasons why associations or organizations should be in continuous contact with government, this particular need for information and consultation to influence government policy is probably the most important. . . .

What is of the greatest value is for the minister to be apprised of the impact of the legislation from the particular viewpoint of the group concerned. Legislation must of necessity speak generally, but there may be special cases which persons in a particular industry or group might recognize more easily than can someone in government, surveying industry or the community generally.

Equally, it is of greater value to have positive alternative suggestions with respect to carrying out the general purpose of the statute rather than negative dissent only. . . .

. . . if there has not been . . . general public discussion preceding legislation, it is important that the particular interest be brought to the attention of departmental officials so that it may be taken into account in policy formulation and it will be useful for the minister also to have these viewpoints so that he may raise them with officials.[11]

The minister's comments relate to policy advice on legislation. Pressure groups are also asked for advice on policy making which occurs in the drafting and amendment of regulations. Frequent illustrations of this type of policy making may be gleaned from the pages of a daily newspaper. For example, it was recently reported that:

Mr. Ross [President of the Independent Petroleum Association of Canada] expects the federal government will invite industry inspection of new regulations and tax changes, as promised, before making its new policies public and binding.[12]

The participation of the Canadian Medical Association and the Canadian Federation of Agriculture in policy making at various levels has already been recounted.[13]

Conflicts between government and pressure groups may range from major disputes over general policy to disagreements over the day-to-day ad-

---

[11] The Honourable Donald S. Macdonald, "Notes for Remarks to the Twenty-Third Session of the Canadian Insitute for Organization Management", President of the Privy Council Press Release, June 19, 1969.

[12] Thomas Kennedy, "IPAC president praises know-how, Arctic effort, despite handicaps", *The Globe and Mail,* Toronto, March 25, 1971, p. B12.

[13] Malcolm Taylor, "The Role of the Medical Profession in the Formulation and Execution of Public Policy", *The Canadian Journal of Economics and Political Science,* vol. 26 (1960), pp. 108-127, and Helen Jones Dawson, "Relations between Farm Organizations and the Civil Service in Canada and Great Britain", *Canadian Public Administration,* vol. 10 (1967), pp. 450-70.

ministration of a regulation. If the conflict centres on a detail of a regulation or on some other minor point that can be settled in private, the administrator must carry the major part of the burden of argument, persuasion and cajolery. When a conflict arises over general policy, however, the political role of the administrator again comes into play.

Civil servants may in the future carry a larger part of the political defence of government policy. They are already expected to be helpful to members of the public and to provide information as a matter of course or on request to news reporters, pressure group officials and Members of Parliament. The decline of civil service anonymity, accentuated by the smallness and intimacy of the political community in Ottawa, will expose the civil servant to a growing number of such requests. He must constantly make judgements on the propriety of a response since the guidelines setting limitations on his discretion are so general. In supplying this information, the civil servant acts as a de facto source of political support for the government. This activity may be characterized as a "passive" political role because it occurs only in response to specific requests.

Civil servants play a more "active" and deliberately political role when they are allowed or even required by their ministers to act as publicists or propagandists to prepare public opinion for a policy change. Under these conditions, civil servants must take the initiative in providing information, especially the "right" information, to the public. This task can be accomplished primarily through civil service testimony in open hearings of royal commissions, government task forces and parliamentary committees. It may also be necessary, however, to take some initiatives to achieve the desired interpretation of this material even by those who are pre-disposed to support the government. To perform this information service effectively, civil servants are obliged to adopt techniques commonly used by professional public relations agencies. For example, in the case of drug prices, the likely policy was opposed by an established, competent pressure group before the government publicly and fully committed itself to a proposal.[14] Civil servants and pressure group officials then acted as the major protagonists and used similar methods to win public support. While the drug prices problem was being investigated by a special committee of the House of Commons, both civil servants and officials of the Pharmaceutical Manufacturers Association of Canada (P.M.A.C.) sought out Members of Parliament to provide them with selected information and refutations of their opponents' arguments. Moreover, both civil servants and pressure group officials gave special briefings to selected journalists who then assisted by presenting one of the sides of the argument and criticizing the other. This was an especially important technique not only because of the readership enjoyed by reporters

---

[14]The following account is based on a variety of documentary sources and on interviews conducted by the author with reporters, Members of Parliament, civil servants in several departments, and officials of several pressure groups. Each assertion here could be supported by a number of independent sources.

who wrote the original stories, but also because of the tendency of the press to reuse information and interpretations *ad infinitum.* In addition, both civil servants and P.M.A.C. officials sought out potential allies, encouraged them to testify before a Commons' Special Committee and provided them with the necessary information and arguments for their briefs. Indeed, it is likely that of those persons and groups not directly representing the pharmaceutical industry, only a very few who testified did so on their own initiative.

This discussion of the recognition of pressure groups and their interaction with civil servants in the policy process describes only part of the whole relationship. One important area, not explored at length here, is the delegation of administrative responsibilities by bureaucrats to pressure group organizations. When a group establishes standards for membership or rules for the self-regulation of its trade or profession, when it answers questions from its membership about the applicability of the law to a particular case, or when it publishes explanations of government policy in its trade or professional journal, it is performing a task that otherwise might be required of civil servants.[15] Yet another significant aspect of the bureaucracy-group system is the etiquette or "rules of the game" accepted by both parties. These "rules of the game" include agreement as to when confidential materials may be exchanged and under what conditions the parties may agree to disagree. In every discussion of such rules of the game the emphasis is on privacy and confidentiality — in short on secrecy.[16] While such secrecy is convenient to the pressure groups, the civil servants and the government, it is probably the government which most demands and enforces it. Civil servants may lose their anonymity but the government insists on retaining its secrets.[17] As suggested earlier, the interaction of civil servants and pressure groups occurs in a context of other relationships; not least among these is the relationship between the government and its civil servants. It is that relationship which probably most effectively governs the interaction of the public and group bureaucracies.

---

[15] The delegation of administration to a pressure group is described in more detail in Malcolm Taylor, "The Role of the Medical Profession in the Formulation and Execution of Public Policy", *The Canadian Journal of Economics and Political Science,* vol. 26 (1960).

[16] Englemann and Schwartz, *Political Parties and the Canadian Social Structure,* pp. 103-4. See also Potter, *Organized Groups in British National Politics,* pp. 230-236, and the complaint against secrecy in S.E. Finer, *Anonymous Empire,* 2nd ed. (London: Paul Mall Press, 1966), pp. 136-145.

[17] For example, after describing her unhappiness about the tactics of the insurance industry lobby against the Canada Pension Plan, Miss LaMarsh suggested to Cabinet that she "would hereafter hear all representations but only when the press was present. Pearson and all my colleagues were appalled." Judy LaMarsh, *Memoirs of a Bird in a Gilded Cage* (Toronto: McClelland and Stewart, 1969), p. 88.

Readings

Anderson, James. "Pressure Groups and the Canadian Bureaucracy. In *Public Administration in Canada,* eds. W.D.K. Kernaghan and A.M. Willms. 2nd ed. Toronto: Methuen Publications, 1971, pp. 370-79.

Aucoin, Peter. "The Role of Functional Advisory Councils." In *Structures of Policy-Making in Canada,* eds. G. Bruce Doern and Peter Aucoin. Toronto: Macmillan, 1971, pp. 154-78.

Axworthy, Lloyd. "The Housing Task Force: A Case Study." In *Structures of Policy-Making in Canada,* eds. G. Bruce Doern and Peter Aucoin. Toronto: Macmillan, 1971, pp. 130-53.

Corbett, D.C. "The Pressure Group and the Public Interest." *Proceedings of the Fifth Annual Conference.* Toronto: Institute of Public Administration of Canada, 1953, pp. 185-95.

Courtney, John C. "In Defence of Royal Commissions." *Canadian Public Administration,* vol. 12, no. 2 (Summer, 1969), pp. 198-212.

Dawson, Helen Jones. "Consumer Association of Canada." *Canadian Public Administration,* vol. 6, no. 1 (March, 1963), pp. 92-118.

Dawson, Helen Jones. "Interest Group: The Canadian Federation of Agriculture." *Canadian Public Administration,* vol. 3, no. 2 (June, 1960), pp. 134-49.

Dawson, Helen Jones. "Relations between Farm Organizations and the Civil Service in Canada and Great Britain." *Canadian Public Administration,* vol. 10, no. 4 (December, 1967), pp. 450-70.

Doern, G. Bruce. "The Role of Central Advisory Councils: The Science Council of Canada." In *Structures of Policy-Making in Canada,* eds. G. Bruce Doern and Peter Aucoin. Toronto: Macmillan, 1971, pp. 246-66.

Doern, G. Bruce. "The Role of the Royal Commission in the General Policy Process and in Federal-Provincial Relations." *Canadian Public Administration,* vol. 10, no. 4 (December, 1967), pp. 417-33.

Doern G. Bruce. "Scientists and Science Policy Machinery." In *Bureaucracy in Canadian Government,* ed. W.D.K. Kernaghan. Toronto: Methuen Publications, 1969, pp. 112-119.

Doern, G. Bruce and Peter Aucoin, eds. *The Structures of Policy-Making in Canada.* Toronto: Macmillan, 1971.

Doerr, A.D. "The Role of White Papers." In *Structures of Policy-Making in Canada,* eds. G. Bruce Doern and Peter Aucoin. Toronto: Macmillan, 1971, pp. 179-203.

Edmonds, J. Duncan and M.K. Pauman. "Business and Government in Canada in the 1970's." *Optimum,* vol. 2, no. 3 (1971), pp. 24-35.

Hanson, Hugh, R. "Inside Royal Commissions." *Canadian Public Administration,* vol. 12, no. 3 (Fall, 1969), pp. 356-64.

Hodgetts, J.E. "Public Power and Ivory Power." In *Agenda 1970: Proposals for a Creative Politics,* eds. Trevor Lloyd and Jack McLeod. Toronto: University of Toronto Press, 1968, pp. 256-80.

Hodgetts, J.E. "Should Canada be De-Commissioned? A Commoner's View of Royal Commissions." *Queen's Quarterly,* vol. 70 (Winter, 1964), pp. 475-90.

Hughes, S.H.S. "The Public Official—Parliament, Public and the Press." *Canadian Public Administration,* vol. 3, no. 4 (December, 1960), pp. 289-98.

Phidd, R.W. "The Role of Central Advisory Councils: The Economic Council of Canada." In *Structures of Policy-Making in Canada,* eds. G. Bruce Doern and Peter Aucoin. Toronto: Macmillan, 1971, pp. 204-45.

Ritchie, Ronald S. *An Institute For Research on Public Policy.* Ottawa: Information Canada, 1971.

Schindeler, Fred and C.M. Lamphier. "Social Science Research and Participatory Democracy in Canada." *Canadian Public Administration,* vol. 12, no. 1 (Winter, 1969), pp. 481-98.

Shoyama, T.K. "Advisory Committees in Administration." *Proceedings of the Ninth Annual Conference.* Toronto: Institute of Public Administration of Canada, 1957, pp. 145-53.

Stanford, Lloyd. "Ivory to Replace Brass?" *Canadian Public Administration,* vol. 12, no. 4 (Winter, 1969), pp. 566-71.

Taylor, K.W. "Pressure Groups in Administration." *Proceedings of the Fifth Annual Conference.* Toronto: Institute of Public Administration of Canada, 1953, pp. 155-206.

Taylor, M.G. "Role of the Medical Profession in the Formulation and Execution of Public Policy." *Canadian Journal of Economics and Political Science,* vol. 26, no. 1 (February, 1960), pp. 108-27.

Taylor, Malcolm G. "Quebec Medicare: Policy Formulation in Conflict and Crisis." *Canadian Public Administration,* vol. 15, no. 2 (Summer, 1972), pp. 211-50.

Thorburn, H.G. "Pressure Groups in Canadian Politics: Recent Revisions of the Anti-Combines Legislation." *Canadian Journal of Economics and Political Science,* vol. 30, no. 2 (May, 1964), pp. 157-74.

Walls, C.E.S. "Royal Commissions—Their Influence on Public Policy." *Canadian Public Administration,* vol. 12, no. 3 (Fall, 1969), pp. 365-71.

Wilson, V. Seymour. "The Role of Royal Commissions and Task Forces." In *Structures of Policy-Making in Canada,* eds. G. Bruce Doern and Peter Aucoin. Toronto: Macmillan, 1971, pp. 113-29.

Wronski, W. "The Public Servant and Protest Groups." *Canadian Public Administration,* vol. 14, no. 1 (Spring, 1971), pp. 65-72.

Chapter Five

Administrative Responsibility

The meanings assigned to the elusive concept of administrative responsibility include, among others, efficiency, effectiveness, responsiveness, integrity and accountability. Any attempt to capture the essence of the concept in a brief statement is, therefore, an impracticable task. A more fruitful endeavour is to explore the means of achieving administrative responsibility through the adoption of instruments to control the exercise of discretionary authority by public servants. The selections in this chapter set out specific proposals for the use of such control devices. The potential utility of an Ombudsman to promote administrative responsibility is examined in Chapter Six.

Eric Hehner begins by describing the scope and the danger of the ever-increasing delegation of legislative and judicial powers to the bureaucracy. Peter Silcox is concerned with the increase in bureaucratic authority resulting from the proliferation of boards and commissions enjoying varying degrees of independence from political control. J.A. Corry sees a threat to individual and collective rights from the expansion of discretionary administrative powers. He contends that application of the rule of law to the contemporary administrative process can achieve the necessary reconciliation of public power and private rights.

14

Growth of Discretions — Decline of Accountability*

Eric Hehner

The functions of the public service have changed in a fundamental way which requires re-appraisal of the positions of Parliament and of the courts of law. This change has happened so quietly that its extent, its basic nature, and its significance to our system of government have not yet been widely recognized. The administrator has gained vastly wider powers and the legislature is losing both knowledge of, and effective control over, the way in which the powers it has conferred are exercised. This has created a new relationship between the individual and the state, and over a period of many years has progressively contributed to the sterilization of Parliament.

Parliament, the public service, and the courts of law were designed for limited functions of government. The ideal of legislation was to be definitive and precise, and to leave little to the imagination or to opinion. Our forefathers undoubtedly fell far short of this ideal, but the ideal was there. The public service performed administrative and service functions. The courts were adjudicators of facts and defenders of injured individuals from other individuals or from the state. Judicial decisions were made under a rule of law with the rules fixed beforehand and equally applicable to all.

Government today is expected to offer direction and to execute policies of a positive nature — to be an active participant in economic and social affairs, not just a writer of rules and an umpire. Had our economic and social structures and the technology on which they in part rest been relatively static, a rule of law as known in the past might have provided an adequate mechanism to enable government to play an increased role. However, the expansion of the scale of economic processes has been great enough to produce differences of nature, not just of size. It has made necessary the use of discretions by governmental authority, which cannot be exercised by Parliament itself.

The activities of government have changed to meet the needs of the times, but our political and legal structure for many years failed to keep pace. There has been increasing delegation of authority by Parliament to the Cabinet, to departments and boards, and to nameless public servants. Since the government is playing a more active and positive role at a time of rapidly

*Eric Hehner, "Growth of Discretions — Decline of Accountability" (updated from an unpublished address delivered to the Ottawa Regional Group of the Institute of Public Administration of Canada on November 24, 1965). The editor extends appreciation to Mr. Hehner for his work in updating this selection.

changing technology, changing patterns of domestic and international trade, and changing social viewpoints, it cannot spell out in statutes all the provisions and exemptions needed to look after the innumerable variations of modern requirements. Our need for greater flexibility in administration has been growing, and the location of responsibility for executive, legislative, and judicial functions has become somewhat vague. The activities of departments of government are no longer separable into neat, mutually-exclusive areas of interest. As the functions and direct participation of government have extended, the machinery of administration has become more complicated and has ceased to be merely administrative.

We have changed the activities of government to an extent that makes even more discretionary powers inevitable. We have provided for many such powers, and at an accelerating pace. However, instead of entering wholeheartedly into the creation of discretions with our eyes open to its implications and needs and simultaneously providing machinery to prevent the abuse of discretionary powers, we tried to pretend that there had been no basic change. We left discretions to be exercised as much in the shadows of secrecy as possible. It has become more difficult to tell where lawmaking stops and administration starts. It has become harder to place responsibility for actions (or lack of them) among the multiplicity of government agencies now involved. Even greater use of discretionary powers may be essential but these powers carry with them potential for abuse unless there are surrounding safeguards.

It became the norm for a statute to delegate authority to make regulations to achieve objectives which have been expressed in very general terms. If regulations extend only to details of mechanical procedures, no real discretionary powers are delegated. However, where the statutory provisions are only a skeleton and it is left to regulations to say "what, where, when, why, how and who," then we have created meaningful discretionary powers and should examine the mechanisms available to review the exercise of these powers. When regulations are issued by the Governor-in-Council, or even by a minister of the Crown, there is at least a degree of accountability for this first step. Where the power is conferred upon a board or commission, review of its exercise becomes more difficult and remote. However, if the discretions have been consciously delegated to a named body directly responsible to the legislature, there is at least a placing of responsibility. If persons or bodies possessed of delegated powers re-delegate them, we come to a state that may be described as "dispersed discretions". When discretionary judgements are not the result of a conscious act which has placed the responsibility upon a named person or body, but are the result of pretending that matters of opinion are matters of fact, we are farther into an area of trouble.

The courts have been the traditional safeguard for the rights of one individual against another or against the state, but the courts were designed to adjudicate matters which at least purport to be issues of fact in relation to pre-established law. Courts lack both the powers and in most cases the capacity to substitute their judgement for opinions which others have been empowered to express. In essence, the traditional courts are incapable of playing a constructive part in the newly developing functions of government, where exercise of discretions is required. For this reason positive action was frequently taken by legislatures to exclude the exercise of delegated discretions from the jurisdiction of the courts, if it was found or suspected that the courts might be in a position to intervene.

The magnitude of the developments described has been generally unrecognized. Most people still think that Parliament makes the laws except for small details; that public servants just administer; and that those exercising delegated discretions are accountable for their actions in fact as well as in theory to the elected representatives of the people. In fact, the rule of law as we knew it until World War II has just about gone and effective accountability to Parliament has been lost over a wide area of governmental activity.

These are not just impressionistic statements. Let us look at some specific examples of this continuing process of growth of discretions. In this paper as originally prepared in 1965, examples were quoted from the Acts of the third session of the 26th Parliament. Updating the examples, the same pattern is still found. The Acts of the third session of the 28th Parliament (October 8, 1970 — January 12, 1972) continued the process of legislating in generalities, leaving the substance to be prescribed by regulations to be administered beyond the control of Parliament. There were 65 public bills introduced in that session which subsequently became law. Many of these were of a mechanical nature such as redefining electoral boundaries and repealing the Leprosy Act, or formalisms such as proclaiming "Pollution Awareness Week", and similar measures of limited interest and content. Of the bills which affected the public at large, the majority conferred new discretionary authority.

Under the Consumer Packaging and Labelling Act (Bill C-180), full power to exempt goods from the application of the Act is delegated to the Governor-in-Council. The labelling requirements that are to apply to goods are to be prescribed by regulations. Thus, in passing the Act, Parliament prohibited the sale or import of goods not packaged in compliance with regulations that had not yet been made and were therefore unknown to Parliament. Similarly, the Act delegates the power of entry without warrant and the seizure of goods at the sole discretion of inspectors in order to enforce regulations made under the Act and therefore unknown to Parliament when the Act was passed.

It should not go unnoticed that the Statutory Instruments Act (Bill C-182)[1], "to provide for the examination, publication and scrutiny of regulations and other statutory instruments", itself created new discretionary powers by authorizing the Governor-in-Council to prescribe by regulation that regulations or classes of regulations need not be examined, published or

---

[1] Canada, *Statutes* (1971).

scrutinized. This the Governor-in-Council subsequently did, in the Statutory Instruments Regulations[2].

Another example is the Clean Air Act (Bill C-224). "Air quality objectives" are left to be "prescribed by the Governor-in-Council". What are to be regarded as "air contaminants" are left to be prescribed by regulation. Those types of operations to be subject to regulation are left to be "specified by the Governor-in-Council". Powers to decide who should be required to conform to standards, who should be exempted, and what the standards should be are also delegated to the Minister. Discretionary enforcement powers are delegated to "inspectors", to be exercised according to what the inspectors "may reasonably believe" to be the facts, or as an inspector "deems necessary".

The Act to amend the Canada Labour (Standards) Code (Bill C-228) had 24 sections. Thirteen of these delegate discretions by reference to "as prescribed by regulations" or the use of similar phrases.

The Unemployment Insurance Act, 1971 (Bill C-229) is an outstanding example. The definition of "insurable earnings" was left to be "prescribed by regulation". What are "excepted employment" and "insurable employment" were left to be defined by regulations which might be general, or restricted to areas in the country, groups of persons, or even applicable only to individual persons. Unemployed persons can be disentitled to benefits by regulation. Wide powers to make regulations are given to the Minister, and the Minister is given power to authorize others to exercise his powers. The Unemployment Insurance Commission is not only given wide powers to issue regulations, but is empowered in turn to delegate its powers to any employees it desires. There are close to 75 references in the Act to the power to make regulations, or requirements to comply with regulations. Without the regulations the Act is hollow.

In addition to legislative acts of this nature, there is the whole area of "Rules, orders, regulations, by-laws or proclamations which are made by regulation-making authorities in the exercise of a legislative power" — commonly known as Statutory Orders and Regulations. In any year these are numbered in the thousands, and not only delegate authority but frequently re-delegate it.

For example, the powers to make regulations provided by the Unemployment Insurance Act, 1971, were promptly and frequently exercised. Authority to exercise judgements and make determinations was extended through the use of such phrases as "in the opinion of the Commission", "approved by the Commission", "in the manner set out in the instructions from the Commission", "may be determined by the Commission". Regulations redefine significant words and phrases from meanings given to them in the statute. There is redelegation of powers, through such phrases as "Where it is established to the satisfaction of an officer of the Department of National

---

[2] SOR/71-592, P.C. 1971-2485, November 9, 1971.

Revenue, Taxation. . . . " The Unemployement Insurance Act, 1971, came into effect on various dates starting in June 1971. In the following 12 months the Unemployment Insurance Regulations were amended 12 times, and the revisions took up about 90 pages of small type in the Canada Gazette. One can appreciate a comment of Mr. Stanley Knowles, M.P., when this series of amendments had barely started:

It is our experience in Parliament time and time again to think we knew what we passed when we gave final approval to a piece of legislation, only to find months later that things were being done or restrictions were being imposed of a kind we did not believe appeared in the bill at all. When we try to find out what happened, we discover that we had given authority to the Governor-in-Council to make regulations for the carrying out of the purposes of the act and that under this authority restrictive regulations were passed, or restrictive definitions introduced of such a nature as to produce quite a different result from the result we thought had been intended. I could give a number of examples. . . . let me give just one, not in order to be contentious, but merely to make my point. Take the new Unemployment Insurance Act. Because we gave the Governor-in-Council the power to define "earnings" we found that things were happening which we did not expect and that in many cases benefits were greatly reduced.[3]

The statutes and regulations used as examples have the merit of being published documents. In addition, there is a large area of unpublished Orders-in-Council and Ministerial prescriptions. There is also the broad field of so-called administrative decisions (or lack of decisions) which are equally exercises of discretion. These are by nature difficult to deal with in public, because they frequently involve decisions relating to private and confidential affairs of individual persons or companies. One can only learn of the details through a confidential relationship to those affected. However, these unpublished Orders-in-Council, Ministerial prescriptions, or administrative decisions are frequently of general application and remain unknown to many persons affected by them because they are not published.

In the last few years it has been more widely recognized that this problem exists, and the first few steps towards doing something about the problem have been taken.

The Parliamentary Special Committee on Procedure and Organization, which reported in December 1964, recognized the joint problems of growth of discretions being exercised by appointed officials and loss of effective control by Parliament. It attempted to deal with the situation by recommending that there be established a Standing Committee on Delegated Legislation. The purpose of this Standing Committee was described as follows:

The function of this Committee would be to act as a watchdog over the executive in its use of the powers conferred by statute, with the duty of reporting to Parliament any tendency on the part of the executive to exceed its authority. The committee's terms of reference should exclude it from considering the

---

merits of or the policy behind delegated legislation, but it would be expected to draw the attention of Parliament to any regulations or instruments which impose a charge on public revenues, which confer immunity from challenge in the courts, which have an unauthorized retroactive effect, which reveal an unusual or unexpected use of a statutory power, or which otherwise exceed the authority delegated by the parent statute.[4]

This recommendation was not accepted by the Government. The flood of unregulated regulations continued and burgeoned.

With the Trudeau administration, there came a change on a number of fronts simultaneously. In September 1968, the House of Commons appointed a Special Committee on Statutory Instruments

... to consider and, from time to time, to report on procedures for the review by this House of instruments made in virtue of any statute of the Parliament of Canada.[5]

In July 1969, the scope of the powers of this Special Committee was extended to permit it, also

to consider and, from time to time, to report on the adequacy of existing statutory authority for the making and publication of Statutory Instruments and on the adequacy of existing procedures for the drafting, scrutiny and operational review of such instruments, and to make recommendations with respect thereto.[6]

This Special Committee did not have powers to review the exercise of delegated authority — merely to recommend what, in its opinion, should be done to deal with this problem.

The report of the Special Committee on Statutory Instruments, presented October 22, 1969, reiterated the importance of the area of delegated legislation, using such phrases as:

... public knowledge of governmental activities is the basis of all control of delegated legislation. For parliamentary democracy is a system of government which requires that the executive be responsible to the legislature and that both be accountable to the people, and there can be neither responsibility nor accountability where there is no knowledge of what has been done ....

Your Committee can agree with the view of Dr. D.C. Rowat that the general tradition of administrative secrecy is based on an earlier system of royal rule in Britain that is unsuited to a modern democracy in which the people must be fully informed about the activities of their government ....

Your Committee's contention is, therefore, that there should be, as a general rule, public knowledge of the processes of delegated legislation, before, during, and after the making of regulations, and that any derogation by government from this rule requires justification.[7]

---

[4] *Debates* (Commons), December 14, 1964, p. 988.

[5] *Ibid.,* September 30, 1968.

[6] *Ibid.,* July 10, 1969.

[7] Canada, *Third Report of the Special Committee of the House of Commons on Statutory Instruments,* October 22, 1969.

The Committee made extensive recommendations (23 in number). Some were subsequently accepted by the Government, othere were not. Among those *not* accepted was that the Committee "be reconstituted in the next session to allow further consideration of certain matters referred to in this Report". Of those recommendations that were accepted, it can be said that the period of gestation between acceptance in principle and subsequent action was lengthy, and in some cases the offspring were stillborn.

It took eight months before there was a government statement on the Committee's recommendations which had been tabled in the House of Commons in October 1969. In June 1970 the President of the Privy Council stated government policy and intentions as follows:

Due to the nature of the committee's recommendations it is not practical, nor is it reasonably possible, to proceed with their implementation by any one means. Rather, implementation of the committee's recommendations will require action of three different kinds: first, legislative action by Parliament to replace the existing Regulations Act by a new statutory instruments act; second, a number of cabinet directives to implement several of the recommendations which cannot be dealt with by general legislation and, third, amendment of the Standing Orders for the purpose of establishing a scrutiny committee to review regulations.

The government accepts fully the principle that both Parliament and the public are entitled to be fully informed of, and to have convenient access to, regulations and other instruments made under the authority of Acts of Parliament. The legislation and other measures that will be proposed by the government will be guided by this paramount principle, and only demonstrably necessary and carefully defined exceptions to the general requirements of the law relating to the examination, registration and publication of such instruments will be permitted.[8]

There had already been a positive step in a related area through the introduction in March 1970, of a bill to establish the Federal Court of Canada, to replace with extended powers the Exchequer Court. This measure, which was proclaimed effective June 1, 1971, repealed provisions in many statutes which had specifically prohibited appeals to the Courts against procedures, or from findings, of a number of semi-judicial boards and tribunals. This measure now affords protection against arbitrary action, and the failure of such boards or tribunals to proceed in a judicial manner. However, it does not, of course, empower the court to substitute its judgement for that of the bodies empowered to exercise discretions.

In November 1970, Bill C-182, "to provide for the examination, publication and scrutiny of regulations and other statutory instruments" was introduced, and in January 1971, it was referred to the Standing Committee on Justice and Legal Affairs. The Hon. John Turner, then Minister of Justice, restated government intentions as being those previously stated by the President of the Privy Council:

---

[8] *Debates* (Commons), June 16, 1970.

1. To issue Cabinet directives "to deal with departmental directives and guidelines and the conferring by legislation of regulation-making powers".

2. To replace the existing provisions for scrutiny and publication of regulations by a new and broader Statutory Instruments Act.

3. To provide a parliamentary committee to review statutory instruments.

The Cabinet directives are said to have been issued, but what they said cannot be reported. When a question on this matter was addressed to the Privy Council office, access to them was denied. The official reply was that they are confidential, "They are not in the public domain".

Bill C-182 received Royal Assent May 19, 1971, and came into force January 1, 1972, together with regulations made thereunder. Adequate comment on the Statutory Instruments Act and the regulations thereunder is not possible within the scope of this article. However, two points should be noted. It would be an error to think that the requirements of the Act extend to all of the multitude of orders-in-council, rules, orders, regulations, by-laws, proclamations — call them what you will — which affect the rights and responsibilities of individuals. The statute applies only to certain regulations as defined in the Act — in essence those "made in the exercise of legislative power", or those "for the contravention of which a penalty, fine or imprisonment is prescribed by or under an Act of Parliament". This leaves out a substantial area of the exercises of administrative discretions. The Act also applies only to those regulations (as defined) made subsequent to its passage; it leaves untouched the thousands of pre-existing regulations.

With respect to the "scrutiny committee", motions to establish a Standing Committee on Regulations and other Statutory Instruments, as a Joint Committee of the House of Commons and the Senate, were introduced and adopted in the Senate on October 12, 1971, and in the House of Commons on October 14, 1971. However, it was not until March 1972 that the Senate named its members of the Joint Committee, and the House of Commons did likewise. There was then official silence.

The powers — if any — of this Committee were never specified. It was not instructed to do anything. All it is empowered to do under the Statutory Instruments Act is to look at those new statutory instruments which are not withheld from inspection. There is nothing which says what the Committee can do after such review. In spite of repeated enquiries and references to inaction from government as well as opposition members, when the 28th Parliament was dissolved, and its Committees died with it, the Joint Committee on Regulations and other Statutory Instruments had still never met. The 29th Parliament is still to be elected at the time of this writing. Whether the Standing Joint Committee on Regulations and other Statutory Instruments will be an active or a passive body in the next Parliament, is still to be seen.

Perhaps what has happened has been inevitable; it may even be desirable — but not as long as we pretend that nothing has really happened to change the old order. If we permit the proliferation of powers—dispersed discretions—

without setting up an effective mechanism to supervise the exercise of these powers, a free community will not long survive. Unless we find some way of bringing Parliament back into the picture, its individual members, legislating only in generalities and without effective means of seeing how their servants are acting, are reduced to comparative impotence.

Delegated legislation is sufficiently significant that it deserves a special mechanism for review of its exercise. Unless members of Parliament fulfil this function, Parliament as we have known it will become relatively impotent. Some public servants have questioned whether members of Parliament can be expected to approach review of the exercise of discretions in a non-partisan manner. They seem to feel that politicians will refuse to distinguish between the essentially political acts of determining policy and voting for legislative programmes, and the essentially non-partisan function of studying how powers delegated by legislation are being exercised. Perhaps the question might be phrased, "Can members forget party politics long enough to be objective in protecting the rights of the individual to the end that there is equal justice for all, and efficient, non-discriminatory application of the law?" This is a function which the courts cannot fulfil in relation to the exercise of delegated discretions. If members of Parliament cannot, or will not, do this job through committees established for this purpose, then we should at least abandon the pretence that they are able to do so now, even with the new Statutory Instruments Act.

15

The Proliferation of Boards and Commissions*

Peter Silcox

The expansion of government activities has had three important results. First, the contacts between governments, government and non-governmental organizations, and government and the general population have all been made much more complex. Second, far more professionals and specialists have been

*Peter Silcox, "The Proliferation of Boards and Commissions", in *Agenda 1970: Proposals for a Creative Politics,* eds. Trevor Lloyd and Jack McLeod (Toronto: University of Toronto Press, 1968), pp. 115-34. Reprinted and abridged by permission of the author and publisher.

brought into government and, because many of their activities are difficult for the layman to understand, the problem of political control has become more complicated. Third, new administrative forms, whose relationship to the normal departmental structure is difficult to work out, have proliferated.

Many of these changes have been brought about by political parties explicitly committed to the proposition that big government poses a threat to the best interests of society. This general view has also been shared by a large majority of the population, at least in North America. Despite these general outlooks popularly elected governments have gone on expanding their activities and there can be no doubt that they have done so, as they themselves claim, under pressure from public opinion. Practically every group in society demands government protection or assistance in its "special" case *despite* the fact its members share the general feeling of disquiet about the expanding role of government. This ambivalence has had an important effect on politicians when they have considered the best administrative structure for dealing with new governmental responsibilities. The semi-independent public agency has a number of attractive features for them. It can give the appearance of being a politically independent corporate body allowed to operate in the manner of the allegedly efficient profit-maximizing private corporation. This structure also has the advantage of making it easier to give interested groups a partnership role in the government's work. In general there can be little doubt that, whatever the realities behind the form, the use of this type of agency does appear to the public to depoliticize the government's role and also to some extent conceal the overall expansion of its power and influence.

Three types of government intervention and agency can be distinguished. First, departments directly under the day-to-day control and supervision of a member of the government. Second, semi-independent public agencies created and given policy goals by the government, which retain some control of the general size and shape of their administrative structure. Third, government-assisted bodies dependent, often to a considerable degree, on government assistance and financial help but not created by an official government initiative; these have a much larger degree of control over their long-term aims and have considerable independence of outside control in organizing their internal organization and procedures.

There are a very large number of semi-independent agencies in existence at both the federal and provincial levels in Canada. Most of them have been established in the past twenty-five years. Among the approximately fifty agencies at the federal level, the most notable group is that of Crown corporations. A number of these, like Air Canada and the CNR, are as large or larger than the most important departments, and others, like the War Veterans Allowance Board, are of more limited significance. In Ontario, there were about fifty "ministerial agencies" in 1968. Some examples of Ontario semi-independent agencies are Ontario Hydro, the Health Insurance Commission, and the much smaller Ontario Highway Transport Board and the Ontario Racing Commission.

The founders of semi-independent agencies have given all kinds of reasons for setting them up. They range in sophistication from C. D. Howe's explanation that a comission should take the form of a corporation because that's the way they are operated around Ottawa to the administrative-technical accounts found in textbooks on public administration. These books explain that the semi-independent form is most useful when, first, the type of administrative flexibility associated with private corporations demands the avoidance of many of the administrative control procedures used in the departmental structure; second, the direct interference of politicians with the day-to-day operations is to be minimized; third, the co-operation of specialists who are often unfavourably disposed to the idea of becoming civil servants is required; fourth, swift action is needed in areas in which the departments have no previous experience.

To bring some order into the chaos of the new areas of government activity, students and administrators have classified agencies according to administrative-technical criteria. Two standard criteria have been used:

1. Type of activity, which has led to the establishment of sub-classes such as proprietary, administrative, judicial, quasi-judicial, and so on.

2. The extent of direct government control as attested to by formal provisions establishing the agency; its freedom in raising funds and the security of tenure of its directors for example. This type of classification can be seen in the Canada Financial Administration Act of 1951.[1]

These classifications appear neat and definitive and they have a kind of non-political air about them acceptable to many public administrators. They are also almost useless if one is concerned with the question of how political power is exercised and the determination of the nature and extent of political responsibility. However, there is evidence to show these arguments often are in the minds of politicians establishing semi-independent agencies, but they are not as decisive as public statements would have us believe. The sceptical political scientist who investigates this area soon discovers that a far wider range of considerations, mostly of a personal and political nature, come to the fore. He is forced to remember that politicians have been at work. The political scientist discovers that within the departmental framework he can find branches and divisions which carry on activities of a commercial nature and that numerous ordinary civil servants are daily exercising judicial or quasi-judicial functions which seem no different from those assigned to semi-independent agencies. Then too, he discovers that all the formal protections for the independence of these agencies do not in practice protect them from the interference of politicians if a determined minister believes that the political credit of the government he serves is at stake. Formal prescriptions are a poor guide in attempting to determine who is responsible for the politically significant decisions taken in the area of concern of a semi-independent agency.

---

[1] See A.M. Willms, "Crown Agencies", p. 28.

All these considerations lead to the suggestion of a different or additional set of reasons why the semi-independent form is sometimes attractive to politicians and a very different system of classification follows from it. The overall expansion of government activities has brought governments more regularly into contact with each other, with privately operated public service organizations, and with powerful pressure groups. Their partnership in particular areas has often been consummated in semi-independent public bodies. Partnership may be desirable for a number of reasons. It may lead to greater efficiency, allow a government to limit its financial commitment or general political responsibility, or it may be the necessary price for active co-operation and political neutrality.

The creation of a semi-independent agency provides the opportunity for a government to minimize its financial support for a particular service from general taxation. Often such agencies are given the responsibility of being as financially self-sustaining as possible. Thus the collection of fees, charges, or contributions can be used to free the government from the financial burden. Contributions collected on a monthly basis by the Ontario Health Insurance Commission are quite clearly a simple poll tax, but they can be disguised as a form of insurance payment to an agency similar in appearance to a private insurance company. People in general are much less hostile to this kind of payment than to a simple poll tax or other regressive tax.

At a more immediately personal level a semi-independent agency might be established to remove from the area of responsibility of a particular minister a new service which the Cabinet feels he is ill fitted to handle. One might also be established as a separate empire for a particularly powerful government supporter with a desire to press ahead in a given area. The desire to impress a special geographic area with the government's interest in it can sometimes be served by the creation of a development agency directed by local notables. Establishing agencies free from restrictions on hiring and firing partially makes up for the reduction of patronage caused by the merit system.

The most relevant classification of agencies will relate to the location of the effective political power to dictate the policies of the agency, to alter its form, or to prescribe its internal procedures. This criterion suggests that semi-independent agencies may be of three types.

1. Subordinate agencies: in relation to which one government has the effective power to set the policies, appoint and replace the directing board or commission, dictate the internal procedures, and change the legislation governing the agency's organization and powers.

2. Government partnership agencies: in this case none of the above changes can be made without changing the essential nature of the agency, unless the approval of governmental partners has been given, even if one level of government has statutory power over the agency.

3. Government group partnership agencies: where the government is inhibited in exercising any binding formal powers over the agency by the

political requirement of satisfying the powerful groups that any proposed changes are not inimical to their interests. It might then be useful to classify agencies in each group according to "type of activity" or other more formal criteria.

This classification, like any other, is not a neat and tidy one. Some agencies may be difficult to fit into it with any certainty, and the same agency might be in different classes at different times. Its advantages are that it does take into account the question of where effective power to command the agency lies, and therefore where effective responsibility for its exercise should be fixed, and that it is not dependent on the purely formal criteria which are such a poor guide to the actual relationships between administrative bodies.

The conventional theory of the means for protecting the public interest assigns important roles to the government, the elected representatives of the people, and the group of individuals directing the agencies. The minister concerned has a number of tasks. It is his responsibility to lay down publicly the general role the government envisages for the agency and thus the general line of policy it must follow. He usually appoints board or commission members, and has final power of approval over investments, decisions, regulations, and procedural rules. With these responsibilities, and the knowledge gleaned from exercising them, the minister can ensure that the agency's work is co-ordinated with that of his own and other government departments. He can also answer in public, and in the legislature in particular, for the agency in those fields where he has responsibility. The task of the board is to use its specialist knowledge to run the day-to-day activities in an efficient manner, and to make decisions within the general policies laid down by the minister with the public interest in mind and without reference to any political considerations. The guarantee that they will concern themselves with the public interest lies in the appointment of honest, intelligent men, whose independent position safeguards them from immediate political pressures. The role of the legislature is to oversee the government's exercise of its responsibilities by using numerous opportunities open to it under the procedures of the legislature. Members can question the minister concerned, debate the regular reports made by the agency which are tabled in the assembly, and scrutinize and debate all legislation concerning the agency brought before the house. The legislature might also keep a more detailed check on these matters through the work of legislative committees. The legislature's responsibility is, of course, to ensure that all activities of the agency are in conformity with the public interest, but its specific control is confined to the area for which the minister is directly responsible.

This is all very comforting to the average citizen. With all these varied groups hard at work to serve the public interest, the problems of co-ordination, public responsibility, and protection of the individual citizen's interests, all seem certain to be solved. But unfortunately it is not necessarily so. Immediately we begin to investigate the actual system, we find serious discrepancies between the theory and the practice.

How do we define general overall policies? Do ministers always declare them? What assurances have we that the minister is satisfied with limiting his interference in the operation of the agency to those powers given to him under the legislation? Can we be assured that any powers of financial supervision, for example, will not be used to determine the scale and direction of day-to-day activities? In the case of agencies where more than one governmental level is involved, how do we know that the responsible representatives will agree on the general lines of development the agency should take? Is the minister knowledgeable enough and well disposed enough to other departments to ensure active efficient co-ordination of government policies? Where agencies involving co-operation with groups are concerned, is the minister more likely to be interested in pacifying important political interests than serving the public good? None of these questions can be answered in the affirmative with any confidence. But have no fear. Remember, the minister is dealing with politically disinterested boards and commissions, and the legislature has an alert eye on him.

Let us look at the boards and commissions and the legislature, then for confirmation of this. First, the boards. The first thing we notice here is that there are a number of different categories of members, and one cannot always be confident of their independence. Some members are civil servants whose position or career prospects are directly dependent on the minister. Some are members of the legislature, although none seem to be members of political parties which oppose the government. Some have long records of political service to political parties or, to be more precise, to the party in power. Some are representatives of other governments or of non-government organizations. A minority are independent-minded experts with no political record. They are a very mixed bunch, and no board or commission is made up exclusively of one type of member. The one thing they have in common is that all were appointed originally by politicians and ultimately all of them can be removed by the same people who control the legislature, whatever kind of tenure they might have.

Studies of the performance of legislative assemblies in the exercise of the responsibilities assigned to them under the conventional theory have reached conclusions that members are not well informed about the work of semi-independent agencies. There is a paucity of information, the members are very busy and have no adequate assistance in researching areas outside their most immediate political concerns, or they are complacent purveyors of the conventional theory.

The ,proliferation of semi-independent public agencies has led to three major problems which must be solved if the public interest is to be protected. First, the maintenance of efficiency requires that their activities be co-ordinated with those of other government bodies. Second, the protection of the right of citizens to have a say in how the government uses its powers requires that there be adequate opportunities for meaningful and informed discussion of their work. Third, the relations between the individual citizen and the agency must be conducted in such a way as to ensure that the former is aware of the reasons for decisions which affect him and is satisfied with the fairness of the procedures which have been followed. All of these problems occur in all public bureaucracies, but they are more acute in this sphere because physical and organizational separation from the departmental structure prevents the normal operation of the methods designed to overcome them.

The prime cause of these extra difficulties is the lack of readily available information on the exact relation of these agencies to the political executive and on their policies and practices. For example, it is impossible to judge if an individual citizen is being unfairly treated unless the aims, general policies, and procedures of an agency have been fully discussed and understood by a significant section of the public. Its conduct in individual cases can only be assessed against this general background. The failure to grasp this simple point has led to far too many cases in which there has been ill-informed criticism of particular agencies.

What changes then are necessary to ensure that the public interest is more adequately protected? The answer must, of course, vary with the type of agency; however, one major innovation is necessary which affects all of them. Far more studies of individual boards and commissions must be made and published. This means that academic investigators must be encouraged to take an interest in the field and their work must be facilitated by giving them free access to relevant material. If this is done, the complacency engendered by the conventional theory of control will quickly be dispelled. Disclosure alone will not deal with the problems I have outlined, but it is the necessary starting point in the search for solution.

Subordinate agencies are the first group we have to discuss. They range from departmental corporations, acknowledged in most cases to be part of the departmental structure, to quasi-judicial bodies with a reputation for their independence from political control. The one feature that these diverse agencies have in common is effective subordination to a minister, which means that a minister can get his own way over the policy the agency follows or the manner in which it is implemented without coming into direct conflict with powerful interest groups that have an institutionalized role in its work or with another level of government. The minister may in fact choose to give the subordinate agency a good deal of independence but he knows that he has the power to dominate, and so do those who direct the particular agency. Often this situation allows a minister to exercise power informally while stressing in public the formal limitations on his responsibility.

In this situation it is clearly the responsibility of the legislature to see that the government acts in the public interest. The link between power and responsibility is as clear as it is in the case of government departments. Modern legislatures are ill fitted at present to undertake the work of checking the work of departments, let alone the extra work involved in doing the same for subordinate agencies. The essential changes are not procedural: they are a willingness on the part of governments to make a clear statement of their policies and to lift the cloak of administrative secrecy, together with the provision of vastly improved facilities to the opposition for the collection of information and its expert assessment.

The most important single reform is the creation of a system of small specialist committees of members sitting not for just one session but throughout a parliament, with an expert staff partially under the control of opposition members. A committee without expert staff for the minority party is like a bird without wings. It has no hope of checking on the work of departments bulging with specialists under the command of the minister. For the same kind of reasons a committee on commissions, with or without a staff, is bound to be of very limited value. How can such a committee carry out a useful investigation of dozens of unrelated semi-independent agencies, let alone check how successfully they have co-ordinated their work with related agencies? The work of any board or commission must be investigated at the same time as that of related departments.

In the case of government partnership and government-group partnership agencies the effective political power, and therefore political responsibility of a single minister is less easily fixed. The independence of these bodies is real because it is based not on formal considerations but on effective political power. In this situation special procedures may be developed which will more effectively result in the protection of the public interest. Two methods commend themselves to this writer: the "watchdog" continuous consultative committee and the committee of investigation. In both cases the "watchdogs" must have teeth. They must be chosen in part by people other than the concerned minister and they must have a specialist staff.

The consultative committee should have a continuous existence; it should have a small, partly expert membership, the assistance of staff, the power to summon papers and persons, and the right to publish reports at will. It might facilitate its work if a central office of consultative committees was established. With these facilities it could provide, as legislative committees should in their areas of responsibility, a continuous commentary on the work of the agency and a centre where a citizen could take his complaints for discussion and if necessary for investigation. There might be some utility in attaching the office to that of the ombudsman, where that office exists. This would make the office's role more easily understood by the public and might lead to administrative efficiency by bringing together the staffs of offices with a similar role in the political system. It must be stressed, however, that the consultative committee should be concerned with general review as well as individual complaints.

An alternative or supplement to the consultative committee may be a periodic investigation by a small expert committee. Such an investigation if done on a regular schedule would have the advantage of being able to make a long-term assessment of the agency's work and of its success in co-ordination and dealing with the general public. In addition it might have some utility in checking the tendency of all administrative bodies to linger on in their old form long after it has ceased to be the most suitable one for the job.

Semi-independent agencies are public bodies, spending public money and using coercive powers in the name of the protection of the public interest. This circumstance gives the public the right to know precisely how they are spending the money and using the power. Then too, isn't the essence of responsible government the right of every citizen to have the information necessary to judge how the government is exercising its responsibilities? The special control procedures suggested here might serve to dissuade politicians from using the semi-independent form. If this did happen it would have the desirable effect of reducing the complexity of the public bureaucracy.

The legislature, equipped for its task in the way we have recommended, together with the other committees, would publicize the work of semi-independent agencies and provide the information on which the public could judge the extent to which they are serving the public interest, however that might be conceived by different people. The individual citizen would know where to go to get advice from informed people and whom to complain to if he was dissatisfied by his treatment at the hands of an agency. There would also be a considerable impetus to co-ordination if there was a real chance that political capital might be made out of a government's failings on that score.

16

The Administrative Process and the Rule of Law*

J. A. Corry

The collectivist society, as we now have it, cannot regulate itself in anything like the degree that the individualistic society was self-regulating. It must be extensively regulated by government. Nor can we settle for the regulatory structure we now have. The social revolution is not over yet. There will be much more directing, confining, channelling, and accommodating to be done through public law of novel kinds.

---

*J.A. Corry, "The Future of Public Law", in *Changing Legal Objectives,* ed., R. St. J. Macdonald (Toronto: University of Toronto Press, 1963), pp. 16-36. Reprinted and abridged by permission of author and publisher.

We came into the social revolution of the twentieth century with constitutions whose main lines were fixed in an individualistic society. We have retained them nearly unchanged in the formal sense. The leading principles of the constitutions of the United States, Britain, and Canada are stated today in nearly the same terms as 70 years ago. Inevitably, the revolution has subjected them to very great strains, strains that have been met in two main ways.

First, we have enlarged out of all recognition the scope of action and the work of the executive. Note its vast growth in numbers, the sweep of its powers, and the experts and specialized skills of every kind that it has at its beck and call. We have tried to meet the constitutional strains by the elaboration of the administrative process.

Second, while the leading principles of the constitutions stand unchanged in form, their content has been considerably modified. Parliament is still formally supreme but the substance has changed in the last 100 years. It is the ruling majority party in the House of Commons that is supreme. It is often said today that the executive, the Cabinet, has succeeded to the supremacy of Parliament. Such judgements rest on superficial analysis. For example, when, after the Canadian election in 1962, it was seen that there would not be a party with a clear majority in Parliament, a shudder went through the nation. When, a few weeks later, the Prime Minister reshuffled his Cabinet, no one saw this action as having any very great bearing on our fate. What really counts in the long run is the electorate or the organizations that can mobilize its votes. In fact, the political party with a majority in Parliament is just another of the massive organizations that dominate our lives.

The judiciary has continued substantially unchanged in numbers, organization, and procedure. Neither in Britain nor Canada has it been equipped with secretarial and expert assistance in any remote way commensurate with the complexity of the society whose troubles come before it.

The rule of law is still a leading principle but its content too has changed. In a host of matters, citizens can no longer require officials to answer according to the ordinary law. Very often they cannot get their quarrels with officialdom before the ordinary courts, but deal with a variety of tribunals, boards, and ministers empowered to determine many rights and duties of the citizens.

However, the rule of law still means in substance as well as form something of vital import. Even when the citizen is exposed at the extreme to an exercise of administrative discretion, there must be a law somewhere that authorizes that discretion to be exercised. We are not yet by any means victims of executive caprice.

In the past 70 years, we have been moved by a powerful urge for social justice of a higher order than the wide individual liberty of the nineteenth century gave any promise of ensuring. Hence the existing support for limiting substantive rights. But no principle of social justice to which we have given support requires us to deny a fair hearing to those whose rights are awaiting sentence by public authority. Actually, in the last few decades, the Anglo-American instinct for fair play has been focusing more and more sharply on the procedures of administrative agencies.

The community is ready for leadership that accepts the welfare state and extensive regulation of economic life but insists on standards of scrupulous fairness in administrative action. The key to the future of public law among us is the durability of the temper that demands both substantive fair chances for all and procedural fair play for all. If the temper and spirit can be made to stick, the Anglo-American genius for devising procedures to accomplish desired ends and to secure cherished values can be counted on to give flesh to the spirit and to preserve an individualistic cast in our public law.

We cannot reverse the administrative process and force it to retreat. Nor can we stop it in its tracks. It is the necessary instrument of big government just as big government is the inevitable consequence of big industry, concentration of economic control, concentration of the physical productive facilities, and concentration of populations in big urban areas. We can try to improve the administrative process, refine it, and civilize it in detail. We can try to counterbalance the executive and the administration by strengthening Parliament and holding ground for law and for the judicial process.

How to set the scales in counterbalance is the question. In big government, the executive must be central: it must govern because neither Parliament nor the judiciary can govern under any form of organization. It must co-ordinate and integrate the vast activities of government that are always threatening to get out of joint. To do this job, it must be able to foresee, to forecast, and to plan. It must be supported by a civil service of strong integrity, high managerial ability, and a great range of scientific knowledge and skill. However, the executive does not need a free hand. Indeed, it works best under a firm control in which its scope is defined and its authority related to its essential function. The authority must be clear enough that the executive knows its limits and yet is confident of itself within those limits. We must balance external control and internal drive.

The responsibility for this task falls to Parliament and the courts. At present, both are badly equipped for the job. Every body of organization that tries to influence events equips itself with specialized committees, staffs, and secretariats. Every body, that is, except legislatures and courts! In our puzzling over legislative and judicial control of administration, we have put too big a share of our attention on the rules and principles to be applied to the controlling and not enough on the organization needed to apply the rules and principles effectively.

The main elements of what Parliament needs are clear enough: first, specialized standing committees whose membership and terms of reference are so arranged that each committee will focus its surveillance on a particular area of administration; second, sufficient access to expert staff that each committee can become thoroughly knowledgeable about the area of administration committed to it. Ministerial responsibility is a vital principle in our constitutional system. It is widely believed to have become a sham. This view is wrong. Just as crime is news, so are the occasions when ministerial responsibility falters. Ministerial responsibility does maintain administrative discipline over a great range of situations. The purpose of a revamped committee system is to put the House of Commons in a position to enforce it more steadily and with a fuller understanding of what is involved.

What supporting organization is needed for the judiciary is a much more difficult question, and without further study, it would be rash to make definite proposals. The organization, and, to some extent, the principles and rules that sufficed for judicial review of administrative activity in the days of *laissez faire* will not hold a proper balance between external control and internal drive in the administrative structures of the late twentieth century.

In the world in which we are going to live, I see no escape from legislatures giving discretionary powers to ministers, authorizing them to cut into private rights. Equally, I see no reason why a legislature should grant such powers without also securing to the persons affected the right to notice and such fair hearing as the circumstances will allow. The real outrage of administrative action is not that our rights are circumscribed by public authority but that, in a variety of matters, it is done without the right to a hearing.

For believers in the rule of law, the unfettered administrative discretion is the most alarming kind of power to face. On the other hand where the legislature confers on an executive agency power to decide specialized issues according to rule or by a standard of some objectivity, there is less reason for concern because the government has conceded that its action is to be confined by an announced principle. There are now a great many such powers in the hands of boards, tribunals, and other executive agencies.

Most of the new law that keeps social change from being disruptive is going to be public law, made by legislatures or by executive bodies under delegated legislative powers. Neither common law nor its near relation, long-standing custom, will be as central to our lives as they were until yesterday. Much of the interpretation and application of the public law, call it judging, will be in the hands of executive agencies, boards and tribunals. One reason is the sheer bulk of the decisions that have to be made. Another is that public law has to be actively and continuously administered if it is to achieve its purposes. The judging has to keep pace with the administering because neither the regulators nor the regulated know what to do at the next stage except as informed by the current judging of the issues that arise. Such boards and tribunals are not common law courts but they can be made to be courts in an adequate sense if they are competently staffed by men of integrity following a fair procedure.

Many of them may be far from this standard now, but lawyers have spent too much time attacking them root and branch on grounds of principle and not enough in concerted pressure on governments to improve the quality of their procedure and personnel. Seeing that there is no early hope of reducing the number of executive agencies making decisions affecting private rights, we should be urging governments ceaselessly on a number of points. First, wherever possible, such agencies should be confined in their decisions by rule or objective standard. Second, as soon as governmental policy in a given area can be articulated in rules and standards, unfettered administrative discretion in the area should be reduced or abolished and an agency confined by rule or standard should take its place. Third, the personnel and procedure of such agencies must be made good enough to carry the essentially judicial functions they are performing. Fourth, something like the Council of Tribunals in Britain but with rather wider terms of reference should be set up for continuous study in detail of what is needed to civilize the administrative process. Fifth, governments should submit periodically to independent inquiries into the operation of the administrative process.

The effective action that is needed must be taken by governments themselves. I do not underestimate the difficulties. Always being saddled with new duties before it has put in good order what it is already doing, government is always short of time for thought about administration. Barely able to deal with clamorous immediacies, it is cool to demands that it re-think and reorganize on a wide front. Faced with the vested interests of civil servants in the existing ways of doing things, it knows that new departures would have to overcome bureaucratic rigidities. Suspicious — and not always without reason — that lawyers will want to judicialize administration beyond what is really workable and so create a new kind of rigidity, it is reluctant to consult freely on what the rule of law can be made to mean for our generation. Always conscious that government must govern, the executive labours to get as much freedom of action as it can and shies, for the most part, at proposals to overhaul the administrative process.

The obstacles can be overcome if we push for overhaul in a persistent, concerted way. There is a striking parallel. At the turn of the century, the patronage system dominated civil service appointments in North America and was the source of corruption and scandalous inefficiency in government. There was formidable opposition to reform both in legislatures and governments. Yet within a generation, the civil service reform movement, pushed by determined men and backed by an awakened public opinion, brought legislatures and governments to set up career civil services. Not only was this reform a good thing but it came to be recognized by everybody that democratic government could not have survived without it.

A new kind of reform is just as vital in our own day. We cannot abolish the administrative process. So we must constitutionalize it. This cannot be done entirely or even mainly by restraints imposed from the outside. Judicial review of administrative action, appeals from executive agencies to the courts on points of law, and administrative courts of appeal are important as restraints, keeping the administration within its allotted sphere and reminding it that there are short, sharp limits to arbitrariness within that sphere. Even the ombudsman may have his place in a system of restraints. I do not deprecate any of these controls. But they *are* on the fringes and can deal with only a tiny fraction of the multitudinous administrative decisions that have to be taken. Moreover, they deal with them only after the damage has been done.

The relationship of courts and administration should not be one of rooted antagonism. In their salutary confining and corrective role, the courts should come with an understanding of broad policy and of the inherent complexities of administration. This much the administration is always entitled to expect. It is vital that the courts should play their role with sympathy as well. But government and administration cannot expect sympathy unless administration recognizes that in pressing public claims against private interests, it is touching to the quick deep and perennial moral issues, and is thus called on to show all the intelligence, integrity, and fairness that can be mustered.

Readings

Abel, A. "Appeals against Administrative Decision: III. In Search of a Basic Policy." *Canadian Public Administration,* vol. 5, no. 1 (March, 1962), pp. 65-75.

Barbe, Raoul P. "Le contrôle parlementaire des entreprises au Canada." *Canadian Public Administration,* vol. 12, no. 4 (Winter, 1969), pp. 463-80.

Cheffins, R.I. *The Constitutional Process in Canada.* Chap. 3., Toronto: McGraw-Hill, 1970.

Dussault, René. *Le Contrôle Judiciare de l'Administration au Québec.* Quebec: Les Presses de l'Université Laval, 1969.

Dussault, René. "Relationship between the Nature of the Acts of the Administration and Judicial Review: Quebec and Canada." *Canadian Public Administration,* vol. 10, no. 3 (September, 1967), pp. 298-322.

Dussault, René and Roger Bernatchez. "La fonction publique canadienne et québécoise. *Canadian Public Administration,* vol. 15, no. 1 (Spring, 1972), pp. 74-159 and no. 2 (Summer, 1972), pp. 251-374.

Fera, Norman. "Review of Administrative Decisions under the Federal Court Act." *Canadian Public Administration,* vol. 14, no. 4 (Winter, 1971), pp. 580-94.

Gelinas, André. "Judicial Control: Great Britain and Canada." *Public Law,* vol. 140 (Summer, 1963), pp. 140-71.

Gelinas, André. Les parlementaires et l'administration au Québec. Quebec: Les Presses de l'Université Laval, 1969.

Hawkins, Freda. *Canada and Immigration: Public Policy and Public Concern.* Montreal: McGill-Queen's University Press, 1972.

Hehner, Eric. "The Public Servant and the Legalistic Mentality." *Canadian Public Administration,* vol. 13, no. 4 (Winter, 1970), pp. 324-30.

Hendry, James McL. "Some Problems of Canadian Administrative Law." *Ottawa Law Review,* vol. 2 (Fall, 1967), pp. 71-86.

Hull, W.H.N. "The Public Control of Broadcasting: the Canadian and Australian Experiences." *Canadian Journal of Economics and Political Science,* vol. 28, no. 1 (February, 1962), pp. 114-26.

Kersell, J.E. *Parliamentary Supervision of Delegated Legislation: the United Kingdom, Australia, New Zealand and Canada.* London: Stevens & Sons Limited, 1960.

Lawford, H.J. "Appeals against Administrative Decisions: I. The Function of Judicial Review." *Canadian Public Administration,* vol. 5, no. 1 (March, 1962), pp. 46-54.

Mallory, J.R. "Parliamentary Scrutiny of Delegated Legislation in Canada: A Large Step Forward and a Small Step Back." *Public Law* (Spring, 1972), pp. 30-42.

McAllister, G.A. "Administrative Law." *Canadian Bar Journal,* vol. 6 (November, 1963), pp. 439-534.

Musolf, L.D. *Public Ownership and Accountability: the Canadian Experience.* Cambridge, Mass: Harvard University Press, 1959.

Chapter Six

Issues in Canadian Public Administration

Certain public policy issues have special relevance for the powers, rights, freedoms, and working conditions of public servants. The articles in this chapter present the opposing arguments on each of six major issues. Analysis of these issues will be better informed if based on a reading of the articles on organization, personnel, finance, politics, and responsibility included in earlier chapters.

P.K. Kuruvilla weighs the benefits of bilingualism in the federal public service against the cost in financial and other terms. Gérard Veuilleux outlines the organization and issues involved in federal-provincial administrative liaison. E.P. Laberge deals with the highly controversial issue of the government's policy on collective bargaining and the right to strike. W.D.K. Kernaghan examines the problem of reconciling the extension of political rights to public servants with bureaucratic neutrality and anonymity. Then, Paul Thomas evaluates the conflicting views on the issue of administrative secrecy. Finally, Donald Rowat describes the institution of the Ombudsman and assesses its existing and potential adaptation to Canadian governments.

17

The Issue of Bilingualism in the Public Service of Canada

P.K. Kuruvilla

The problem of bilingualism in Canada's public service is two-fold. It involves the creation of an administrative milieu in which the French and English languages can co-exist. It also involves the adaptation to a *bilingual* country of a public service now staffed primarily with *unilingual* French - and English-speaking officials.

To maximize employee participation and performance in the public service, administration must be conducted in the language in which employees have the greatest facility. Similarly, the absence of linguistic barriers facilitates communication between the government and the public; it enables citizens to exercise greater influence and control over the public service; and it permits them to compete on an equal footing for public service positions. Moreover, equal status for the French and English languages may promote administrative responsibility in the sense of a responsive and representative public service.

For most of Canada's history, the status of the French language in the federal bureaucracy has been greatly inferior to that of English. The British North America Act does not require the use of French in the public service and for all practical purposes English has been the only working language within departments, agencies, and the armed forces. Government communication with the general public has been conducted almost entirely in English. Furthermore, French Canadians have been inadequately represented in the public service, especially at the higher levels where key policy recommendations are formulated.

Canada's Royal Commission on Government Organization reported in 1962 that the country's bilingual and bicultural character was not sufficiently reflected in the federal public service and that French Canadians could not therefore participate on an equal basis with English Canadians.[1] The Commission recommended that active measures be taken to develop bilingual capacity among government employees and to attract into the public service highly qualified French Canadians who were capable of advancing to senior ranks.[2]

---

[1] Canada, *Royal Commission on Government Organization,* vol. 1 (Ottawa: Queen's Printer, 1962), pp. 265-67.

[2] *Royal Commission on Government Organization,* p. 267.

In April, 1966, Lester Pearson, then Prime Minister, announced a new government policy on bilingualism.[3] He stated that

the government hopes and expects that, within a reasonable period of years, a state of affairs in the public service will be reached whereby:

1. It will be normal practice for oral or written communications within the service to be made in either official language at the option of the person making them, in the knowledge that they will be understood by those directly concerned.

2. Communications with the public will normally be in either official language having regard to the person being served.

3. The linguistic and cultural values of both English-speaking and French-speaking Canadians will be reflected through civil service recruitment and training.

4. A climate will be created in which public servants from both language groups will work together toward common goals, using their own language and applying their respective cultural values, but each fully understanding and appreciating those of the other.

The Prime Minister also asserted that bilingualism must be conceived as a long-term programme and should be introduced gradually in a manner which would not inflict injustice on anyone, particularly those who have devoted many years of their lives to the service of their country.

The Public Service Employment Act,[4] passed in 1967, went some distance toward improving government communications with the public in both official languages. Section 20 of the Act provides that

employees appointed to serve in any department or other portion of the Public Service, or part thereof, shall be qualified in the knowledge and use of the English or French language, or both, to the extent that the [Public Service] Commission deems necessary in order that the functions of each department, portion or part can be performed adequately and effective service can be provided to the public.

The Royal Commission on Bilingualism and Biculaturalism which was appointed in 1963 reported on the federal administration in 1969. Among the broad terms of reference of this Commission was the instruction "to report upon the situation and practice of bilingualism within all branches and agencies of the federal administration . . . and in their communications with the public and to make recommendations designed to ensure the bilingual and basically bicultural character of the federal administration".[5] The general conclusions of the Commission were as follows:

---

[3] *Debates* (Commons), April 6, 1966, pp. 3,915-17.
[4] *Statutes of Canada* (1967), c. 71.
[5] Canada, *Royal Commission on Bilingualism and Biculturalism,* Book 3A, part 2 (Ottawa: Queen's Printer, 1969), p. 352.

1. The French language should increasingly become a language of work in the public service.

2. The atmosphere of the public service should represent the linguistic and cultural quality of Canadian society, and Canadians whose mother tongue is French should be adequately represented in the public service — both in terms of numbers and levels of responsibility.

The most significant recommendations of the many specific ones the Commission made for the federal administration were that the federal government establish separate French-language administrative units in government departments and Crown agencies, that appointments at the highest levels of the public service be administered so as to ensure balanced participation by Anglophones and Francophones, that all positions throughout federal departments and Crown agencies be classified as to language requirements and that these requirements be taken into account in the determination of remuneration, that the Public Service Commission's Language Training Directorate establish courses to improve the use of French in the federal administration, that the process of testing and selecting candidates for federal departments and Crown agencies take into account the differing linguistic and cultural attributes of Francophone and Anglophone applicants, and that the office of a Commissioner of Official Languages be created to safeguard the linguistic rights of the public as well as of public servants.[6]

In July, 1969, the federal Parliament unanimously approved the *Official Languages Act*[7] which incorporates most of the major recommendations of the Commission and is the most memorable landmark in the history of bilingualism in the Canadian public service. First, it makes the English and French languages the official languages of Canada and assures equal rights and privileges as to their use in federal institutions. Secondly, it provides that each department, crown corporation, and other agency must adopt measures to ensure that "the public can obtain available services from and can communicate with it in both official languages." Thirdly, it stipulates that areas where the official linguistic minority forms at least 10 per cent of the total population must be designated as federal bilingual districts for purposes of bilingual services. Fourthly, it provides for the appointment of a Commissioner of Official Languages with responsibility for overseeing the application of the Act and for ensuring the equal status of French and English in federal institutions.

The Department of the Secretary of State, the Treasury Board and the Public Service Commission are the primary administrative units involved in the development and coordination of bilingualism in the federal administration. It is the activities of the Public Service Commission in the area of

---

[6] *Royal Commission on Bilingualism and Biculturalism,* pp. 265-92.
[7] *Statutes of Canada* (1969), c. 54, s.2.

bilingualism, however, that have been the focus of much controversy and have received most of the publicity in the media.

To help achieve the government's bilingual objectives, the Public Service Commission has, among other measures, established a comprehensive language training programme which, from humble beginnings in 1964, expects to have an enrolment of 10,000 by 1973.[8] Through both language training and recruitment, the Commission hopes by 1975 to reach the following percentage targets for bilingual employees in federal bilingual districts:

Occupational Category	Target for 1975
Executive	60%
Administrative and Foreign Service	50
Scientific and Professional	15
Technical	15
Administrative Support	35
Operational	15

At the end of 1971, the Commission was on target for all categories except the Executive group.[9]

The central recommendation of the Royal Commission on Bilingualism and Biculturalism affecting the public service was that French-language administrative units be created. In 1971, the government established 457 of these units on an experimental basis. The units are spread throughout 39 departments and involve 29,000 employees. Communications within each unit and with other departments are conducted in French but communication with the English-speaking public is in English.[10]

Despite these vigorous and costly efforts to bring about a bilingual public service, several problems remain. Most Canadians appear to support both the goal of merit in the public service and the goal of a unified public service providing equal opportunity to all citizens. In practice, however, these goals are seldom compatible with one another in so far as achieving equal opportunity for French - and English-speaking Canadians in the public service, both in terms of numbers and levels of responsibility. This situation has given rise to a variety of problems and protests.

First of all, the policy of assigning additional credit for bilingualism in public service recruitment and promotion has been vehemently opposed by many public servants from English Canada and by the major public service staff associations. They also fear that the policy of assigning an increasing number of senior positions to French Canadians will seriously undermine the merit system of recruitment and promotion, and so prejudice the careers of

---

[8] John J. Carson, "Bilingualism in the Public Service", *Canadian Public Administration,* vol. 15, no. 1 (Summer, 1972), p. 193.

[9] John J. Carson, "Bilingualism in the Public Service", p. 193.

[10] *Globe and Mail,* August 18, 1971.

unilingual English-speaking public servants. They believe that French Canadians might be hired merely because they are French-speaking without due regard to the need for French in the positions involved or the real merit of the candidates.

The government and other spokesmen for bilingualism contend that it is not necessary for every public servant to become bilingual. Rather, both the French and English languages should be employed at the highest echelons of the public service where the values and attitudes of both the French and English cultural groups may contribute to policy formation and implementation. Although it may be necessary to speak both languages to qualify for certain positions below the top levels, the vast majority of officials will probably continue to speak only one language.

Secondly, there are numerous criticisms of the introduction of French-language administrative units. These include the views that the truly bilingual employees in any unit may find themselves acting merely as translators, that when promotions within the units are made the merits of those outside the units may be ignored, that the operation of the units will lead to costly duplication of work and to inefficiency resulting from inevitable breakdowns in communication, and, finally, that language ghettos may develop which will exacerbate the divisions already existing between the two language groups in the public service.

It is too early yet to evaluate accurately the validity of these criticisms. It is noteworthy that the Public Service Commission, which assisted in the establishment of the units, predicted that they will benefit the government in two ways:

1. They will enhance the recruitment of young unilingual Francophones to the national capital by offering them the possibility of initially working in their mother tongue (a privilege hitherto only available to young Anglophones).

2. They will provide those thousands of Anglophone public servants who have devoted so many hours to learning the other language with a badly needed post-training facility to crystallize and solidify their newly acquired skills in an actual work situation.[11]

A third argument frequently presented by critics of current efforts to achieve a bilingual public service, especially through recruitment of French-speaking Canadians, is that the French-Canadian educational system does not yet produce a sufficient number of graduates with the required training and qualifications.

There is some merit in this argument. As recently as 1969, the Royal Commission on Bilingualism and Biculturalism reported that there was

little indication that the relative lack of Francophones among the profes-

---

[11] See John J. Carson, Chairman, Public Service Commission, Letter to the Editor on "Bilingualism", *The Globe and Mail,* July 8, 1970.

sionals and other qualified personnel can be eased quickly. The demand is so great that chances of hiring qualified Francophones away from other employers are small. . . . There have been recent efforts to increase immigration of qualified people from France but, as far as we can foresee, the Public Service's intake of Francophone graduates will continue to be largely limited to the output of French-language universities in Canada.[12]

Moreover, the French-language educational system has traditionally emphasized such subjects as law, classics and religion at the expense of economics, commerce and the natural sciences. Yet the greatest demand in the public service is for scientists, qualified professionals, managers, technicians and skilled workers.[13] In addition, French-language university and college graduates have been less motivated than their English-language counterparts to join the public service.[14]

It is significant, however, that for some time now the educational system in Quebec has been going through a period of modernization. The number of professionally qualified Francophones among potential recruits to the federal public service is therefore being progressively increased.

Some opponents of the government's policy on bilingualism contend that this policy works an injustice on linguistic groups in Canada whose mother tongue is neither French nor English. Spokesmen for this point of view argue that the cause of Canadian unity will not be served by programmes which replace injustice to French Canadians with injustice to "other Canadians."[15]

However, the claims of other cultural communities for linguistic rights do not have the same historic or legal status as those of the French and the English. Although "other Canadians" form a significant proportion of the total population, they do not constitute a homogeneous language group. Indeed, they are divided into numerous, relatively small linguistic groups scattered throughout the country. Furthermore, it may be argued that immigrants with mother tongues other than French or English should be prepared to recognize the supremacy of the language of Canada's "founding races".

Finally, bilingualism in the public service has been attacked on economic terms as being too expensive. Advocates of this argument state that the enormous financial expenditures and the inevitable delays in administrative transactions that will result from bilingualism will probably outweigh the possible advantages of a bilingual public service. Although the cost of the government's programmes to promote bilingualism in the country and in the public service in particular is difficult to measure precisely, the expenditure is very great. The government is committed to allocate 300 million dollars over a

---

[12] *Royal Commission on Bilingualism and Biculturalism,* Book 3, p. 183.

[13] *Royal Commission on Bilingualism and Biculturalism,* pp. 186-187.

[14] *Royal Commission on Bilingualism and Biculturalism,* p. 195.

[15] See Royal Commission on Bilingualism and Biculturalism, *A Preliminary Report* (Ottawa: Queen's Printer, 1965), pp. 50-55 and Book 4. Also *The Cultural Contribution of Other Ethnic Groups* (Ottawa: Queen's Printer, 1969).

three-year period from 1971 to 1974 for its support of bilingualism in the schools of the provinces.[16] In addition, 25 million dollars has been allocated to promote bilingualism in the federal public service during the fiscal year 1972-1973. This latter amount does not take account of the enormous cost of the time public servants spend learning French or English rather than performing their regular duties.[17]

Thus, on economic and other grounds, bilingualism in Canada's public service remains an extremely contentious issue. Official spokesmen for the Cabinet and the Public Service Commission contend, however, that the benefits of their policies on bilingualism are now becoming evident. Given the government's enormous financial, political and administrative investment, the problem appears to be "how best to" rather than "whether to" achieve a bilingual public service for Canada.

18

Federal-Provincial Administrative Relations in Canada

Gérard Veuilleux

Canadian history and geography have determined that the political organization of the country be of the federal form. Thus, in 1867, two levels of government were established and each level—the federal and the provincial—was allocated certain responsibilities. However, what was a reasonable delineation of powers and responsibilities in 1867 proved to create over the years certain imbalances and frictions. Normally, it could be expected that such problems could be rectified by securing amendments to the Constitution. But constitutional amendment is a necessarily slow process, especially in Canada where the British North America Act does not provide for its amendment by any domestic legislative authority. The mechanism which was

---

[16]See *The Globe and Mail,* September 10, 1971, for the announcement by Gerard Pelletier, the Secretary of State.

[17]The *St. Catharines Standard,* July 29, 1972.

found to reduce the rigidity inherent in our Constitution was intergovernmental cooperation.[1]

Canada's Fathers of Confederation had envisaged that some areas would require intergovernmental cooperation and so assigned immigration and agriculture as areas of concurrent jurisdiction under the Constitution. But with the large expansion in the responsibilities assumed by the public sector, especially since the Second World War, governments realized that in a modern federal state it was no longer possible for each level of government to stay strictly within its own sphere of jurisdiction. The policies and programmes of one level of government affect in varying degrees those of the other level. For example, provincial education measures influence federal employment policies and the latter have an impact upon provincial welfare programmes. Thus, the advent of the welfare state has extended de facto (although not de jure) jurisdictional concurrency into most areas of governmental activities. The need for intergovernmental coordination and consultation has, therefore, greatly increased.

Machinery for Intergovernmental Liaison

The development of machinery for federal-provincial relations has passed through three major stages since Confederation.[2] The first stage (1867-1887) involved cooperation between the federal government and the provincial Lieutenant-Governors. During the second stage (1887-1937), provincial Premiers supplanted the Lieutenant-Governors, and about 1920, departmental ministers joined the Prime Ministers and Premiers in the conduct of federal-provincial relations. Then, as the nature of public affairs became more complex and "expert" advice was required, a third major period of cooperation began (1937-today) in which administrative officials became increasingly active participants.

Formal Relations

The *formal* arrangements for administrative liaison have expanded to cover most areas of government activity. The organization of these arrangements is similar in each area. A Ministerial Conference is at the top, under which a senior intergovernmental committee—normally at the deputy minister level—operates and to which a plethora of specialized committees is answerable. This flat, hierarchical structure in each sector of government activity is used more at the administrative than at the ministerial level. Moreover, the participants in each area tend to operate somewhat independently of those in other areas.

The machinery for intergovernmental administrative relations may be described in various ways. Institutions for federal-provincial cooperation, of

---

[1] For a more detailed and complete treatment of federal-provincial administrative relations in Canada, see my book entitled *Les Relations Intergouvernementales au Canada, 1867-1967* (Montreal: Les Presses de l'Universite du Quebec, 1971).

[2] Veuilleux, *Relations Intergouvernementales au Canada,* Part 1.

which there were about 170 in 1967, may be *grouped into categories* such as federal-provincial committees, interprovincial committees, advisory councils, and so on.[3] The various cooperating bodies may also be *classified by areas of government activity* using Statistics Canada's functional classification of government expenditures.[4] This approach illustrates the ubiquity of the machinery and the relatively greater use of cooperative arrangements in such areas as general government, health and social welfare. By looking at *the levels at which the committees operate,* some light may be shed not only upon the participants involved, but also upon the areas of growth over the years. A four level hierarchical classification — Minister, Deputy Ministers, Directors, Professional and Technical — has been used,[5] as well as the simpler and less arbitrary two tiers — Ministerial and Administrative.[6] Finally, a descriptive analysis has been attempted by compiling *the frequency of intergovernmental meetings* in each area of activity.[7] The purpose of this method is to illustrate the degree of correlation between the frequency of the meetings and the areas of greatest jurisdictional overlapping.

Informal Relations

The number of federal-provincial conferences and committees and the frequency with which they meet should not necessarily be viewed as proportional to their importance. Often, the most useful form of liaison is the informal one. Every day there are innumerable contacts between ministers and officials of both levels of government. These contacts take several forms depending on the nature and importance of the question at hand. Communications can take the form of a telephone conversation, an exchange of correspondence, or a personal visit. The extent of informal contacts depends on such factors as the people involved, their length of time on the job, the significance of the issue, and even the distance from Ottawa of the province concerned. Informal communications provide the oil that keeps the formal machinery operating more smoothly.

Organization Supporting the Machinery

This whole network of federal-provincial formal and informal administrative liaison requires that each government have organizational structures to support it and make it work. Although the consequences of inadequate internal coordination cannot be precisely measured, cases have frequently arisen in which a position taken by a minister at one conference has not been consistent with the position taken by his Premier or Prime Minister at another

---

[3] See, for example, "Federal-Provincial Administrative Liaison in Canada", in *Public Administration in Canada,* 2nd ed., eds. W.D.K. Kernaghan and A.M. Willms (Toronto: Methuen, 1971), pp. 128-30.

[4] Veuilleux, *Relations Intergouvernementales au Canada,* part 2, c.1.

[5] Edgar Gallant, "The Machinery of Federal-Provincial Relations", Canadian Public Administration, vol. 12, no. 4 (December, 1965), pp. 515-26.

[6] Veuilleux, *Relations Intergouvernementales au Canada,* part 2, c. 1.

[7] *Ibid.,* p. 90.

conference. The obvious need for internal coordination has been met in varying degrees by different governments.

The organizational units assisting the *federal* government in the conduct of federal-provincial relations operate at two levels — the political and the administrative. At the *political* level, the federal government has a Cabinet Committee on Federal-Provincial Relations. This Committee is chaired by the Prime Minister and meets at regular times each week to consider most new policies or amendments to existing policies having federal-provincial implications. The Committee not only acts in an advisory capacity vis-à-vis the whole Cabinet but can also take specific decisions on its own. At the *administrative* level, the federal government has two main units with general responsibilities for federal-provincial relations: the Federal-Provincial Relations Secretariat in the Privy Council Office and the Federal-Provincial Relations Division in the Department of Finance. While the delineation of responsibilities between these two units is not always clear-cut, in general, the Privy Council Office is concerned more with obtaining an overview of departmental activities in the field of federal-provincial relations and with servicing the Cabinet Committee. The Department of Finance is more concerned with the financial aspects of such relations, e.g. equalization, tax-sharing, shared-cost, opting-out arrangements, and fiscal coordination.

Like the federal government, some provincial governments have at the *political* level a Cabinet committee on federal-provincial relations. In the *administrative* sphere, most provinces have separate units of one form or another for federal-provincial co-operation. Ontario, for example, has a Federal-Provincial Affairs Secretariat within its Treasury and Economics Department. Quebec, Alberta and Newfoundland have full-fledged departments of intergovernmental affairs.

The Issues Raised

The machinery for federal-provincial relations described above has served and continues to serve some very useful purposes in Canada. Nevertheless, the development of these arrangements and the manner in which federal-provincial consultation has been conducted have received some criticism.

General Development

It is often argued that the machinery for federal-provincial liaison has developed in a haphazard way and in the absence of an overall policy as to the long-term goals and purposes this machinery is to serve.

Short-term circumstances do appear to have dictated the development of this machinery to a substantial extent. The result is not only that committees have tended to proliferate but that they have done so mainly in one direction — at the technical level. Many committees established to deal with a particular problem have taken on a life of their own. They have acquired a distinct existence and operate more or less independently of one another. The consequence has been that the machinery for federal-provincial liaison has grown in such a compartmentalized and fragmented manner that some have likened it to the detached parts of a complex puzzle or to an ever-lengthening freight train with not all the box cars hitched up firmly enough.

As early as 1957, recognition of such problems led to the suggestion that "it might be a good rule to require each committee, council or conference, every five years or so, to submit a written apologia for its continued existence, and perhaps we might find a panel of Devil's Advocates to review these sub-missions."[8] This proposal was meant to be interpreted not only to suggest a mechanism to prevent the undue proliferation of federal-provincial com-mittees, but also to oblige governments to maintain the internal coordination necessary for the effective conduct of intergovernmental cooperation.

Conduct of Meetings

The two main criticisms of the general conduct of federal-provincial meetings are that they are held in camera and that the arrangements made between governments tend to limit the sovereignty of Parliament.

In Camera Meetings

The practice of holding federal-provincial meetings in camera is probably the result of the way federal-provincial liaison has developed in Canada. Intergovernmental liaison, especially since the 1950's, has developed more rapidly at the technical level than at the ministerial level. Since very few ob-jected to the officials meeting in camera, the practice became more or less institutionalized and was continued when the ministers held their meetings. It was then that Opposition members and reporters began to criticize the practice and to allege that the public had a "right to know" what was being discussed and what agreements were being reached.

The holding of federal-provincial meetings in camera has been justified on the grounds that meetings remove some of the "politics" and favour more pragmatic and statesmanlike discussions. Politicians may take a more flexible and less "political" posture than if the discussions are open to the public. Indeed, the concept of "diplomacy" has been used to describe the functioning of federal-provincial liaison[9], and diplomacy is most effectively conducted in private.

The validity of these arguments for in camera meetings was challenged by the results of the Confederation of Tomorrow Conference of November, 1967, which was open to the public. It is notable that less than three weeks later the federal and provincial governments agreed to open to the public some sessions of the Federal-Provincial Conference on Housing and Urban Development. Recognition of the great educational benefits of public conferences seemed to influence the First Ministers (i.e. Prime Ministers and Premiers) who have

---

[8] K.W. Taylor, "Coordination in Administration", *Proceedings of the Ninth Annual Conference, 1957* (Toronto: Institute of Public Administration of Canada, 1957), p. 259.

[9] See, for example, the title of Richard Simeon's book, *Federal-Provincial Diplomacy* (Toronto: University of Toronto Press, 1972).

held some of their subsequent meetings, notably those on the Constitution, in public.

Given these conflicting views, a logical formula for the future may be to continue to hold meetings in camera at the public servants' level, but to hold conferences partly or wholly open to the public at the ministerial level, subject to the decisions of the ministers attending the conference.

Parliamentary Sovereignty

The charge is often made, especially by Opposition members, but also by the press, that federal-provincial conferences have become a third tier of government or a sort of super Parliament where firm commitments on matters of policy are made. It is argued further that while in theory Parliament and the provincial legislatures must approve all such agreements, in practice this amounts to nothing more than rubber-stamping. Both federal and provincial Opposition parties complain that their legislative role on federal-provincial matters is being usurped by federal-provincial conferences and that they cannot influence (through amendments) a federal-provincial policy or programme proposed by their particular government.

It is important to note that federal-provincial conferences are not decision-making bodies. Rather, they seek to achieve a consensus on certain issues. Each government remains free to accept or reject[10] the consensus since it is not legally binding until it is submitted and approved by the legislatures involved. However, once a government has agreed to abide by a consensus and submits it to the legislature for approval, the role of the Opposition parties appears to be limited. While a government can accept an Opposition amendment to a policy or programme *not* involving other governments, it is more difficult to agree to amend a policy or programme which *does* involve other governments because this would constitute a direct challenge to the "agreed consensus". A government would presumably wish to consult those other governments party to the consensus before accepting any amendment.

It is notable that this constraint applies not only to Opposition parties but to governments as well. It is difficult for a government unilaterally to amend a policy or programme affecting other governments without appearing to challenge the agreed consensus. Such a government would, no doubt, wish to consult the other governments concerned. Thus, one could say that federal-provincial programmes are a form of contractual obligation imposing limitations upon the sovereignty of both the federal Parliament and the provincial legislatures. This very same situation has existed for a long time with regard to international relations and treaty implementation. One must conclude, therefore, that the limitations placed by federal-provincial programmes upon the sovereignty of Parliament and the legislatures are "one of those inconveniences which are the price of federal government".[11]

---

[10] The most recent example of this is the rejection of the Victoria Charter by the Province of Quebec in 1971.

[11] K.C. Wheare, *Government by Committee* (London: Oxford University Press, 1955), pp. 5-6.

Conclusions

The machinery for intergovernmental relations was quite slow to develop in Canada because the management of public affairs was not very complex until the beginning of the twentieth century. It soon became evident to the provinces, however, that this form of cooperation permitted only the federal government to exert influence. The classical form of federalism, with a division of powers between the federal government and the constituent units of the federation, evolved into cooperative federalism involving continuing consultation and compromise between both levels of government. Intergovernmental liaison has also become much more significant and complex as a result of the increasingly frequent meetings, not only at the political level between First Ministers or Cabinet Ministers, but particularly between public servants at various levels of the administrative hierarchies.

19

Collective Bargaining in the Public Service of Canada*

E. P. Laberge

The Public Service Staff Relations Act, which came into force in Canada on March 13, 1967, changed the relationship between the Federal Government and its employees from a traditional concept based on paternalism to a more equalitarian one. Parliament, acting on the advice of the Preparatory Committee on Collective Bargaining, approved the principle of collective bargaining and adopted the Act which gave public servants the right to negotiate wages and conditions of employment with the employer on a basis comparable with the private sector. It is reasonable at the present time to examine some of its results and attempt to determine what impact this original legislation may have had on the employer, the employees, employee associations and the community at large.

*E.P. Laberge, "Collective Bargaining in the Public Service of Canada", *International Review of Administrative Sciences,* vol. 36, no. 3 (1970), pp. 227-33. Reprinted and abridged by permission of the author and publisher. The editor extends appreciation to Mr. Laberge for his work in updating this selection.

The Preparatory Committee on Collective Bargaining, which made its report to the Government in 1965, recommended the establishment of collective bargaining for the employees of the Federal Government of Canada. The number of employees in the Government of Canada at the time the Preparatory Committee began its deliberations in 1963 was slightly over 200,000. The number had increased to 245,000 in 1967, bringing in its wake a variety of administrative problems which made the introduction of collective bargaining more urgent and at the same time more complicated. In addition to this explosive factor, it was found that the classification system of the Canadian public service was archaic and totally inadequate for use in the context of collective bargaining. Some way had to be found to make it flexible enough, but contained within a framework that permitted meaningful bargaining. A revision was indispensable if proper units were to be established for purposes of collective bargaining. A new classification pattern was devised which consisted of five operational categories divided into 72 occupational groups. This total was subsequently increased to 81. In addition, there was an executive category consisting of top management for which bargaining was not envisaged.

Institutions Concerned with
Employee Relations in the Public Service
Basically four branches of the Canadian Government share some of the responsibilities of employee relations, although not in equal amounts nor in the same contexts. First is the Public Service Staff Relations Board established in 1967. With the introduction of the collective bargaining legislation, the Pay Research Bureau, which was created in 1957 and attached to the Public Service Commission, was transferred to the administrative jurisdiction of the Public Service Staff Relations Board. Its job is to conduct objective and impartial research to obtain information on rates of pay, employee earnings, conditions of employment, and related practices to meet the needs of the parties for bargaining in the Public Service.

The second is the Public Service Commission which was established under the Civil Service Amendment Act of 1908; its primary function has been to uphold the merit principle. Other functions have from time to time been grafted onto the Commission such as classification, pay research, certain types of appeals and training. The first of these functions was withdrawn from the Public Service Commission and placed under the control of the Treasury Board in 1967 while the operational aspects of classification were decentralized to the Departments; the second was placed under the jurisdiction of the Public Service Staff Relations Board while functions concerning the maintenance of the merit system were left to the Public Service Commission. Appeals on promotions, for instance, are heard by the Public Service Commission instead of forming part of the grievance procedure under the Public Service Staff Relations Act.

The third is the Treasury Board which was established on July 2, 1867, as a committee of Cabinet. Its main functions are to advise Cabinet on financial policy and screen all projects, requests and decisions having financial implications. In this manner, the Treasury Board becomes involved in personnel as well as financial policies because pay rates, classification, establishments and certain conditions of employment have financial connotations. The role of the Treasury Board grew steadily over the years but was expanded at a considerable rate after the publication of the Glassco Commission report in 1962 and the report of the Preparatory Committee on Collective Bargaining in 1965. The principle responsibility added to the Treasury Board in 1967 was that of representing the Government at the bargaining table. A few branches of the Public Service specifically designated in Part II of Schedule A of the Act are, however, exempt from this coverage. The most important branches thus exempt are: The Defence Research Board, the Fisheries Research Board, the National Film Board and the National Research Board. These branches negotiate directly with the bargaining agents certified by the Public Service Staff Relations Board. The central and strategic position occupied by the Treasury Board and the mass of knowledge and information made available to it concerning personnel and financial policy made it the obvious choice for this task.

Fourth and last is the Department of Labour. Although the responsibility of the Department of Labour has to do with labour relations in the private sector concerning areas in which Federal laws are applicable, certain public corporations fall within its scope. This is the case of Air Canada, the Canadian National Railways, Polymer Corporation and others whose activities are more closely allied to the private sector.

The Public Service Staff Relations Act

The Public Service Staff Relations Act provides for the establishment of a system of collective bargaining for the employees of the Federal Government of Canada and gives its employees the legal right to use, in certain circumstances, means long recognized in the private sector to enforce their demands.

The preamble of Bill C-170 which became the Act, described it as:

A measure to provide for the establishment of a system of collective bargaining applicable to the Public Service of Canada and for the resolution of disputes that may arise in the negotiation or conclusion of collective agreements applicable to such employees; to establish a process for the presentation of grievances of employees; to provide for the establishment of a board to be known as the Public Service Staff Relations Board which shall be responsible for the administration of the said measure and to provide further for the constitution and appointment of such other authorities, officers and employees as are required in connection with the administration of said measure.

The major responsibilities of the Public Service Staff Relations Board are the determination of the appropriate bargaining units, the certification of bargaining agents, investigation of complaints against alleged violations of certain provisions of the Act, declarations regarding the lawfulness of strikes, the determination of questions of law and jurisdiction arising out of arbitration and adjudication proceedings, as well as giving consent to prosecution in the courts of law on violations of the Act. Broad regulatory authority relating to certification, the presentation of grievances and grievance adjudication are also invested in the Board. Senior management, the Royal Canadian Mounted Police and the Armed Forces are excluded from the operation of the Act.

Various opinions have been expressed about this law, some favourable and others skeptical. In spite of some adverse criticism, it seems obvious that the government has established a workable system of collective bargaining for the Public Service, if we accept the opinion of Mr. C. A. Edwards, President of the Public Service Alliance of Canada, who said on January 24, 1969, at a conference of the Public Personnel Association in San Francisco:

I want to state unequivocably that, in my opinion, it is a good law designed primarily for employees of our Federal Government. This does not mean that I agree with every clause, or that we did not seek changes prior to passage, or that we would not seek changes now. We did and we would, but in general terms, the law has provided a good system of collective bargaining for public employees of our Federal Government.

The Public Service Staff Relations Act has now been operative for five years and opinions have been expressed about its appropriateness from various sources. Public servants individually and staff associations have complained that certain items may not be negotiated according to the law. For example, the classification of employees is not a matter subject to negotiation. Section 7 of the Act reads: "Nothing in the Act shall be construed to affect the right or authority of the employer to determine the organization of the Public Service and to assign duties to and classify positions therein". Others would like to have items now covered by the Public Service Employment Act concerning appointments, promotions and appeals, as well as matters covered by the Superannuation Act, made subject to negotiation. Some criticism was levied against the Treasury Board as representative of the employer in negotiations concerning the length of time needed to arrive at an agreement. On the other hand, the employer has reacted much in the same manner as employers in the private sector concerning the maintenance of management rights. Fears were expressed concerning possible stoppages of work in areas of the Public Service that are considered essential. These fears have thus far not been generally justified; the notable exceptions have been the Post Office employees and the air traffic controllers. The principle and application of collective bargaining in the Public Service of Canada is still, after five years, so comparatively new that a final assessment of its function is not yet possible. Many facts and results are known while other elements of the system must be reviewed at some future date to determine their validity and effectiveness.

Dispute Settlement

The Public Service Staff Relations Act sets out procedures for certifying bargaining agents, negotiation procedures, and dispute and disagreement settlement procedures. It allows the certified bargaining agent the right to choose between conciliation with the right to strike, or settlement of disputes by binding arbitration. It provides the means for the appointment of conciliators and conciliation boards in the case of election to proceed by conciliation and arbitration tribunals where binding arbitration is chosen as the means of settlement. It is the right of the bargaining agent on behalf of employees to specify what method will be followed before notice is given to bargain. In addition, the law provides for the establishment of adjudication tribunals to settle grievances during the life of an agreement when the several steps of the grievance procedure have failed to produce an understanding between the parties.

Employees may not strike if their duties are such as to affect the safety or security of the public. Strikes are also illegal during the effective life of an agreement or an arbitral award, these being legally acceptable only as a means to secure more favourable wages or conditions of work during the negotiation process when the medium of conciliation has been chosen in preference to that of binding arbitration.

The traditional power of the employer to make unilateral decisions about rates of pay and terms and conditions of work has been eroded. Employees in the Federal Government of Canada are now in the position to challenge the Government effectively through the collective bargaining process which eventually leads to the signing of an agreement. Bargaining rights are granted to employees on certification of their bargaining agent. This is a right which government employees enjoy without first having to obtain recognition from the employer, as is the case in the private sector and where national and provincial labour boards may play a part.

Application for certification may be made by an employee organization or a council of employee organizations. Before certification is granted, the Public Service Staff Relations Board must be satisfied that a majority of the bargaining unit wish that organization to represent them as their bargaining agent. The bargaining agent so named is given the exclusive right to bargain collectively with the employer on behalf of the employees in the bargaining unit. A bargaining unit is described in Section 2(e) of the Act as "a group of two or more employees that is determined, in accordance with this Act, to constitute a unit of employees appropriate for collective bargaining". This definition is then equated by the Public Service Staff Relations Board to one of the occupational categories and groups stated in the classification system mentioned earlier, in respect of which relationships as to wages and conditions of work exist in fact. The Board must ensure that within a particular bargaining unit all employees are of the same occupational category.

The section of the Act which is perhaps the most original and interesting is that which gives the certified bargaining agent the exclusive right to choose between binding arbitration, or conciliation with the possible use of the strike weapon to strengthen his position. However, this choice must be stated before negotiations begin. "For the purpose of facilitating the specification by a bargaining agent of the process for resolution of any dispute to which it may be a party in respect to that bargaining unit, the Board shall, upon request to it by the bargaining agent, by notice require the employer to furnish to the Board and the bargaining agent a statement in writing of the employees or classes of employees in the bargaining unit whom the employer then considers to be designated employees" (Section 36(2)). These employees, though members of the bargaining unit, do not have the right to strike should negotiations break down. The statement or list may be challenged by the bargaining agent, in which case the Public Service Staff Relations Board makes the final decision. This information gives the bargaining agent the advantage of knowing in advance which of its members could legally strike and, of course, it gives it the choice of the means of settlement which it might consider most advantageous.

Although conciliation is not binding and the choice of this process may eventually lead to a strike by employees of a bargaining unit who are not designated employees, it should be noted that prior to resorting to the establishment of a conciliation board either the employer or the bargaining agent may request the Public Service Staff Relations Board to appoint a conciliator to assist the parties in reaching agreement. The conciliator may make suggestions only. Nothing he states to the parties is binding. "Where the employer or a bargaining agent advises the Board by notice in writing of the inability of the parties to reach agreement on any term or condition of employment that may be embodied in a collective agreement and that it desires the assistance of a conciliator in reaching agreement, the Chairman may appoint a conciliator who shall forthwith after his appointment confer with the parties and endeavor to assist them in reaching an agreement" (Section 51). "The conciliator shall, within fourteen days from the date of his appointment or within such period provided as the Chairman may determine, report his success or failure to the Chairman" (Section 53).

A conciliation board consists of three members and its terms of reference are fixed by the Chairman of the Public Service Staff Relations Board. The terms of reference set forth those matters on which the conciliation board shall report its findings and recommendations. The conciliation board must permit the evidence of both parties to be recorded and its report must be submitted within fourteen days after the terms of reference are received, unless otherwise extended by the Chairman of the Public Service Staff Relations Board or by agreement of the parties involved. The Chairman of the Public Service Staff Relations Board may direct the conciliation board to reconsider and clarify any portion or all of its report. The Chairman must forward a copy of the report to each of the parties and may even publish it if he so wishes. A strike may be lawfully declared if seven days have elapsed following the receipt of the conciliation board report by the Chairman of the Public Service Staff Relations Board. Also, if a request for a conciliation board was made and denied by the

Chairman, a strike may take place lawfully as soon as the parties are notified of the Chairman's intention not to establish such a board.

Arbitration, if selected by a bargaining agent as a means of settling a dispute during the contract negotiation, is binding on both sides. Before the appointment of an arbitration tribunal either party may request the Public Service Staff Relations Board to nominate a conciliator to assist them in reaching an agreement in the normal manner. If he fails to accomplish this the only recourse left is arbitration. Subject to any rule of procedure made by the Public Service Staff Relations Board an arbitration tribunal may determine its own procedures, but it must give both parties the opportunity to present evidence and make submissions. The award of the arbitration tribunal is signed by the chairman, with no report or observations made by any of the members. The decision of the tribunal is made by a majority vote of its members with the chairman making the decision whenever a division takes place. The decision of the tribunal is final. Arbitral awards may deal with rates of pay, hours of work, leave entitlement, standards of discipline and other terms and conditions of employment. No arbitral award shall, however, deal with the standards, procedures or processes governing the appointment, promotion, demotion, transfer, lay-off or release of employees or with any term or condition of employment that was not a subject of negotiation.

Grievances

The Act also has unique provisions in that portion dealing with grievances and the grievance procedure. The grievance procedure differs from practices in other jurisdictions since it establishes a statutory grievance process that is a right of employees even though a bargaining agent has not yet been certified or a contract negotiated. The presentation of grievances through the usual process is also open to employees who are not entitled to collective bargaining under the Act (employees who have been declared to be in managerial or confidential positions). Public Service employees are allowed to submit grievances on a wide range of matters relating to their terms and conditions of employment. Employees in industry by contrast may submit a grievance concerning the interpretation of the contract or application of a collective agreement only after it has been entered into by the union and the employer. In their case there can be no grievance if there is no agreement. There are overriding conditions limiting the types of grievances that may be processed under the Act, i.e. no grievance may be submitted if there is some other form of redress under another Act of Parliament. This means that a grievance cannot be submitted if the complainant is dissatisfied concerning the result of a promotional competition, since this matter is governed by an appeal procedure under the Public Service Employment Act. Also, for the present at least, no grievance concerning classification can be entertained because classification is not a matter subject to negotiation.

Grievances concerning the interpretation of a collective agreement or an arbitral award may only be made with the consent of the bargaining agent for the bargaining unit to which the collective agreement or arbitral award applies. Although a grievance may be processed through a maximum of four steps in the grievance procedure, not every grievance need go as far as adjudication (this term is usually referred to as arbitration in the private sector). Those that may be referred to adjudication are grievances that have been processed through the final level of the process and have not been satisfactorily resolved insofar as the employee is concerned. Adjudications are final and binding. The only material restriction imposed on adjudicators or adjudication boards is that they cannot render decisions which would make it necessary to amend any article of an existing agreement or arbitral award, and much less a law or statute.

Public and Employee Reactions

What was expected of this new legislation, particularly by the employees? No doubt a great number felt that the law would provide early and easy answers to their long standing grievances. This law, like most social enactments, will not provide all the answers until enough time has passed to iron out the wrinkles, identify the shortcomings, and correct them with amended legislation.

The most obvious deficiencies appear to be in the restrictions or exemptions imposed by the law concerning what is negotiable and what is not. The tendency over the years undoubtedly will be a liberalization of the items subject to negotiation in such areas as selection, transfers, lay-offs, promotions, demotions, training and classification. These items, with the exception of training and classification, are tied to the merit system which is strictly under the jurisdiction of the Public Service Commission and regulated by the Public Service Employment Act. The principle involved in these restrictions is that they cover action that an apellant may take under other statutes, or that they form part of management rights. Amendments to the Public Service Staff Relations Act may be introduced in Parliament at some future date to change this situation and allow negotiation of at least some of these items, as well as entertain all types of grievances from persons who believe themselves to have been treated unjustly.

What has been the impact of collective bargaining on both sides? It has without doubt created a new era in employer-employee relations. Public employees feel they are no longer second-class citizens in a country where collective bargaining has been practised in the private sector for almost half a century. They have gained equality with their counterparts in a society that has otherwise admitted frequent manpower interchanges between both sectors. The employer for his part has established a channel of communications with employees far in advance of the previous system when unilateral decisions were made concerning wages and conditions of employment. In addition, grievances are now aired before they are given an opportunity of growing into greater sources of discontent and frustration. Finally, the government can assure the people that greater stability in service to the public can be achieved if the employees of the Government are given the means of settling disputes and grievances within the context of the collective bargaining legislation. The public need not fear greater disruption of service under the rule of law than through illegal slowdowns and strikes.

20

The Political Rights and Activities of Canadian Public Servants*

W. D. Kenneth Kernaghan

Until the 1960's, the approach of the Canadian federal and provincial governments to the extension of political rights to public servants was much less progressive than that of many other industrialized, democratic states. Despite the loosening of restraints on the political activity of Canadian federal employees in recent years, the conclusion of a comparative study conducted by a United States Government commission in 1967 was that

Canadian restrictions of the political activities of civil servants have been stricter than those found in other British Commonwealth nations of comparable development, such as Australia and New Zealand, and are presently far stricter than the regulations in Great Britain itself.[1]

This paper will provide an inquiry into the theoretical debate on the granting of political rights to government personnel; a comparative analysis of the legal regulations in certain foreign states and Canadian provinces; and an examination of the evolution of political rights at the federal level of government in Canada.

In its application to the public service, the term *political rights* generally encompasses the rights to vote, to campaign in support of a candidate, to attend political meetings, to stand as a candidate in federal or provincial elections, to hold local office and to appeal against dismissal arising from real or

* W.D.K. Kernaghan and A.M. Willms, eds., *Public Administration in Canada,* 2nd ed. (Toronto: Methuen Publications, 1971), pp. 382-90. Reprinted and revised by permission of the publisher.
[1] United States, *Report of the Commission on the Political Activity of Public Personnel,* vol. 2 (Washington, D.C.: United States Government Printing Office, 1968), p. 162.

alleged political activity. In addition, the citizen's crucial right to freedom of expression on political matters touches on the propriety of a public servant's action in criticizing government policy in the press or from the platform and in disclosing official information without authorization.

The dilemma posed by the question of political rights for government personnel is the need to reconcile the necessity for the political neutrality and administrative impartiality of public servants with the demand for equal rights for all citizens in a democratic state. The traditional arguments promoting the extension or limitation of the political rights of government employees purport to benefit the general citizenry, the political heads of executive departments, political parties and the public servants themselves.

Opponents to broadening the range of political rights assert, first of all, that overt political partisanship among government employees undermines public confidence in the impartial conduct of the nation's business. Moreover, they contend that the unabated expansion of the bureaucracy's influence in the policy-making process requires a public service free of political bias. Governments can discharge their responsibilities effectively and efficiently only if the bureaucracy is divorced from partisan affiliation since the political executive, who relies on administrative subordinates for counsel and policy implementation, must be assured of their integrity and loyalty. It may be argued further that government employees should not publicly criticize government policy, whether this criticism is based on knowledge available to the general public or on information available to public servants by virtue of their official position. Certainly, in the interests of state security, governments must impose heavy penalties on public servants who make unauthorized use of official documents. Another common argument for the restriction of political rights is that in accepting the advantages of security and generous fringe benefits accompanying government employment, public servants can realistically be expected to relinquish certain political rights enjoyed by other citizens. Finally, public servants must be protected against financial exploitation or coercion by a superior with party affiliations who can affect his subordinates' prospects for promotion.

On the other hand, advocates of the emancipation of public servants from political restraints are motivated in large part by the political sterilization of an increasing percentage of the population as the number of public servants continues to expand.[2] In a democratic society, the isolation of such a substantial proportion of the population from political activity must be offset by substantive and demonstrable benefits to the public interest. An especially powerful argument for the removal of political restrictions is that the public services contain a concentration of the best educated and best informed persons in the country. As a consequence of excessive limitations on the political rights of

---

[2] The number of public servants at all levels of Canadian government today amounts to about one sixth of the total labour force. See my article "An Overview of Public Administration in Canada Today", *Canadian Public Administration*, vol. 11, no. 3 (Fall, 1968), pp. 292-93.

public personnel, the nation may be deprived not only of an articulate and knowledgeable expression of views on public issues but also of talented persons reluctant to accept employment which restricts their political activities. In addition, political parties may be obliged to exclude from active party membership and possible candidature persons whose intimate acquaintance with governmental problems is invaluable to the formulation of party policy.

The solution to this conflict between administrative nonpartisanship and the enjoyment of political rights is not a simple weighing of these opposing theoretical considerations or the application of one or the other set of arguments to particular countries. In practice, it is common for governments to evolve a position of compromise between the unworkable extremes of unrestrained political activity and absolute political sterilization. The measure of political activity accorded government employees in democratic societies may be depicted along a continuum between these two extreme poles.

On this continuum, the status of public servants in the United States approaches the extremity of complete exclusion from political activity. The *Hatch Act* of 1939 and its amendment in 1940[3] severely restrict the political activities of more than 4.5 million public servants at the federal, state and local levels of govenment.[4] The provisions of this federal statute apply to employees of state and local governments working on programmes financed wholly or in part by federal loans or grants.

The narrow range of permissible political activities under the Act includes the right to vote; the right to express views "on all political subjects and candidates"[5]; membership in political party clubs and attendance at political rallies and conventions; voluntary contributions to political parties and organizations; wearing political badges and displaying political stickers and signs on a car or at a home; participation in local non-partisan elections; and full political activity on matters "relating to constitutional amendments, referendums, approval of municipal ordinances, and others of a similar character".

A wider range of prohibited activities includes standing as a candidate for federal, state or local office; organizing or holding office in a political club; serving as a speaker, delegate or alternate to a party convention; campaigning actively for a political party or candidate through public speeches, the distribution of literature, the circulation of nominating petitions or participation in parades; engaging in official or partisan activity at the polls on election day or transporting voters to the polls; and soliciting political contributions. The penalty imposed for violation of these prohibitions is removal from office or suspension without pay for a minimum period of 30 days.

---

[3] 53 United States, *Statutes,* 1147 (1939) and 54 United States, *Statutes,* 767 (1940).

[4] *Report of the Commission on the Political Activity of Public Personnel,* vol. 1, p. 11.

[5] The United States Civil Service Commission has explained that this right "is subject to the prohibition that employees may not take any active part in political management or in political campaigns". *Political Activity of Federal Officers and Employees,* United States Civil Service Commission (Washington, D.C., May, 1966), pamphlet 20, p. 12.

The Commission on the Political Activity of Public Personnel, appointed jointly by the President and both Houses of Congress in 1966, presented a three-volume report recommending the removal of many of the existing barriers to political activity.[6] The implementation of these recommendations would help to eliminate numerous abuses of the *Hatch Act* which have arisen partly from uncertainty among public servants as to the permissible and proscribed activities under the Act. One of the central proposals of the Commission was that "the law regulating political activity of government personnel should specify in readily understandable terms those political activities which are prohibited, and specifically permit all others."[7]

The British Government's attitude on the issue of political activity for public servants brings their position closer to the pole of unrestrained political activity. Yet this general statement must be severely qualified since a substantial number of British civil servants are barred from all but the most limited political activity. Following an evolution over 80 years in the direction of extending the scope of political activity, a reconciliation of views contained in the Masterman Committee Report[8] with the counter-proposal of the staff side of a Whitley Council Committee led to the adoption in 1953 of a differentiated system of political rights for civil servants.[9]

The entire body of British civil servants was divided into three major categories labelled *politically free, intermediate* and *politically restricted* depending on their influence on policy making and their occupational relationships with the public. The politically free category comprises all employees working in the industrial civil service and those in the non-industrial civil service falling within the manipulative grades of the post office and the minor grades of messengers and cleaners. These civil servants are free to participate fully in national and local political activities although they must submit their resignations before nomination day if they stand for election. Moreover, they may be subsequently reinstated to the civil service on the fulfilment of certain conditions. The intermediate category embraces those civil servants performing clerical and typing responsibilities. These employees may take part in all political activities except candidacy for Parliament. Their political activities are subject, however, to the granting of departmental permission "according to the degree and nature of the conduct with the public involved"[10] and to the acceptance of a code of discretion. The politically restricted category includes all other civil servants, that is, those falling with the executive, the professional, the scientific and technical, and the administrative grades. Members of this restricted category will normally be permitted to take

---

[6] See especially vol. 1, *Findings and Recommendations.*

[7] *Findings and Recommendations,* p. 4.

[8] Great Britain, *Report of the Committee on the Political Activities of Civil Servants* (London: His Majesty's Stationery Office, 1949), Cmd. 7,718 (June, 1949).

[9] *The Political Activities of Civil Servants* (London, Her Majesty's Stationery Office, 1953), Cmd. 8,783 (March, 1953). See also *Establishment Circular* 26/53 (Treasury, August 14, 1953).

[10] *The Political Activities of Civil Servants,* sec. 37(b).

part in local political activities which are not associated with national political organizations. The political activities of this group are subject both to the acceptance of a code of discretion and the obligation to inform the department of election to a local government office.

The location of Canada's federal public servants on the continuum of political activity lies between the positions of the United States and Great Britain. Only during the decade of the 1960's did Canada take the progressive measures necessary to achieve this status.

For 40 years following Confederation, the Canadian federal government was plagued by a heritage of patronage from the pre-Confederation era of colonial rule. The practices of appointment for party service, the use of government employees to promote partisan objectives, the holding of office at pleasure and rotation in office brought the government to the verge of the United States *spoils system.* Little advance toward the elimination of the evils of patronage was made before the *Civil Service Amendment Act* of 1908[11] which applied the merit principle to the inside service (civil servants in Ottawa) and imposed the penalty of dismissal for political activity. Patronage in the outside service continued apace, however, and the device of making temporary appointments on political grounds to the inside service almost destroyed the merit system during the following decade.

Then, in 1918, a new *Civil Service Act*[12] extended the merit system. Provision was made for admission by competitive examination to both the inside and outside services. The prohibition against political activity was reinforced by vesting exclusive power of appointment and promotion in the Civil Service Commission rather than in the politicians. Section 55 of the Act, which stood unaltered for 43 years, stated:

1. No deputy head, officer, clerk or employee in the Civil Service shall be debarred from voting at any Dominion or provincial election if, under the laws governing the said election, he has the right to vote; but no such deputy head, officer, clerk or employee shall engage in partisan work in connection with any such election, or contribute, receive or in any way deal with any money for any party funds.

2. Any person violating any of the provisions of this section shall be dismissed from the Civil Service.

Although the enforcement of the Act diminished substantially the magnitude of partisan political activity among government employees, Dawson wrote as late as 1936 that "political patronage is still the great enemy of civil service efficiency in Canada".[13]

Nevertheless, the effect of patronage on appointments to positions falling under the authority of the Civil Service Commission gradually dwindled to the

---

[11] *Statutes,* 7-8 Edw. VII, c. 15.

[12] *Statutes,* 8-9 Geo. V, c. 12.

[13] R.M. Dawson, "The Canadian Civil Service", *Canadian Journal of Economics and Political Science,* vol. 2 (August, 1936), p. 291.

point where by 1960, Hughes, then chairman of the Commission, could write that

> *... no one will seriously contend that the influence of political patronage in the recruitment and selection of public employees is not on the decline. Even in those jurisdictions where there are no statutory safeguards against its operation, there is a general inclination to avoid it and at the very least to pay lip-service to the principle of appointment and promotion by merit.*[14]

In making reference to "those jurisdictions where there are no statutory safeguards," Hughes was alluding to the large numbers of public servants working in government positions and agencies which had over the years been exempted from the application of the inflexible and overcentralized controls of the *Civil Service Act.* Indeed, in 1960, only 131,953 persons out of a total civilian public service of 344,362 (less than 40 per cent) were subject to the provisions of the Act, including the restrictions on political activity.[15] Although the acceptance of the merit principle by exempt groups varies from agency to agency, political appointments and activities have been more common outside the confines of the *Civil Service Act.*

Also in 1960, the federal government, by Order-in-Council, conceded a public servant the legal right to participate in political movements and elections at the local level of government "if he has been granted leave without pay to do so or if his Deputy Minister finds that holding such office will not prevent the civil servant from properly discharging his duties. . . ."[16] A federal public servant may in addition receive leave without pay if he wins election to a full-time municipal office.[17]

The Province of Saskatchewan long preceded the federal government in removing certain deterrents to the political activity of public employees. As early as 1947, the Saskatchewan government bestowed on its employees generous political privileges. *The Public Service Act*[18] provides that no public servant may engage in political activity during working hours; use his authority to coerce any other employee into political participation or to make financial contributions to any political party; or indulge in political activities which might "impair his usefulness in the position in which he is employed". Aside from these minor restraints, the province's public servants are free to take part in political activity outside their regular working hours. Furthermore, a government employee who wishes to stand for public office may have 30 days leave of absence without pay before election day.

---

[14] S.H.S. Hughes, "The Public Officials — Parliament, the Public and the Press", *Canadian Public Administration,* vol. 3, no. 4 (December, 1960), p. 295.

[15] Civil Service Commission, *Annual Report,* 1960 (Ottawa: Queen's Printer, 1961), Appendix B, *Composition of the Public Service as of September 30, 1960,* p. 34.

[16] *Public Office — Municipal or Civic,* P.C. 1960 — 1121, August 12, 1960 (Ottawa: Queen's Printer).

[17] *Civil Service Regulations,* c. 71. *Canada Gazette,* vol. 96, no. 7 (Ottawa: April 11, 1962), p. 396.

[18] Saskatchewan, *Revised Statutes,* 1965, c. 9, sec. 52.

The 1958 *Report of the Civil Service Commission on Personnel Administration in the Public Service*[19] (the Heeney *Report*) proposed few modifications in federal legislation affecting political activity. The *Report* included proposals that public servants be permitted to act as poll officials under specified conditions and that a commission of inquiry be established to consider alleged instances of political partisanship. The revision of the *Civil Service Act*[20] in 1961 retained the longstanding prohibition against partisan work but incorporated the recommendation of the Heeney *Report* that an alleged violation of political activity be the subject of an inquiry. In all provinces except Saskatchewan, Ontario and Quebec, legal regulations or established practices affecting political activity are today identical or very similar to the federal procedure as is existed under this 1961 Act. The federal government was upstaged by the 1963 amendments to Ontario's *Public Service Act*[21] which liberalized previous regulations in the realm of political activity for a large proportion of the province's employees. Any public servant, other than deputy ministers and certain designated senior officials, may be a candidate or actively support another candidate for election to municipal office providing that such activity does not adversely affect the employee's performance on the job; does not harm the interests of the Crown; and is not affiliated with a provincial or federal political party. The employee shall, however, be granted a leave of absence without pay to stand for provincial or federal election or to campaign openly and to solicit funds in support of a provincial or federal party. An Ontario public servant who resigns on winning election may be reinstated if he ceases to be a political representative within five years and applies for reappointment within the subsequent three months.

According to the terms of the Quebec *Civil Service Act*,[22] a provincial civil servant may participate in federal or provincial political activities only on resignation from the civil service. If defeated in an electoral contest, the civil servant is entitled to reappointment to the service.

On the basis of the recommendations of a joint committee of the House of Commons and the Senate on employer-employee relations in the federal public service,[23] significant alterations in federal legislation regulating political activities were incorporated in the *Public Service Employment Act*.[24] Public servants are now permitted to attend political meetings and to contribute money to a candidate's campaign or to party coffers. The Public Service Commission has authority to approve requests for leave of absence without pay to enable any employee to seek nomination and election to federal, provincial or municipal office. These requests may be denied if the employee's usefulness would be impaired by such activity. Furthermore, in the event of

---

[19] (Ottawa: Queen's Printer, December, 1958), pp. 93-4.
[20] Canada, *Statutes*, c. 57.
[21] Ontario, *Statutes*, 1961-1962, c. 121 as amended by *Statutes*, 1962-1963, c. 118.
[22] Quebec, *Statutes*, 1965, c. 14.
[23] Ottawa, Queen's Printer, 1966-67.
[24] Canada, *Statutes*, 1966-67, c.71.

election to office, the employee automatically vacates his position.[25] Under section 32(6) of the Act, the Commission may conduct an inquiry into alleged contraventions of the regulations and recommend dismissal of an offending employee only if an "allegation is made to the Commission by a person who is or has been a candidate for election".

The very general language of the statute and the inadequacy of its coverage provides little specific direction to federal employees and leaves much discretion as to acceptable and forbidden political activities to the Public Service Commission. For example, the Act makes no reference to membership in political parties. In practice, however, federal employees may hold "inactive membership" in a political party, that is, they may be seen at party gatherings and rallies but may not be heard.

None of the Canadian legislation on political activity discussed to this point has treated the critical and delicate issue of the right of public servants to freedom of expression on political matters. The traditional, but informal, practice has been that government employees should maintain "a certain reserve" in their discussion of public questions. In 1965, a federal government actuary was dismissed for his public denunciations of the *Canada Pension Plan* which at the time was being debated in the House of Commons. The Appeal Board upheld the dismissal primarily on the grounds that the employee had special responsibilities "as a member of the civil service to uphold the constitutional laws and traditions and as an employee to refrain from conducting himself in a manner that would destroy his harmonious relationship with his employer". In addition, the Board noted that the employee's conduct in making "the representatives of the press and the public . . . witnesses to the unedifying spectacle of a senior civil servant attacking government policy . . . tended to make the discharge of the government's functions more difficult".[26]

The unauthorized disclosure of information by public servants is ordinarily regulated by the initial oath or affirmation of office and secrecy.[27] Severe penalties may be imposed under the *Official Secrets Act*[28] on government employees who make unauthorized use of official information, particularly the communication of a "code word, pass word, sketch, plan, model, article, note, document or information" to agents of a foreign power.

Comparative analysis indicates that the gradual extension of political rights to certain groups of government employees is not likely to injure the

---

[25] For an account of the extent of the political activity of federal public servants, see the section on "Political Involvement" in the annual reports of the Public Service Commission of Canada.

[26] "Appeal of Mr. John W. Kroeker, Actuary 6 (Senior Actuary) against decision of Superintendent of Insurance to recommend dismissal under Section 60 of the Civil Service Act", INS-A-20, April 9, 1965, pp. 22-23.

[27] The federal wording is as follows: "I, (A.B.) solemnly and sincerely swear (or affirm) that I will faithfully and honestly fulfil the duties that devolve upon me by reason of my employment in the Public Service and that I will not, without due authority in that behalf, disclose or make known any matter that comes to my knowledge by reason of such employment. (In the case where an oath is taken add, 'So help me God'.)" Schedule C of the *Public Service Employment Act.*

[28] Canada, *Revised Statutes,* 1970, c. 198.

public interest through the reintroduction of appointment and promotion on partisan grounds. Canadian federal and provincial governments may benefit not only from granting a broader range of political rights but from a more explicit legislative statement of permissible and prohibited political activites. Canadian governments may also evaluate the procedure of differentiating among public servants for purposes of political activity based on the British or the Ontario model.

The federal government and certain provincial governments have moved a long way in the direction of an appropriate balance between the political neutrality and the individual rights of government employees. Yet, in a comparative context, not only with Great Britain but with several developed countries in Western Europe and Asia, Canadian laws and practices appear unduly restrictive. The accumulation of much more empirical data on the extent of political activity at all levels of Canadian government is essential, however, before further legislative modifications are made.

21

The Issue of Administrative Secrecy in Canada

Paul Thomas

The reconciliation of secrecy, publicity and privacy in governmental affairs is a formidable task. The challenge is to strike an appropriate balance among several elements — the necessity for a measure of administrative secrecy, the extension of government information services, the need for reliable information on which to base public policy decisions, and the demand that individuals be protected against misuse of such information.

The single most important cause of increased government secrecy in Canada during this century appears to be certain traditions of cabinet-parliamentary government. Under our fused executive-legislative model of government, the Canadian bureaucracy is accountable to the legislature only indirectly through the Cabinet. The bureaucracy is sheltered from parliamentary control and supervision by the doctrines of Cabinet and Ministerial responsibility. If public servants were to accept the direction of the legislature or its committees, responsibility would be blurred because neither the Cabinet nor Ministers could be held responsible for administrative acts which they did not initiate or approve. In theory, Ministers are responsible for all activities of their departmental officials; public servants are impartial, anonymous and cannot engage in political controversy. It follows, therefore, that the counsel Ministers receive from public servants must be confidential. The advice offered, the alternatives evaluated and the final determinants of policy choices are not open to examination by any body outside the executive branch. The whole ideology of Cabinet government, then, protects the policy-making function of government from public scrutiny.[1] It is significant, also, that the courts have ruled in numerous cases that the executive officer concerned is the sole judge as to whether the public interest would be damaged by the release of information. Thus, a tradition of secrecy has become deeply engrained in the executive branch of the Canadian government.

It has become clear, however, that the doctrine of ministerial responsibility does not correspond to political reality. The practice now appears to be that the government, particularly the Prime Minister, decides largely on political grounds whether administrative mismanagement or abuse warrants a Minister's resignation. Certainly, the number of such resignations in Canada has been very small. The notion underlying the concept of ministerial responsibility, that the Minister is or can be aware of all actions taken by his administrative officials, is simply a fiction. Many decisions, including some of a controversial nature and some with significant political implications, are taken without his knowledge. Moreover, responsibility is further diffused through the developing practice of "contracting out" research and service activities to private institutions which can be held accountable only in a narrow auditing sense.

The contention is frequently made that administrative secrecy is essential to efficient and effective administration. It is suggested that the interchange of opinions and information preceding a policy decision must take place in private so that public servants will feel free to present unpalatable facts and unpopular arguments to political superiors. K.W. Knight has suggested that if the executive branch operated in a goldfish bowl of publicity, administrative officials might begin to write for posterity or simply rely heavily on oral communication.[2] Public servants would be dragged into the political fray when the Opposition parties decided to make political capital out of cases where a Minister rejected the advice of his experienced and expert officials.

Actually, the consequences of greater access to government documents may not be as destructive of administrative vitality as suggested by advocates of frank, private communication among public servants and their political masters. Donald C. Rowat has argued persuasively that officials are likely to

---

[1] For a strong critique of this ideology, see Brian Chapman, *British Government Observed* (London: Allen and Unwin, 1963).

[2] K.W. Knight, "Administrative Secrecy and Ministerial Responsibility", *Canadian Journal of Economics and Political Science,* vol. 32 (February, 1966), pp. 78-80.

give more considered judgements if they know they are writing for the public record.[3] It may be argued, also, that fears about public servants writing for history or not writing at all are largely false because public servants are required to record the bulk of administrative information and this requirement can be extended by legislation. To understand whether the Minister has chosen the proper course of action or whether his department is operating efficiently and effectively, Parliament must know what information is available and on what basis a decision was taken.

The period of the "cold war" did much to heighten secrecy as it relates to the security of the state. *The Report of the Royal Commission on Security (Abridged)*[4] did not offer much hope to proponents of greater access to administrative records. The Commission admitted the vagueness of present classification procedures and the many complaints about overclassification of documents, but could not recommend a better system. It did note that departments should be constantly reminded of the value of downgrading the classification of documents. The Commission also recommended that more attention be paid to the "need to know" principle, i.e., the dissemination of security information only as far as necessary for the conduct of business.

In May, 1969, the Prime Minister announced that departmental files would be available for research and other use after thirty years, with the exception of those documents whose release "might adversely affect Canada's external relations, violate the right of privacy of individuals, or adversely affect the national security".[5] The Royal Commission on Security reported that there seemed to be no alternative to the thiry-year rule, but that some material (mainly intelligence and security files) should be permanently withheld. The whole tenor of the *Report* led James Eayrs to comment that "it has pushed us back into the murk of administrative secrecy of which other countries are working free".[6]

The disclosure of some categories of information having no connection with national security could damage the national interest. With the growth of government economic regulation, much information of a private, confidential nature has been collected with the understanding that this information will be kept secret. The detailed records which the government now keeps on business firms contain such material as financial data and trade secrets which, if disclosed, could injure both the firms and the national interest. Thus, a substantial measure of ordinary business secrecy has been incorporated into the procedures of executive departments. It is also government policy to deny public access to personnel records containing the background and evaluation files on federal public employees. Similarly, records on individual Canadians

[3]Donald C. Rowat, "Administrative Secrecy and Ministerial Responsibility: A Reply", *Canadian Journal of Economics and Political Science,* vol. 32 (February, 1966), pp. 77-84.
[4]Canada, *Report of the Royal Commission on Security (Abridged)* (Ottawa: Queen's Printer, 1969).
[5]*Debates* (Commons), May 1, 1969, pp. 8,199-200.
[6]*Toronto Star,* July 8, 1969.

are kept confidential because of growing concern about invasion of individual privacy.[7] Canadians are now required to pour out an almost continuous stream of information for government files — records for birth, marriage, health services, the census, assessment, taxes, licenses and so on. However valuable such information may be for the development of public policy, the capacity of government data banks to track an individual's file from cradle to grave is an ominous potential threat to personal freedom.

The large size, complexity and specialization characteristic of modern bureaucracies also contributes to the development of administrative secrecy. Much of the internal communication of the public service is considered privileged material. The Prime Minister has indicated the government's intention to issue an order-in-council regarding access to records, but, for the present, access remains a matter for departmental discretion.

In 1969, the Task Force on Government Information Services recommended that the government provide much more information to Canadians as the foundation for fulfilling their right to "full, objective and timely information."[8] Among the Task Force's many recommendations was the suggestion that a central resource organization, to be known as Information Canada, be "assigned the function of public advocate in matters of access to federal information and timeliness of replies to citizens' queries".[9] Through the establishment of Information Canada in 1970, the government attempted to centralize and coordinate the information flow from a central point in the bureaucracy. It is notable that Information Canada functions not only to inform the public of the services offered by various government departments, but also to enhance the public image of these departments. It has, therefore, a vested interest in releasing only that information which brings credit to departments.

The Task Force suggested that the government provide more informative replies to Parliamentary questions and that for this purpose guidelines be prepared for departmental officials.[10] Also, access of mass media representatives to government information should be increased, both by releasing more documents and by improving channels of communication between public servants and the Press Gallery.[11]

Several of the Task Force's recommendations amounted to little more than noble sentiments. Indeed, the implementation of all the recommendations would only have resulted in marginal improvements because they did not deal directly with the interrelated issues of ministerial responsibility, bureaucratic neutrality and secrecy. Nevertheless, not even the modest

---

[7] See J.M. Sharp, "The Public Servant and the Right to Privacy", *Canadian Public Administration,* vol. 14, no. 1 (Spring, 1971), pp. 58-64.
[8] Canada, *Report of the Task Force on Government Information Services,* vol. 1 (Ottawa: Queen's Printer, 1969), p. 54.
[9] *Ibid.,* p. 59.
[10] *Ibid.,* pp. 63, 64.
[11] *Ibid.,* p. 65.

recommendations of the Task Force were acceptable in their entirety to the government. The Prime Minister stated that the government accepted the philosophy of the Report and promised to implement most of its recommendations.[12] The government rejected, however, the suggestion that a government agency be created to defend the public's "right to know" on the grounds that this function belonged to Parliament.

Critics of the extent of administrative secrecy in Canada contend that the federal government has relied on tradition and constitutional doctrine to suppress a large volume of information that in other countries would automatically be made public. They suggest that Canada look to such countries as Sweden and the United States as models of more open administration and of a more realistic approach to administrative secrecy.[13]

At present, access to much information is restricted unless and until cause is shown why it should be made public. This is wrong in principle in that it is contrary to democratic theory; it is dangerous in practice because it will not contribute to intelligent policy-making in the long run. To break through the veil of secrecy surrounding much of the government's activity, there should be a complete reversal of the present approach: information should be made available unless cause can be shown why it should be kept secret.

The greater the amount of secrecy, the greater is the temptation to base decisions on a limited number of premises or objectives. The Canadian public in general, and Parliament in particular, lack sufficient information to participate adequately in policy formation or to conduct an intelligent review of executive performance. If the public and Parliament are going to contribute ideas and opinions to the public policy process and to hold the government accountable, a dramatic change in the existing balance among publicity, secrecy and privacy in Canadian government is essential.

---

[12] *Debates* (Commons), February 10, 1970, pp. 3,405-6.
[13] See, for example, Donald C. Rowat, "How Much Administrative Secrecy?" *Canadian Journal of Economics and Policial Science,* vol. 31, no. 4 (November, 1969), pp. 484-93; and *Report of the Task Force on Government Information Services,* vol. 2, pp. 27-34.

22

A Federal Ombudsman for Canada?*

Donald C. Rowat

In 1963 and 1964 two cases of individual grievance against government administration shocked the public and promoted the idea of an ombudsman, or citizen's defender against bureaucratic abuse. The first was a case of administrative bungling in which a seaman with an excellent record was discharged from the Royal Canadian Navy for no apparent reason. After much prodding from the Opposition, the government finally revealed that he had been judged a security risk because of an allegation that his uncle had been a Communist candidate in a recent federal election. Upon further investigation it proved to be a case of mistaken identity: although the candidate had the same last name as the seaman, he was not the seaman's uncle.

The second came to be known as the "blood bomber" case. On August 24, 1964, a man threw a carton of cow's blood from the gallery onto the floor of the House of Commons. It turned out that he was the head of "Underdog," an organization to help mistreated people. He had done this to dramatize the plight of a man with a grievance against the government: the man complained that he was wrongly suspected of being a Communist because the RCMP refused to acknowledge his earlier activities as an undercover agent, and he could find no way to have his case investigated. Two days later, in reply to a question from the floor of the House, the Minister of Justice stated that he was in favour of considering the idea of creating the office of Ombudsman.

The reason for giving the idea favourable consideration was the realization that in the modern bureaucratic state there are many cases of this kind that never come to light and are never remedied. The office of Ombudsman, which had recently been created in a number of other democratic countries, seemed eminently suited for investigating such cases. The Ombudsman is an independent officer of Parliament who investigates and remedies grievances against bureaucratic action. The office originated in Sweden in 1809. It spread to Finland in 1919, to Denmark in 1953, and then to Norway and New Zealand in 1962. At the time of the seaman and "blood bomber" cases, a proposal for the office in Britain was being actively discussed.

Even before the revelation of these cases, the idea had received considerable publicity in Canada. Articles in learned journals and popular magazines had advocated ombudsmen for Canada at both the federal and

*Donald C. Rowat, "Whatever Happened to the Federal Ombudsman?" *Saturday Night,* vol. 86, no. 10 (October, 1971), pp. 17-20. Reprinted and abridged by permission of the author and publisher.

provincial levels of government, and private members' bills providing for the appointment of an Ombudsman had been introduced annually in the House of Commons since 1961. In 1964, a graduate student at Carleton University made a survey of members of the House of Commons and found that the great majority of those who replied were in favour of an Ombudsman because their own facilities for handling grievances were inadequate.

At about the same time, a committee of the House of Commons took up the idea and received evidence from expert witnesses, including Sir Guy Powles, the Ombudsman for New Zealand. In February, 1965, it recommended that the office be created, and in April, 1965, the Pearson government announced that the Ombudsman idea would be referred to a new royal commission being set up to study administrative bodies. Thus it appeared that the ombudsman plan was well on the way to being adopted. The royal commission was never appointed, however, and no action has been taken to implement the parliamentary committee's recommendation.

Meanwhile, the idea has spread rapidly in other countries and among the Canadian provinces. Shortly after the Pearson government dropped the idea, the British government established an ombudsman plan and appointed Sir Edmund Compton, the retiring Auditor General, as Britain's first Ombudsman, officially known as Parliamentary Commissioner for Administration. His office was so successful that the government of Northern Ireland created a similar office in 1969 for its own departments, and appointed Sir Edmund to the post. It also created the office of complaints commissioner for other public bodies and for local governments.

Perhaps the most remarkable spread of the ombudsman idea has occurred in the United States. In 1966 the word "ombudsman" was practically unknown in the United States. Since then, ombudsman plans have been proposed for all levels of government in the United States, and for school boards, universities, public corporations and private associations. Versions of the scheme have been adopted by local governments, and bills providing for it have been introduced in the legislatures of most states. Two states have actually adopted a plan based on the New Zealand version: Hawaii in 1967 and Nebraska in 1969. Also, more than fifty universities in the United States have appointed ombudsmen to investigate student complaints. Bills to create a federal Ombudsman have been before the United States Congress for several years, and the United States civil service commission has recently created a complaint office for civil servants.

The plan has also spread rapidly in other countries. Versions of it have been adopted in Guyana and Mauritius (1965), Tanzania (1966) and, more recently, Ghana and Israel. Ghana's 1969 constitution provides for an Ombudsman, and a bill to implement this provision was placed before Parliament in 1970. Israel has a version of the plan based on the state comptroller's office, which has been handling complaints from the public for many years. Early in 1971 this function was made explicit by an amendment to the state comptroller law, which named him also as public complaints commissioner.

The world-wide spread of the idea leads me to believe that a tentative prediction I made in 1965 (as the conclusion to my book *The Ombudsman*) may not be far off the mark: "The ombudsman institution or its equivalent will become a standard part of the machinery of government throughout the democratic world."[1]

Though the Trudeau government has chosen to ignore this remarkable spread of the ombudsman idea in other countries, its refusal to be influenced by the rapid spread and success of the scheme among Canada's provinces is even more surprising. By now, six provincial governments have adopted the plan. Two of these plans, in Alberta and New Brunswick, have been in effect since 1967. Two others, for Quebec and Manitoba, were adopted in 1969, and are already in operation. Legislation for the other two, in Nova Scotia and Newfoundland, was passed in 1970, and the Ombudsman for Nova Scotia has already been appointed. It is likely that Saskatchewan and Ontario will also create the office within the next year or two.

All of the provincial plans have common features based on the New Zealand model. In each, the Ombudsman, like an Auditor General, is considered to be an officer of the legislature, and can be removed only by it. He is intended to be non-partisan, so that he is interested neither in embarrassing nor in protecting any particular party in power. Thus, he can be trusted on all sides—by citizens, politicians and civil servants. He receives complaints direct from the public and has the power to investigate those that may be justified. In order to protect civil servants from the publicity of unfair allegations, investigations are conducted in private. If the Ombudsman discovers an administrative error or abuse, he will request that remedial action be taken by the department concerned. He has no power to enforce his decisions, but he can publicize instances where action has not been taken. Thus his key weapons are persuasion and publicity. An important aspect of his work is that he exonerates civil servants in cases where unfair accusations have been made, and thus supports the public's truct and confidence in the civil service.

A key feature of the office, like that of the Auditor General, is the Ombudsman's annual report to the legislature. Besides outlining the action he has taken in particular cases, it makes recommendations for improving the civil service and amending unfair laws. The annual reports of the provincial Ombudsmen who have been in office for more than a year are available to the public and make fascinating reading.

Anyone who has doubts about the value of the Ombudsmen has only to read their accounts of some of the real grievances for which they have provided a remedy. The 1968 report of Alberta's Ombudsman, Mr. McClellan, reveals cases of many persons who had been found unfit to stand trial or found "not guilty" of criminal charges by reason of insanity, and who had been subsequently detained in a mental hospital by order of the provincial government. Some of these persons had been detained for periods of over twenty years,

---

[1] D.C. Rowat, ed., *The Ombudsman* (Toronto: University of Toronto Press, 1965), p. 292.

in one case twenty-seven years, without ever having had a review of their mental situation by an independent body. Successive governments were not even made aware that these people were being detained at the government's pleasure. He came to the conclusion that this situation was wrong and that their cases ought to be reviewed periodically.

A typical example of Ombudsman Flemington's work in New Brunswick is the case of a teacher who complained that she was unable to collect her pension when she wished to retire six months before the minimum age, after teaching for nearly thirty years. The regulations provided that she could not retire on pension unless she was either sixty or too infirm to work. Although physically sound, she felt psychologically unable to continue teaching. Dr. Flemington felt that the rules were too rigid and unfair in her case. On his recommendation she was granted a full pension and the regulations were reviewed by the government.

Louis Marceau, Quebec's public protector, discovered during his first year in office that a social welfare court order had kept a mentally ill eighteen-year-old in prison for two years, although the youth had been convicted of no crime. The reason was that health department officials had neglected to admit him to a psychiatric hospital where he could receive help. Thanks to the intervention of Dr. Marceau, this negligence was rectified. Dr. Marceau also discovered that a complainant was still waiting for his final payment six years after his property had been expropriated by the government. As soon as the public protector looked into the matter, the long-standing balance was quickly paid.

Although Quebec's public protector has been in office for only about two years, in that time he has become very visible to the Quebec public. Early in 1969 he handled a complaint from an imprisoned FLQ terrorist about his treatment by jail officials. Dr. Marceau found the complaint justified and remedial action was taken. At the time of the political kidnappings in the fall of 1971, he again came into the news through his willingness to investigate the numerous complaints by people who were temporarily arrested under the War Measures Act for suspected or possible membership in the FLQ. On his recommendation, the Quebec government agreed to pay the complainants for damages suffered as a result of the arrests.

In view of the obvious success of the ombudsman plan at the provincial level, the federal government's refusal to accept it is strange. This is doubly so because the government has already provided a precedent for it and has accepted the basic idea (though on a very limited scale) in the powers granted to the recently appointed commissioner of official languages. He is empowered to investigate complaints against federal offices for not dealing adequately with the public in both English and French. Like an Ombudsman, he may also recommend remedies and, if they are not accepted, may report the matter to Parliament.

The provincial Ombudsmen have no power to review complaints against the thousands of administrative decisions that are made annually by federal civil servants. Yet the need for the institution at the federal level is just as great as in the provinces and greater than in some other countries. For one thing, the liberties of the citizen are not yet entrenched in the Canadian constitution. The federal government has few administrative tribunals for appeal, and has inadequate legislative controls over administrative procedure. There are many regulatory boards and commissions with power to decide cases but no provision for appeal to the courts. Canada has antiquated laws on crown privilege, expropriation and government liability. Unlike other Commonwealth countries, the Canadian Parliament has no special grievance committees for settling individual complaints. And the methods of appeal to the courts are costly, complex, and slow. So the courts are not a suitable instrument for settling minor grievances against bureaucratic action.

Robert Thompson, Conservative member for Red Deer and former leader of the Social Credit party, deserves credit for keeping the subject alive in the federal Parliament. He has presented a bill based on the New Zealand model to each session of Parliament since 1963. In recent years he has also presented a second bill containing a less far-reaching but also less effective proposal. This would give the Ombudsman's function to the Auditor General, who would be allowed to investigate only complaints received through members of Parliament.

The few reasons that the Trudeau government has given for refusing to consider the ombudsman plan do not make much sense. In reply to a question in the House of Commons about the idea, the Prime Minister gave the answer that the Minister of Justice acts as the Ombudsman. This shows a complete misconception of the office. Its main purpose is to provide an investigator who is completely independent of the Ministers, since they are the ones responsible for directing the civil service. Former Justice Minister John Turner stated that the question of setting up the institution would have to wait until a detailed review had been conducted of administrative procedures and methods of appeal. Yet experience elsewhere has shown that, regardless of how good the procedures or avenues of appeal provided by the administration, an independent office standing outside the civil service is still needed as an instrument to build public trust.

A standard argument against the ombudsman proposal is that he is not needed very badly: citizens' rights seem to be adequately protected already, and one doesn't "hear about" very many cases of people who have received unfair or distressing treatment. The objectors forget that, since administrative action is secret, the great majority of such cases do not come to light. Only some of the most serious ones, either through good fortune or the strenuous efforts of the complainant, happen to be revealed. Since they concern isolated individuals, often they are not widely publicized by the press and are soon forgotten by the public. There are countless others that are never brought to light, in some of which the aggrieved person may suffer years of heartbreaking frustration. On the basis of experience in the provinces, one can estimate that the total caseload of an ombudsman plan at the federal level would be several thousand complaints a year. Even if only a few hundred of these were found to be justified, their remedy would be well worth the plan's relatively low cost. And the very existence of the plan would prevent many cases of maladministration and misconduct.

Clearly, the federal government needs a strong ombudsman institution with wide scope. What should be the nature of this office?

I have argued that a single Ombudsman would be overloaded at the federal level. More suitable would be a collegial body, or complaints commission. Tanzania's version of the ombudsman plan is a three-man commission. In Sweden the load of the Ombudsman for civilian affairs had become so heavy by 1968 that his office and the separate office of Ombudsman for military affairs were replaced by a joint body of three ombudsmen who share their work. It is true that the single parliamentary commissioner in Britain has been able to manage satisfactorily, but this is mainly because he can take up only complaints that have been referred to him by members of Parliament. This restriction has greatly reduced the number of complaints, but it has also severely limited the effectiveness of the plan.

The proposed complaints commission should be enabled to delegate to some of its senior officers the power to investigate and make recommendations on minor cases. The commission should travel about the country, either singly or as a group, in order to make its existence known and to receive complaints orally. This is done by the commission in Tanzania and is an important reason for its success. Hawaii's Ombudsman, too, has begun a programme of visits throughout the islands. In addition, it might be desirable to set up regional offices across the country. Quebec's public protector has already set a world-wide precedent for this by opening a regional office in Montreal.

Another suggestion is that the commission should offer to receive complaints by telephone and to produce its own written version of these complaints. This would be of great assistance to complainants, especially those who are poor and illiterate. Hawaii's Ombudsman has done this and has found that about 70 per cent of his complaints are received by telephone, about 20 per cent through visits, and only about 10 per cent by mail. In contrast to New Zealand's Ombudsman, who charges a fee for each complaint, he even accepts complaints in the form of long-distance collect calls.

By now the need for and the success of the ombudsman scheme have been amply demonstrated not only in other countries but also at the provincial level in Canada. Canada's provinces have been in the forefront of the spread of the institution from Scandinavia to the rest of the world. Indeed, the provincial plans in Canada have been so successful that they now serve as prototypes for other countries. Surely it is time for the federal government to create an even more sophisticated version of the plan.

Readings

Abel, A. "Administrative Secrecy." *Canadian Public Administration,* vol. 11, no. 4 (Winter, 1968), pp. 440-448.

Blackburn, G.A. "A Bilingual and Bicultural Public Service." *Canadian Public Administration,* vol. 12, no. 1 (Spring, 1969), pp. 36-44.

Burns, R.M. "The Machinery of Federal-Provincial Relations: II." *Canadian Public Administration,* vol. 8, no. 4 (December, 1965), pp. 527-34.

Canada. Civil Service Commission. *Report of the Preparatory Committee on Collective Bargaining.* Ottawa: Queen's Printer, 1965.

Canada. Department of Labour. "The Public Service Staff Relations Act." In *Public Administration in Canada,* eds. W.D.K. Kernaghan and A.M. Willms. 2nd ed. Toronto: Methuen Publications, 1971, pp. 305-12.

Canada. National Joint Council of the Public Service. *The National Joint Council of the Public Service of Canada, 1944-1964.* Ottawa: Queen's Printer, 1964.

Canada. *Royal Commission on Administrative Classification in the Public Service, Report.* Ottawa: King's Printer, 1946.

Canada. Royal Commission on Bilingualism and Biculturalism, Report. Book 3, Part 2. *The Federal Administration.* Ottawa: Queen's Printer, 1967.

Canada. Task Force on Government Organization. *To Know and Be Known.* Ottawa: Queen's Printer, 1969.

Carson, John J. "Bilingualism in the Public Service." *Canadian Public Administration,* vol. 15, no. 2 (Summer, 1972), pp. 190-93.

Cloutier, Sylvain. "Senior Public Service Officials in a Bicultural Society." *Canadian Public Administration,* vol. 11, no. 4 (Winter, 1968), pp. 393-406.

Cole, Taylor. *The Canadian Bureaucracy and Federalism 1947-1965.* Denver, Colorado: University of Denver Press, 1966.

Coté, E.A. "The Public Services in a Bicultural Society." *Canadian Public Administration,* vol. 11, no. 3 (Fall, 1968), pp. 280-90.

Dwivedi, O.P. and J.P. Kyba. "Political Rights of Canada's Public Servants." In *Contemporary Issues in Canadian Politics,* eds. Frederick Vaughan et al. Toronto: Prentice-Hall, 1970, pp. 230-39.

Frankel, S.J. *A Model for Negotiation and Arbitration between the Canadian Government and its Civil Servants.* Montreal: McGill University Press, 1962.

Gallant, Edgar. "The Machinery of Federal-Provincial Relations: I." *Canadian Public Administration,* vol. 8, no. 4 (December, 1965), pp. 515-26.

Gallant, Edgar. "The Secretariat of the Constitutional Conference." In *Bureaucracy in Canadian Government,* ed. W.D.K. Kernaghan. Toronto: Methuen Publications, 1969, pp. 47-50.

Kernaghan, W.D.K. "The Political Rights and Activities of Canadian Public Servants." In *Public Administration in Canada,* eds. W.D.K. Kernaghan and A.M. Willms. 2nd ed. Toronto: Methuen Publications, 1971, pp. 382-90.

Knight, K.W. "Administrative Secrecy and Ministerial Responsibility." *Canadian Journal of Economics and Political Science,* vol. 32, no. 1 (February, 1966), pp. 77-84.

Kwavnick, D. "French Canadians and the Civil Service of Canada." *Canadian Public Administration,* vol. 11, no. 1 (Spring, 1968), pp. 97-112.

MacFarlane, R.O. "Freedoms and Limitations of the Public Servant." *Canadian Education,* vol. 11 (September, 1956), pp. 65-71.

Mundell, D.W. "Ombudsman for Canada." *Canadian Bar Journal,* vol. 7 (June, 1964), pp. 179-209.

Prémont, Jacques. "Publicité de documents officiels." *Canadian Public Administration,* vol. 11, no. 4 (Winter, 1968), pp. 449-53.

Robertson, Gordon. "Official Responsibility, Private Conscience and Public Information." *Optimum,* vol. 3, no. 3 (1972), pp. 5-18.

Rowat, Donald C. "Administrative Secrecy and Ministerial Responsibility: a Reply." *Canadian Journal of Economics and Political Science,* vol. 32, no. 1 (February, 1966), pp. 84-7.

Rowat, Donald C. "An Ombudsman Scheme for Canada." *Canadian Journal of Economics and Political Science,* vol. 28, no. 4 (November, 1962), pp. 543-56.

Rowat, Donald C. "How Much Administrative Secrecy?" *Canadian Journal of Economics and Political Science,* vol. 31, no. 4 (November, 1965), pp. 479-98.

Rowat, Donald C. *The Ombudsman.* 2nd ed. Toronto: University of Toronto Press, 1968.

Rowat, Donald C. "Recent Developments in Ombudsmanship." *Canadian Public Administration,* vol. 10, no. 1 (March, 1967), pp. 35-46.

Rowat, Donald C. and Henry Llambias. "The Ombudsman in Canada." In *The Ombudsman,* ed. Donald C. Rowat. 2nd ed. Toronto: University of Toronto Press, 1968, pp. 186-93.

Santos, C.R. "Public Administration as Politics." *Canadian Public Administration,* vol. 12, no. 2 (Summer, 1969), pp. 213-23.

Sharp, J.M. "The Control and Accessibility of Private Data Held in the Federal Public Service of Canada." *Optimum,* vol. 2, no. 3 (1971), pp. 6-17.

Sharp, J.M. "The Public Servant and the Right to Privacy." *Canadian Public Administration,* vol. 14, no. 1 (Spring, 1971), pp. 58-64.

Sheppard, C.A. "An Ombudsman for Canada." *McGill Law Journal,* vol. 10, no. 4 (1964), pp. 291-340.

Simeon, Richard. *Federal-Provincial Diplomacy: The Making of Recent Policy in Canada.* Toronto: University of Toronto Press, 1972.

Smiley, Donald V. "Public Administration and Canadian Federalism." *Canadian Public Administration,* vol. 7, no. 3 (September, 1964), pp. 371-88.

Smiley, D.V. "The Structural Problem of Canadian Federalism." *Canadian Public Administration,* vol. 14, no. 3 (Fall, 1971), pp. 326-43.

Vachon, Gérald-P. "Collective Bargaining in the Federal Public Service: Experience and Prospects." In *Public Administration in Canada,* eds. W.D.K. Kernaghan and A.M. Willms. 2nd ed. Toronto: Methuen Publications, 1971, pp. 313-317.

Vaison, Robert A. "Collective Bargaining in the Federal Public Service: the Achievement of a Milestone in Personnel Relations." *Canadian Public Administration,* vol. 12, no. 1 (Spring, 1969), pp. 108-22.

Veuilleux, Gérard. *Les relations intergouvernementales au Canada, 1867-1967.* Quebec: Les presses de l'Université du Québec, 1971.

Index